THIS IS LIFE

By PAUL C. HEUBACH
Dean of Theology, Walla Walla College
Pastor of the College Church

"He who is following the divine guidance has found the only true source of saving grace and real happiness, and has gained the power of imparting happiness to all around him. No man can really enjoy life without religion. Love to God purifies and ennobles every taste and desire, intensifies every affection, and brightens every worthy pleasure. It enables men to appreciate and enjoy all that is true, and good, and beautiful."—*Messages to Young People,* p. 264.

"Christ made it possible for all who will to have the life that measures with the life of God."—*Ibid.,* p. 17.

REVIEW AND HERALD

Washington, D.C.

DEDICATION

To my wife and two daughters and all the young people in my classes through the years who under God have taught me much about life.

Copyright © 1957 by the

Review and Herald Publishing Association

The Bible texts in this book credited to Moffatt are from *The Bible: A New Translation* by James Moffatt. Copyrighted 1922, 1935, 1950, by Harper and Brothers. Used by permission.

The Bible texts in this book credited to Phillips are from *The Gospels Translated Into Modern English*, by J. B. Phillips, copyright 1952 by the Macmillan Company; and *Letters to Young Churches*, by J. B. Phillips, copyright 1947 by the Macmillan Company. Used by permission.

PRINTED IN U.S.A.

JANUARY

Life Through the Knowledge of God   *January 1*

THIS IS LIFE

And this is life eternal, that they might know thee the only true God, and Jesus Christ, whom thou hast sent. John 17:3.

Everyone wants to live—truly live, and not just merely exist. There is a song that goes like this: "I love life, so I want to live."

Some can sing this song zestfully, having found the joy of living. Others must sing it doubtfully, for they are not sure. Some would sing it wishfully, wishing it were true but feeling that the song is not for them. Some may not be able to sing it at all, for somehow they have lost the joy of living. Yet down deep in their hearts, even they do not want to die.

How shall we get the most out of life? What can we do to drink of life's fullness here and to be sure of life hereafter? For our answer, why not go to Him who is the source of life? Jesus said, "And this is life eternal, that they might know thee the only true God, and Jesus Christ, whom thou hast sent" (John 17:3).

"This knowledge is the secret spring from which flows all power."—*Counsels to Parents and Teachers,* p. 406.

This is the knowledge that "transforms man into the image of God. It gives to man the mastery of himself, bringing every impulse and passion of the lower nature under the control of the higher powers of the mind. . . . It brings him into communion with the mind of the Infinite, and opens to him the rich treasures of the universe."—*Christ's Object Lessons,* p. 114.

Let us, this new year, seek this knowledge, that we may truly live. A fitting prayer to begin the year would be the words of that well-known and loved hymn: "We have not known Thee as we ought, nor learned Thy wisdom, grace, and power; the things of earth have filled our thought, and trifles of the passing hour. Lord, give us light Thy truth to see, and make us wise in knowing Thee." Amen.

Life Through the Knowledge of God *January 2*

NOT IN WISDOM, POWER, OR RICHES

Thus saith the Lord, Let not the wise man glory in his wisdom, neither let the mighty man glory in his might, let not the rich man glory in his riches. **Jer. 9:23.**

"Wisdom! Power! Riches! If only I had these, I could truly live." So think wordly men. But these, apart from God, bring no lasting joy and happiness. The story is told of a sailor on a sinking ship laden with gold, in the days of the Spanish conquests. The captain had ordered every man to abandon ship. As he made his final round to see that no one was left on board, he came upon a man sitting on one keg of gold nuggets, with another hacked open before him.

"What in the world are you doing here, man? Don't you know the ship is sinking?" shouted the captain.

"Yes, sir," the man replied, "but I don't care. I've been a poor man all my life, and at least I'm going to die rich."

What does it profit a man if he gain the whole world and lose his own soul? Riches, apart from God, only make slaves of men. They take possession of men instead of being possessed by them. They give men a false sense of superiority, and this keeps them from the joy of unselfish service, which is the law of life. Power, apart from God, leads to destruction, for without God, men are not able to control and channel it aright. Wisdom, apart from God, makes men more clever sinners. These three, in themselves, are not evil. To the man with a true knowledge of God and a heart surrendered to Him, all three—wisdom, might, and riches—become servants for the welfare of man and the glory of God. This is life.

The more we understand and know God as He really is, the more like Him we shall want to become. We shall want to be loving and kind as He is. We shall want to use good judgment in all our decisions, and above all, we shall want to be clothed in His righteousness.

Life Through the Knowledge of God *January 3*

But in the Knowledge of God Is Life

But let him that glorieth glory in this, that he understandeth and knoweth me, that I am the Lord which exercise lovingkindness, judgment, and righteousness, in the earth: for in these things I delight, saith the Lord. Jer. 9:24.

Those things which seem to count so much in life from the human point of view alone, namely, wisdom, power, and riches, are not the things about which we should glory. Experience shows that these three, apart from God, bring no lasting happiness. In our text today Jeremiah tells us what really counts, and what it is in which we can truly glory. It is in knowing God.

Now, why is this true? First of all, to know God enables us to see the things of life in their true perspective. Second, the things most valuable in life are the things of the heart—fellowship and love. We were made that way. The true joy of living comes with communion and fellowship with those we love. To know God is to love Him. To love Him is to love others. In this, then, we may glory. And third, the knowledge of God makes us wise unto salvation. This makes for a more satisfying life here, and eternal life hereafter. The things of earth are soon to pass away, but the things of God are eternal.

Jeremiah brings to light three characteristics of God that He delights in displaying. They are loving-kindness, judgment, and righteousness. Our God is a God who loves and who is kind, One who uses good judgment in His dealings with men and nations, and One who is righteous, who always does the right thing because He is right. All three go together. One without the other two would not be completely satisfying. In all three characteristics He takes great pleasure, because these make for fullness of life.

Let us pray that God will keep us from being blinded by the false and the spurious and from becoming enamored of the wisdom and power and riches of the world apart from God, and let us know Him whom to know is life eternal; for in the knowledge of God, there are these three: true wisdom, true power, and true riches.

Life Through the Knowledge of God January 4

THE BEGINNING OF TRUE UNDERSTANDING

The fear of the Lord is the beginning of wisdom: and the knowledge of the holy is understanding. Prov. 9:10.

How is it that the fear of the Lord is the beginning of wisdom? Would not a knowledge of facts come first, and be most important in the *beginning* of wisdom? Not so. Before one can truly understand, he must know more than mere facts. Facts are like beads, you need a string to put them on. Two men may observe the same facts and come to two different conclusions. And why? Because each interprets the facts in different ways, on the basis of different premises. For example: Two men may observe the Grand Canyon of the Colorado River. One comes to the conclusion that this canyon must be millions of years old. He reaches this conclusion on the basis of the premise that "changes have always taken place as they are now going on." The second man, observing the same facts, comes to the conclusion that here is evidence of the Flood. In the natural phenomenon associated with the Grand Canyon he sees the marvelous work of the Creator. He comes to this conclusion on the basis of the premises laid down in the Word of God.

We need to come to the observation of facts with the correct postulates, if we would come to correct conclusions. That is why the beginning of wisdom is to know and understand God. In His Word we find those principles that give us true wisdom and understanding.

Knowledge apart from God tends to make skeptics of men, because the more we know, the more ways of interpreting what we know become possible, and the less sure we are as to which is correct. But knowledge gained from the observation of facts in the light of the premises laid down in God's Word, leads to an understanding that gives security and peace of mind. More than this, a true knowledge of God leads us to Him. This is our greatest need.

Let us pray that God will lead us to see the things of this life in their true relationship, to interpret what we see in the light of God's Word, and, more than that, to know Him personally.

Life Through the Knowledge of God *January 5*

PERTAINING TO LIFE AND GODLINESS

According as his divine power hath given unto us all things that pertain unto life and godliness, through the knowledge of him that hath called us to glory and virtue. **2 Peter 1:3.**

Since man is not just a physical animal, but a spiritual being as well, he is not satisfied with knowing facts alone. He is concerned with values and meaning.

There are four levels of knowledge. The first is that of facts; the second, the principles governing these facts. The third is the level of moral values; and the fourth, that of moral principles. To illustrate: One may know all the facts about an airplane. He may understand all the principles governing these facts. But that is not enough. What the airplane is *for* is more important, and the principles that govern its use are most important. An airplane has moral significance only as it affects the relationships of moral beings to one another and to God. How the airplane is used is determined by man's needs coupled with his sense of values. And it is here that the knowledge of God comes in and provides man with a true scale of values and a revelation of correct moral principles. A knowledge of God then makes all knowledge on the first two levels meaningful.

Our text today indicates that through the knowledge of God we are given all things that pertain unto life and Godliness. "Higher than the highest human thought can reach is God's ideal for His children. Godliness, Godlikeness, is the goal to be reached."—*Education*, p. 18. This goal can be reached only through a correct knowledge of God. We read in *The Ministry of Healing*, page 409: "Like our Saviour, we are in this world to do service for God. We are here to become like God in character, and by a life of service to reveal Him to the world. In order to be co-workers with God, in order to become like Him and to reveal His character, we must know Him aright."

May God grant us today a true sense of values, and make us more like Him, so that He may fulfill His purpose for our lives.

Life Through the Knowledge of God January 6

THE SOUL THIRSTS FOR GOD

As the hart panteth after the water brooks, so panteth my soul after thee, O God. **Ps. 42:1.**

Every person has certain great soul thirsts—some things for which he longs, which he deeply desires. The greater the soul, the more and greater are these thirsts. The number, quality, and intensity of these are the measure of the man.

These thirsts arise from basic human needs common to all. In addition to thirsts and desires arising from physical needs, there are those arising from the need for self-realization and those arising from the need for love, fellowship, recognition, and response. The desire to be accepted by, to feel a part of, to have the sense of belonging to, someone else is basic. We were created for fellowship, and the thirst for social approval is one of the most dynamic forces in human experience.

Then, there is the thirst for meaning. We want to know the reason for things. This need manifests itself early in life. Parents are plagued daily with the questions "Why, Mommy?" "Why, Daddy?" Older ones, too, question, "Why, oh, why, must this happen to me?"

Again, there is the thirst for beauty—the thirst that arises from man's aesthetic needs. This thirst distinguishes man from animal. This is a longing satisfied only by open spaces, a glorious sunset, beautiful flowers, inspiring music, works of art, et cetera.

In addition to these, and deeper than any other longing, is the longing for God. Hearts heavy with past sins and mistakes seek forgiveness and peace. The soul thirsts for fellowship with its Maker.

These are the longings put into every heart by the Creator Himself. He made provision for all these needs in Eden when Adam and Eve were first brought into existence, and He wants to supply your needs and mine.

May your thirst for fellowship with Him be satisfied today.

Life Through the Knowledge of God   *January* 7

Personal Fellowship With a Living God

My soul thirsteth for God, for the living God: when shall I come and appear before God? Ps. 42:2.

Deep in the hearts of men and women is a great soul thirst that many misinterpret. To some, the great thirst is the thirst for gold—more and more money, things material, possessions, properties, et cetera. They are like the farmer in the days of Jesus who said, "I will pull down my barns, and build greater."

To others, the great thirst is for pleasure. They are always looking for excitement—new and different ways of having fun, with more and greater thrills. Just to go places, see things, and do things. Ah, that would satisfy!

Some even thirst for revenge, thinking that only thus can satisfaction be gained. Some long for escape from reality. "Oh that I had wings like a dove! for then would I fly away, and be at rest" (Ps. 55:6).

Actually, however, underlying all these is the thirst for God. Many are totally unconscious of this thirst. Many deny this thirst or refuse to admit it. They feel it is a sign of weakness, or fear that it may disturb some pet pleasure.

On the other hand, some misunderstand God. Having false conceptions of His character, they have developed an attitude of fear, rebellion, or even hate. For some, the thirst for God is only periodic. They are conscious of this thirst only when they are in trouble.

However, down deep in every heart, irrespective of race or color, there is a searching after the living God. We were created for fellowship with our Creator, and we can never be completely satisfied until we find that fellowship.

Fellowship can be experienced only with living, loving beings who understand one another. That is why David said, "My soul thirsteth for God, for the *living* God." He wanted a personal encounter with the living God. This is what you and I desire. May God grant us that experience today.

Life Through the Knowledge of God January 8

GOD'S INVITATION

Ho, every one that thirsteth, come ye to the waters, and he that hath no money; come ye, buy, and eat; yea, come, buy wine and milk without money and without price. Isa. 55:1.

Today we have the invitation from God Himself to let Him satisfy the thirsts of the soul. These thirsts, and particularly the great thirst after God, in the depths of human hearts cannot be quenched by substitutes. Solomon attempted it. In Ecclesiastes 2 he tells how he tried pleasures abundant, built houses, planted vineyards, made gardens and parks, brought in slaves, amassed great possessions, and gathered treasures of every kind. He brought in singers, both men and women, and tried to satisfy every human desire. Yet he concluded by saying, "I hated life, because what is done under the sun was grievous to me; for all is vanity and a striving after wind" (Eccl. 2:17, R.S.V.). After this experience he closed his book by saying that this is "the conclusion of the whole matter: Fear God, and keep his commandments: for this is the whole duty of man" (Eccl. 12:13).

As ends in themselves, and apart from God, the things Solomon tried do not satisfy. It is only in touch with the Divine, in contact with the Source of life, and in harmony with the laws of life, that one finds happiness, peace of mind, and worth-whileness. Thus, the glorious truth is that all our true thirsts are quenched in the quenching of this one great thirst, the thirst for the living God. All basic human needs are met in Him, and they cannot be met apart from Him.

We are not self-sustaining, physically or spiritually. We cannot, within our own selves, quench our thirst for water. Neither can we, within our own hearts, satisfy, apart from God, the deepest longings of the soul. We need something above and beyond ourselves. We have, however, within us that which will respond with ever-increasing delight. And so to the thirsty soul the living God offers living water.

Life Through the Knowledge of God *January 9*

GOD'S PROMISE

And he said unto me, It is done. I am Alpha and Omega, the beginning and the end. I will give unto him that is athirst of the fountain of the water of life freely. Rev. 21:6.

Since God so graciously offers us of the fountain of the water of life, how shall we drink and live?

May I offer just two suggestions here. They are so simple, but so effective. First, simply ask. You remember, Jesus said to the woman of Samaria, "If thou knewest the gift of God, . . . thou wouldest have asked of him, and he would have given thee living water" (John 4:10). How true of us is the statement, "Ye have not, because ye ask not" (James 4:2).

In Chicago, when Foster Coats was editor of the *American,* a millionaire was being sued for divorce. The editor wanted a picture of the woman involved, so he sent his best man to get it. The man failed. Coats ordered more than one man to try. The day passed, and no photograph had been brought in. The reporters tried bribing the servants. A fake telephone repairman went through almost every room in the house without success. The deadline was approaching, and while the newspapermen were talking, a brisk young cub reporter hurried past. Coats then pointed in the youngster's direction, saying, "Send him to bring back a picture of her." Within an hour, he was back with one, and the editor called in the whole staff to hear a real piece of newspaper strategy.

"I asked her for her picture, and she gave it to me," the young reporter said.

So simple; almost unbelievable. Why not ask, then?

Second, drink. Eating and drinking are symbolic of fellowship. It is by taking time for fellowship with the Master—time to commune with Him—that we drink to our soul's satisfaction.

Those who thus drink will be like a watered garden. They will be like a tree planted by the rivers of water. Why not ask and drink today?

Life Through the Knowledge of God *January 10*

PHYSICALLY WE NEED GOD

O God, thou art my God; early will I seek thee: my soul thirsteth for thee, my flesh longeth for thee in a dry and thirsty land, where no water is. Ps. 63:1.

Even physically we need God. It is literally true that in God, our Creator, we live and move and have our being. "The mechanism of the human body cannot be fully understood; it presents mysteries that baffle the most intelligent. It is not as the result of a mechanism, which, once set in motion, continues its work, that the pulse beats and breath follows breath. In God we live and move and have our being. Every breath, every throb of the heart, is a continual evidence of the power of an ever-present God."—*Testimonies,* vol. 8, p. 260.

In the human body, then, we are in touch with the vital force of the universe in its highest physical manifestation. Every time a physician listens to a heartbeat with a stethoscope, he listens to the throbbing, pulsating power of God in the human life. As he checks the nervous system and follows the electric currents of energy through the body, he follows nothing more or less than the path of the power and life of God. As he deals with that system and the organs of sight and hearing, he deals with the avenues to the soul, the means by which God communicates with man.

The relation that exists between the body and the mind is very intimate. When one is affected, the other sympathizes. Physicians everywhere know this to be so true. Our bodies function best in an atmosphere of contentment. A contented mind, a cheerful spirit, is health to the body and strength to the soul. That is why we read, "A merry heart doeth good like a medicine" (Prov. 17:22), and "A sound heart is the life of the flesh" (Prov. 14:30).

It is also true that grief, anxiety, discontent, remorse, distrust, all tend to break down the life forces and to invite decay and death. "A broken spirit drieth the bones" (Prov. 17:22). Many a man's body longs for peace of mind, which God alone can supply.

Life Through the Knowledge of God January 11

THE WHOLE BEING NEEDS GOD

My soul longeth, yea, even fainteth for the courts of the Lord: my heart and my flesh crieth out for the living God. Ps. 84:2.

The whole being cries out after God. This is better understood in the light of the nature of man. Some would compare man to a three-story building, the first floor of which might represent the body; the second floor, the mind; and the third, the spirit. In their minds, each is separate and distinct from the others. This, however, is not a correct concept of man. The Bible teaches us that man is a being in which body and mind and spirit are all fused together.

When God created man, He formed him of the "dust of the ground, and breathed into his nostrils the breath of life; and man became a living soul" (Gen. 2:7). Notice, man became a living soul. He did not receive one. The living soul is not a separate entity, but a living being—a complete whole, made up of body, mind, and spirit. This is clearly manifest in every clinic where body-mind relationships are studied.

In mathematical addition, the whole is equal to the sum of its parts. But although this is true in figures, in man the whole is something more and different from the sum of its parts. Medical men have learned more and more about what each part of the body is for, but few have given enough consideration to what the whole man is for. The Bible teaches us that man was created for fellowship with God. Body, mind, and spirit all function together in making this fellowship with our Creator possible. This makes more meaningful what the psalmist had in mind when he said, "My soul longeth, . . . my heart and my flesh crieth out for the living God" (Ps. 84:2).

May God help us to see that we are made for fellowship with Him and that only in that fellowship can we truly live. May we consecrate body, mind, and spirit to God today.

Life Through the Knowledge of God *January 12*

BEHOLD YOUR GOD

O Zion, that bringest good tidings, get thee up into the high mountain; O Jerusalem, that bringest good tidings, lift up thy voice with strength; lift it up, be not afraid; say unto the cities of Judah, Behold your God! Isa. 40:9.

Today let us listen to the prophet as he bids us, "Behold your God!" In this fortieth chapter of Isaiah, in which our text is found, we have our God portrayed in His great sevenfold capacity.

He is presented here as the All-wise One with whom judgment, knowledge, and understanding originate. In contrast with Him, the nations of earth are as "a drop of a bucket." The whole world is as "small dust," the isles as a "very little thing." Nations are "as nothing," in fact, "less than nothing" before Him. He is also presented as the Creator of the heavens and the earth, to whom we can liken no one. Not only is He Creator, but He is also Upholder, the One in whom we have our strength—who "giveth power to the faint; and to them that have no might he increaseth strength" (Isa. 40:29).

He is again introduced as a great judge, whose reward is with Him. He is the king of the universe, before whom every valley will be exalted and every mountain and hill made low.

The All-wise One, the Creator, the Upholder, the Judge, the King, is also Shepherd and Comforter. Sometimes we stagger at the greatness of God. For us the prophet describes Him as a shepherd who lovingly carries the lambs in His arms and gently leads those that are with young. He presents Him, too, as the Comforter, saying, "Comfort ye, comfort ye my people" (Isa. 40:1).

In other words, He is just the God we need, a God who is strong in power, and who is in perfect control of all the forces of the universe. He is great enough to take care of a universe as vast as ours, and at the same time, He is the kind of God who knows and understands human hearts, who can give comfort where it is needed, and who can lead us as a shepherd leads his sheep. Such is our God.

Life Through the Knowledge of God *January 13*

INTELLECTUAL DIFFICULTIES

Canst thou by searching find out God? canst thou find out the Almighty unto perfection? Job 11:7.

"A boy was born 'mid little things,
  Between a little world and sky—
And dreamed not of the cosmic rings
  Round which the circling planets fly.

"He lived in little works and thoughts,
  Where little ventures grow and plod,
And paced and ploughed his little plots,
  And prayed unto his little God.

"But as the mighty system grew,
  His faith grew faint with many scars;
The Cosmos widened in his view—
  But God was lost among His stars.

"Another boy in lowly days,
  As he, to little things was born,
But gathered lore in woodland ways,
  And from the glory of the morn.

"As wider skies broke on his view,
  God greatened in his growing mind;
Each year he dreamed his God anew,
  And left his older God behind.

"He saw the boundless scheme dilate,
  In star and blossom, sky and clod;
And as the universe grew great,
  He dreamed for it a greater God."

By permission of Lothrop, Lee & Shepard Co., Inc.

Which boy represents your experience?

Life Through the Knowledge of God — January 14

GOD'S WAYS PAST FINDING OUT

O the depth of the riches both of the wisdom and knowledge of God! How unsearchable are his judgments, and his ways past finding out! Rom. 11:33.

A God we could understand would be inadequate for such a universe as ours. The story is told that Augustine was walking along the seashore one day trying to understand God. At this particular time he was concerned about the Trinity. He came upon a little fellow carrying water in a pail from the ocean to a little reservoir he had made. Welcoming a little respite from the strenuous mental exertion, he watched the little fellow for a while and finally asked, "What are you doing, son?" "I am trying to put the ocean in this little lake I made," replied the boy as he went after another pail of water. As Augustine walked on, he said to himself, "That is what I am trying to do. I am trying to get the great ocean of truth into my little mind."

Our text today points out that God's ways are past finding out. This is true, not because He deliberately hides from us to keep us bewildered, but because of our limitations. In every area of knowledge, even in the ways of men, we begin with fundamentals and increase in understanding as the horizons widen before us. The problems become more complex with every new thought. So it is in the knowledge of God and His ways. Solomon tells us the "path of the just is as the shining light, that shineth more and more unto the perfect day" (Prov. 4:18).

In Isaiah 55:8, 9 we read: "For my thoughts are not your thoughts, neither are your ways my ways, saith the Lord. For as the heavens are higher than the earth, so are my ways higher than your ways, and my thoughts than your thoughts." It is true that His ways are higher than ours, but where His ways and ours coincide they are reasonable. "Come now, and let us reason together, saith the Lord" (Isa. 1:18).

Aren't you glad His ways are past finding out? This gives room for growth. And what would we do throughout eternity if we learned all there is to know about God's ways now?

Life Through the Knowledge of God   *January 15*

Ye Shall Find Me

And ye shall seek me, and find me, when ye shall search for me with all your heart. Jer. 29:13.

It is one thing to know *about* God. It is something more to know *Him.* The most important question, then, is "How can I find Him personally?" Our text today is a wonderful promise. "Ye shall seek me, and find me."

Notice first the word "me." "Ye shall seek *me,* and find *me,* when ye shall search for *me.*" Too many of us are so concerned with our own interests that we forget God until sorrow comes. We are like children happy in their play, forgetting all about Mother, or even hoping she won't come to stop their fun. But when it begins to grow dark, then they cry for her.

It is also possible to be so concerned with trying to understand God's ways that we forget to look at God. Paul said, "I know whom I have believed, and am persuaded that he is able to keep that which I have committed unto him against that day" (2 Tim. 1:12). He did not say, "I know *what* I believe and am satisfied that I have the answers to all of life's questions." No, he said, "I know *whom* I have believed." It was his faith in the person of God and fellowship with Him that gave Paul the courage for which he is so noted.

When many disciples walked no more with Jesus because they could not understand His sayings, Jesus asked the twelve, "Will ye also go away?" Peter replied, "Lord, to whom shall we go? thou hast the words of eternal life." That is the secret; when you find the *Person,* nothing else matters.

Notice, too, "Ye shall . . . find me, when ye shall search for me with all your heart." Divided loyalty will not work. We cannot have fellowship with God and harbor evil in our hearts as well. True fellowship is not enjoyed with reservations. When we love with all our hearts, there are no barriers. This kind of fellowship God wants to enjoy with us today.

Life Through the Knowledge of God January 16

THE EARTH IS FULL OF HIS RICHES

O Lord, how manifold are thy works! in wisdom hast thou made them all: the earth is full of thy riches. Ps. 104:24.

Everywhere, God has made Himself known. The earth is full of His riches. If we but look, we shall find. This is so beautifully expressed in the following quotation:

"From the solemn roll of the deep-toned thunder and old ocean's ceaseless roar, to the glad songs that make the forests vocal with melody, nature's ten thousand voices speak His praise. In earth and sea and sky, with their marvelous tint and color, varying in gorgeous contrast or blended in harmony, we behold His glory. The everlasting hills tell us of His power. The trees that wave their green banners in the sunlight, and the flowers in their delicate beauty, point to their Creator. The living green that carpets the brown earth tells of God's care for the humblest of His creatures. The caves of the sea and the depths of the earth reveal His treasures. He who placed the pearls in the ocean and the amethyst and chrysolite among the rocks, is a lover of the beautiful. The sun rising in the heavens is a representative of Him who is the life and light of all that He has made. All the brightness and beauty that adorn the earth and light up the heavens, speak of God. . . . All things tell of His tender, fatherly care, and of His desire to make His children happy."—*The Ministry of Healing,* pp. 411, 412.

Too often we study nature merely to discover the facts about the world in which we live. Or we look upon nature merely as a work of art, to discover its beauty, study its grandeur, or admire its delicate shades of color. In either case, the scientist or the artist may fail to see God. But if, in addition to searching for facts and studying its beauty, we recognize the hand of God, wonderful will be the result. When science and art combine with religion in the study of nature, glorious experiences in fellowship with the Creator will follow.

Life Through the Knowledge of God   *January 17*

Find Him in the Starry Hosts

Lift up your eyes on high, and behold who hath created these things, that bringeth out their host by number: he calleth them all by names by the greatness of his might, for that he is strong in power; not one faileth. Isa. 40:26.

In the days of the French Revolution, when the state was against the church, every minister, priest, and evangelist was driven from his pulpit, and many paid with their lives. Churches were made into stables, and Bibles were burned. The Goddess of Reason was set up, and men were forced to worship her. Men ordained by the council were sent to spy on men who held to their religious beliefs. One man came to the Vaudois valley and found a peasant worshiping God. "You worship Him?" he said. "If there is a God, why doesn't He strike us down for doing wrong? We have burned His churches or made them into stables, and killed His priests." The old peasant, unlettered and unlearned, replied, "Yes, but you have left us the stars." The heavens declare the glory of God. This revelation man cannot erase.

"O God, Thy heavens, in the hush of night,
So awesome, with their galaxies alight,
Stir to their depths our silent, brooding souls,
As, all above, the wondrous scroll unrolls.

"In tones more awesome than the scene we scan
Thy voice bespeaketh, in the heart of man,
A way of life comporting with Thine own,
Who hast not left us in the dark alone.

"O Living Spirit, all our powers reclaim;
Let Thy compassion set our souls aflame;
Form Thou in us a purpose true and pure,
That what we build together may endure. Amen."

—Henry B. Robins

Life Through the Knowledge of God   *January 18*

FIND HIM IN THE FIRMAMENT

The heavens declare the glory of God; and the firmament sheweth his handywork. **Ps. 19:1.**

We have seen God's greatness in the starry heavens. Today let us look closer. Let us see Him in the firmament. The air we breathe, composed of oxygen and nitrogen, is in just the right proportions to be used by the human body. The carbon dioxide released by man and animals is used by plants. Thus, a continuous cycle is set up to sustain all living things on the earth. Only a master mind could have planned such a system.

The firmament also provides an outstanding irrigation system. Just think! It would be a gigantic task for the greatest engineers in the world to free enough of the water in the ocean of its salt to irrigate even a few acres. How shall water be provided for the whole earth? In a marvelous way the sun draws the fresh, sweet water up from the ocean into the heavens, where clouds are formed. These are carried over the earth by air currents, and a delicately controlled and balanced thermal system brings about gradual condensation, causing showers of rain. No wonder we read, "Dost thou know the balancings of the clouds?" (Job 37:16).

That is not all. An excellent system of storage, locks, and canals provides for proper distribution. Snow, formed in the atmosphere, is stored, gradually melting and running into lakes and rivers to water the earth.

As we look for God in the firmament we see Him still more gloriously revealed in the sunset. Here one beholds, as it were, the very robe of the Creator in gorgeous, changing colors such as no royal potentate of earth can ever wear.

Arched in wonderful beauty is the rainbow, which joins the other witnesses in proclaiming glory to His name.

Thus, in the very atmosphere we breathe, in every raindrop that falls, in every ray of sunlight, we see our Father's glory manifest.

Life Through the Knowledge of God   *January 19*

FIND HIM IN THE MOUNTAINS

I will lift up mine eyes unto the hills, from whence cometh my help. My help cometh from the Lord, which made heaven and earth. Ps. 121:1, 2.

In the Revised Standard Version, this text reads, "I lift up my eyes to the hills. From whence does my help come? My help comes from the Lord, who made heaven and earth."

There is something about the mountains that lifts us above the noise of earth, nearer to God. As one puts it:

"Above the clouds, the sun shines and we can see farther than from down below. In town we are circumscribed in thought and vision. Our minds are hindered by the clamor and our minds are shut in by man-made structures that hide the sky. Even the eye of the soul finds it hard to penetrate the murky atmosphere of everyday affairs. But upon the hills the horizon broadens."

I like this prayer written by Grace Noll Crowell. Let us make it our prayer for today.

> "Maker of mountains—
> Creator of their beauty and their might,
> I lift my small and human heart to Thee,
> Fill it, I pray, with something of their might,
> Their steadfastness, their high serenity;
> Sweep it with canyon winds, and wash it clean
> With clear cold water from the eternal snow,
> Let these bright torrents purge it, let all mean
> Desires and passions leave it—let me go
> Back to the lowlands, back to the crowded days,
> Poised and sustained, and ready for my part,
> Let me go back, schooled in the mountain ways,
> Bearing their old vast secrets in my heart. Amen."

—Taken from *Light of the Years*. Copyright 1936 by Harper & Brothers. Used by permission.

Life Through the Knowledge of God **January 20**

FIND HIM IN THE SEA

They that go down to the sea in ships, that do business in great waters; these see the works of the Lord, and his wonders in the deep. Ps. 107:23, 24.

Many a man has found God in the sea because he feared for his life on a sinking vessel. Like Peter, he cried out, "Lord, save me!" But you can find God in the sea in so many positive ways if you look for Him. William Cullen Bryant once wrote:

> "The sea is mighty, but a mightier sways
> His restless billows. Thou, whose hands have scooped
> His boundless gulfs and built his shore, thy breath,
> That moved in the beginning o'er his face,
> Moves o'er it evermore. The obedient waves
> To its strong motion roll, and rise and fall."

You can almost hear God's voice saying, "Thus far shalt thou come, and no farther," as you watch the great waves break upon the shore.

There is a depth to the ocean no man can fathom. And beneath the wild commotion of the billowy foam, there is peaceful stillness, undisturbed by wind and storm. God is like that.

An unknown author has given us another vision of God in the sea, in these words:

> "We can only see a little of the ocean,
>   Just a few miles distant from the rocky shore;
> But out there—far beyond our eyes' horizon,
>   There's more—immeasurably more.
>
> "We can only see a little of God's loving—
>   A few rich treasures from His mighty store;
> But out there—far beyond our eyes' horizon,
>   There's more—immeasurably more."

Let us trust Him today.

Life Through the Knowledge of God   *January 21*

FIND HIM IN THE SANCTUARY

To see thy power and thy glory, so as I have seen thee in the sanctuary. **Ps. 63:2.**

How difficult it is to visualize the invisible! When Israel of old left Egypt and encamped about Mount Sinai, God said, "And let them make me a sanctuary; that I may dwell among them" (Ex. 25:8). In Egypt, Israel had become accustomed to seeing visible representations of deities. Now, they were brought out to worship a God they could not see. It is difficult for people to visualize an invisible God. To them, then, Moses represented God. When he went up into the mountain to commune with God for the people and to receive instructions for them, he was gone forty days. During this time, having no one they could see, they prevailed upon Aaron to make for them a golden calf, which was to represent the God who brought them out of Egypt.

God understood their weakness and their need. In order to help them visualize the invisible, they were instructed to build a sanctuary, and in this sanctuary God would make Himself known. God loves His people. He longs for fellowship with them. For this purpose God created man. Sin has separated man from Him. But, even so, He wants to dwell with His children. That was another reason He wanted them to make the sanctuary—"that I may dwell among them." For this purpose we have the church and its services today.

As a pastor approached the entrance of his beautiful church in one of our large cities, he noticed a little boy with his eye pressed against the crack between the two great doors. Hearing the footsteps of the pastor, the little fellow turned around and said, "Say, Mister, is God in there?" What a wonderful opportunity this was for the pastor to take the little fellow by the hand into the church to tell him about God. God wants to reveal Himself in every sanctuary.

May God grant that every pastor who stands in His place may rightly represent Him, and that every worshiper may see God's power and glory in the church as David saw Him in the sanctuary.

Life Through the Knowledge of God   *January 22*

GOD'S WAY IN THE SANCTUARY

Thy way, O God, is in the sanctuary: who is so great a God as our God? **Ps. 77:13.**

When one reads about the sanctuary in the Old Testament, he is impressed with the many sacrifices that were offered. The questions arise, "How do these sacrifices reveal God? What do they teach us about Him?"

Concerning the circumstances surrounding the first sacrifices, we read in *The Desire of Ages* (1940), page 115:

"With intense interest he [Satan] watched the sacrifices offered by Adam and his sons. In these ceremonies he discerned a symbol of communion between earth and heaven. He set himself to intercept this communion. He misrepresented God, and misinterpreted the rites that pointed to the Saviour. Men were led to fear God as one who delighted in their destruction. The sacrifices that should have revealed His love were offered only to appease His wrath."

God's original purpose in providing the sacrificial system was to teach man, through an object lesson, that sin causes death; that God would provide a substitute—someone to die in his stead; that forgiveness was possible if sins were confessed.

Instead of God's demanding a sacrifice, we see, in the sacrificial service, God Himself the sacrifice. God so loved the world that He gave, not demanded, a sacrifice. The law of self-sacrificing love is the law of life for earth and heaven, of which God Himself is the embodiment. We should be more than willing to sacrifice for Him.

Satan takes the truth, "The wages of sin is death" (Rom. 6:23), and twists it in man's thinking to read, "The wages of God is death," in order that men might hate God or serve Him from fear. God wants men to love Him and to understand that sin brings sorrow, heartache, and death.

In the sanctuary we learn that "the wages of sin is death; but the gift of God is eternal life through Jesus Christ our Lord."

The Father Himself Loves Us

At that day ye shall ask in my name: and I say not unto you, that I will pray the Father for you: for the Father himself loveth you, because ye have loved me, and have believed that I came out from God. John 16:26, 27.

There was once a boy who had the bad habit of leaving the gates and barn doors open when he did the chores. His father would get after him time and again, but the boy seemed unable to learn his lesson.

One evening special activity was scheduled for the boys of the neighborhood. The father gave his son permission to go, after the chores were done. Naturally, the boy was in a hurry and as usual, he left the gate open, as well as the door to the granary. Soon a cow wandered into the granary and began eating grain. Fortunately, the father discovered the cow in time, and after taking care of the cow, proceeded to take care of the boy. On the wall of the granary was a large "black snake"—one of those long flexible whips that some men know how to use. When the boy saw his father reach for the whip, he knew there was trouble. He made for the house as fast as he could go. In the kitchen, then, we have a very interesting scene. We see an angry father, a little sinner, and a loving mother who steps in between to see that the wrath of an angry father might cool a bit before justice is administered.

Many people have such a concept of God. They picture Him as an angry God demanding the blood of the sinner, and then, a loving Jesus steps between. That is not a true picture of God. Our heavenly Father has been misrepresented. Satan has twisted the thinking of men and women to believe that God must be persuaded to have mercy on man, and that God needs to be reconciled to man. It is not God who needs to be reconciled. Man is the one who needs reconciling. "God was in Christ reconciling the world unto himself. . . . Be *ye* reconciled to God" (2 Cor. 5:19, 20).

The Father Himself loves us. Let us respond to His love.

Life Through the Knowledge of God   *January 24*

HIS WAYS ARE JUST AND TRUE

And they sing the song of Moses the servant of God, and the song of the Lamb, saying, Great and marvellous are thy works, Lord God Almighty; just and true are thy ways, thou King of saints. Rev. 15:3.

In the sanctuary we have seen God's desire to dwell with man. We have seen His love manifested in providing a sacrifice—Himself, in Christ, the sacrifice—that we might live. We have seen His wonderful wisdom in providing a mediator, through whom He can reconcile sinners to Himself.

Today, consider another revelation of the character of God in the Day of Atonement, which was part of the sanctuary service. This was a day of judgment. God is a God of judgment. We would not want Him otherwise. God wants this tragic controversy with evil settled in a way satisfactory to all concerned. It will be. There will be a day when God and all His universe will be "at one" again. Atonement means at-one-ment. When it is complete, God Himself will be satisfied, for we read, "He shall see of the travail of his soul, and shall be satisfied" (Isa. 53:11). Man will be satisfied, for all will exclaim, as our text indicates today, "Great and marvellous are thy works, Lord God Almighty; just and true are thy ways, thou King of saints." Even sinners will be satisfied, for "'every knee shall bow to me, and every tongue shall give praise to God'" (Rom. 14:11, R.S.V.).

The whole universe will be satisfied. "Every creature which is in heaven, and on the earth, and under the earth, and in the sea, and all that are in them, heard I saying, Blessing, and honour, and glory, and power, be unto him that sitteth upon the throne, and unto the Lamb for ever and ever" (Rev. 5:13). And when all is over, "affliction shall not rise up the second time" (Nahum 1:9) and "the former shall not be remembered, nor come into mind" (Isa. 65:17). Why not? Because they will have been settled so satisfactorily that no one will ever worry about them again. What wonderful wisdom is manifest in God's provision for the satisfaction of all involved.

Life Through the Knowledge of God *January 25*

GOD DRAWS US IN LOVE

The Lord hath appeared of old unto me, saying, Yea, I have loved thee with an everlasting love: therefore with lovingkindness have I drawn thee. Jer. 31:3.

There are times when we wonder why God allows us to suffer, if He loves us so. Why didn't God destroy Satan in the very beginning and spare us the sickness, disease, and death caused by Satan?

In *The Desire of Ages* (1940), page 759, we have the answer:

"God could have destroyed Satan and his sympathizers as easily as one can cast a pebble to the earth; but He did not do this. Rebellion was not to be overcome by force. Compelling power is found only under Satan's government. The Lord's principles are not of this order. His authority rests upon goodness, mercy, and love; and the presentation of these principles is the means to be used. God's government is moral, and truth and love are to be the prevailing power."

God could have made beings who could do nought but serve Him. But this would never satisfy His heart of love, any more than loving a robot would satisfy our hearts. For this reason He gave creatures the power of choice. Lucifer and his followers chose sin. Suffering resulted.

God wants only the service of love, and only love awakens love. It cannot be commanded or won by force or authority.

Sometimes God uses the motive of fear, temporarily, to keep men from destroying themselves, until He can teach them that He loves them. A father uses the motive of fear to keep a child from running into the street, until he can understand. So God, though unwillingly, has used the motive of fear to keep men from destroying themselves. Sin is self-destructive. Men would destroy themselves if God did not intervene. But He wants us to serve Him, not from fear, but because we know it is the only thing that brings joy and happiness.

When we suffer, He suffers with us. When we get discouraged, He still loves us, for His love is everlasting. Let us respond to His loving-kindness today.

Life Through the Knowledge of God *January 26*

BE STILL AND KNOW

Be still, and know that I am God: I will be exalted among the heathen, I will be exalted in the earth. Ps. 46:10.

"An intensity such as never before was seen is taking possession of the world. In amusement, in money-making, in the contest for power, in the very struggle for existence, there is a terrible force that engrosses body and mind and soul. In the midst of this maddening rush, God is speaking. He bids us come apart and commune with Him. 'Be still, and know that I am God' (Psalm 46:10).

"Many, even in their seasons of devotion, fail of receiving the blessing of real communion with God. They are in too great haste. With hurried steps they press through the circle of Christ's loving presence, pausing perhaps a moment within the sacred precincts, but not waiting for counsel."—*Education,* p. 260.

Let us make the words of Whittier our prayer for the day.

> "Dear Lord and Father of mankind,
>   Forgive our feverish ways;
> Reclothe us in our rightful mind,
> In purer lives Thy service find,
>   In deeper reverence, praise.
>
> .   .   .   .
>
> "Drop Thy still dews of quietness,
>   Till all our strivings cease,
> Take from our souls the strain and stress,
> And let our ordered lives confess
>   The beauty of Thy peace.
>
> "Breathe through the heats of our desire,
>   Thy coolness and Thy balm;
> Let sense be dumb, let flesh retire;
> Speak through the earthquake, wind, and fire,
>   O still small voice of calm!"

Life Through the Knowledge of God

January 27

LIKE A POTTER

But now, O Lord, thou art our Father; we are the clay, and thou our potter; and we all are the work of thy hand. Isa. 64:8.

A common picture of God and His relation to His creatures is that of the potter and the clay. When we think about God as a potter, we think first of His sovereignty. The potter has complete and absolute power over the wheels and the clay. So has God over His universe. All who rebel against this find out sooner or later that it is true. To be God, He must be sovereign. This is both sobering and comforting. It is sobering in that you cannot get away from God. Eventually, all will face this fact—when it is too late. Why not acknowledge Him now and rejoice? It is comforting in that "above the distractions of the earth He sits enthroned; all things are open to His divine survey; and from His great and calm eternity He orders that which His providence sees best."—*The Ministry of Healing,* p. 417.

In the potter-clay picture of God, we see not only sovereignty but also purpose as well. A potter has a purpose for the clay, and he operates the wheels with that purpose in mind. God has an eternal purpose that He is working out through Jesus Christ our Lord—a purpose for the universe and a purpose for every life. It is not always clear what His purpose is, but He is an intelligent, capable workman with the ability to accomplish His purpose. This is comforting.

To know that the Potter is absolute sovereign can be terrorizing, and to know that He has a purpose, and will accomplish that purpose, can lead to fatalism, unless we look at the person of the Potter. It is our loving heavenly Father who is the potter. Our greatest good is His desire and purpose. If you study the foot that turns the wheel and the hand that presses the clay, you will see nailprints there. These are the marks of love. To such a potter we can gladly yield ourselves as clay. Let us make the old familiar hymn "Have Thine Own Way, Lord" our prayer for the day.

Life Through the Knowledge of God January 28

OUR REFUGE AND OUR FORTRESS

I will say of the Lord, He is my refuge and my fortress: my God; in him will I trust. Ps. 91:2.

Isaiah gives us the following picture of God to help us understand Him: "Like as the lion and the young lion roaring on his prey, when a multitude of shepherds is called forth against him, he will not be afraid of their voice, nor abase himself for the noise of them: so shall the Lord of hosts come down to fight for mount Zion, and for the hill thereof" (Isa. 31:4). God is likened to a lion roaring on his prey. When a multitude of shepherds is called out against him, he is "not terrified by their shouting or daunted at their noise" (R.S.V.). A strange picture of God is this. Why did Isaiah not picture God as a shepherd, with a multitude of lions roaring about, in the midst of which he carries the lamb unafraid?

There are times in human experience when God seems lionlike and cruel—times when all the entreaties or shouting of shepherds seem of no avail. He just seems to continue to roar. As the psalmist puts it, "Flood follows flood, as thy cataracts thunder, thy breakers and billows are all surging over me" (Ps. 42:9, Moffatt). These are the times when clouds hang so low on life's horizon that we cannot see the everlasting hills. But these are the very times when we need a God who is strong as a lion—a God who is undisturbed by all the conflicts of earth. It is this concept of God that gives one a security in this world, where nothing seems secure. As our text for today indicates, "God is my refuge and my fortress: . . . in him will I trust."

There is so much that we cannot understand about God. But He understands us. And though we need to think of God as a shepherd in this great controversy between good and evil, we need also to think of Him as a mighty fortress. We need, occasionally, to sing with Luther, "A mighty fortress is our God, A bulwark never failing; Our helper He, amid the flood Of mortal ills prevailing."

Today, ally yourself with Him and be secure.

Life Through the Knowledge of God *January 29*

LIKE A LITTLE MOTHER BIRD

As birds flying, so will the Lord of hosts defend Jerusalem; defending also he will deliver it; and passing over he will preserve it. Isa. 31:5.

Sometimes God is like a lion roaring on his prey. Today's text presents another picture in wonderful contrast. "As birds flying." The word "birds" here, in the Hebrew, is diminutive and feminine; and "flying" is actually "hovering." The picture, then, is one of a little mother bird hovering over her young in the nest. What a contrast! Though God sometimes appears lionlike and cruel, if we could only see, we would find His heart as warm and tender and loving as that of a little mother bird. This is your God and mine. According to our text, it is such a God who defends, delivers, and preserves us.

In this warfare with the forces of evil we need a defense that is sure. We need deliverance, for, already, sin has a hold on us that we cannot break in our own strength. We need also to be kept by His power. Knowing this about God will enable us to trust Him even though we do not always understand.

When Dr. and Mrs. Einstein came to America, the news reporters gathered around Mrs. Einstein. They asked her, "Do you understand the complicated theory of relativity for which your husband is so famous?" "No," replied Mrs. Einstein, with a twinkle in her eye, "I do not understand Dr. Einstein's theory, but I understand Dr. Einstein." So we may not understand God's ways, but we can understand God.

In contemplation of the greatness of God and the vastness of the universe we may wonder, "Does God take notice of me?" Remember, then, the words of Jesus, "Are not five sparrows sold for two farthings, and not one of them is forgotten before God? But even the very hairs of your head are all numbered. Fear not therefore: ye are of more value than many sparrows" (Luke 12:6, 7). Our God, who has a heart as warm and tender as a little mother bird, and who does not forget the tiny feathered creatures, will not forget His children.

Life Through the Knowledge of God   January 30

THOSE WHO KNOW GOD DO EXPLOITS

And such as do wickedly against the covenant shall he corrupt by flatteries: but the people that do know their God shall be strong, and do exploits. Dan. 11:32.

Right in the heart of the complicated prophecy of Daniel 11 is the statement, "The people that do know their God shall be strong, and do exploits." It has always been so. Men and women who have learned to know God have been the men and women who have done things for Him, and whose names are written large in the record that counts.

A vision of God always gives a man strength and true perspective. First, he sees himself as he really is. It was when Job experienced a vision of God that he exclaimed, "I have heard of thee by the hearing of the ear: but now mine eye seeth thee. Wherefore I abhor myself, and repent in dust and ashes" (Job 42:5, 6).

It was when Isaiah saw the Lord sitting on the throne, high and lifted up, that he, too, exclaimed, "Woe is me! for I am undone; . . . for mine eyes have seen the King, the Lord of hosts" (Isa. 6:5). Not only does this vision of God cause us to see our own weaknesses, but it also inspires us to dedicate all our talents to the service of God. So it was that in answer to the question "Whom shall I send, and who will go for us?" Isaiah replied, "Here am I; send me" (Isa. 6:8).

It was when Saul of Tarsus, on the way to Damascus, caught a vision of God in Jesus Christ that he channeled all his energies—once directed against God's people—into the lines of constructive activity for the cause of God.

It is when you and I learn to know the Lord that we, too, will be drawn to Him. In comparison with His character, our own littleness stands out, and we will realize our dependence upon Him. Then, He can take us and use us as He sees fit. Let us dedicate all our talents to His service. Let us be the men and women depicted in the prophecy, and arise and do exploits for God in these great days in which we live.

Life Through the Knowledge of God   *January 31*

INCREASING IN THE KNOWLEDGE OF GOD

That ye might walk worthy of the Lord unto all pleasing, being fruitful in every good work, and increasing in the knowledge of God. Col. 1:10.

This past month we have been thinking about God and about the statement of Jesus, "This is life eternal, that they might know thee the only true God, and Jesus Christ, whom thou hast sent" (John 17:3).

In the things of God, with every new realization comes greater anticipation. For the more we know, the more we see there is to know, and before the earnest seeker for truth there is a continual line of progress.

Every aspect of life is affected when we know the Lord. Our attitude toward sin changes. Too often, human beings love sin and hate God. But when we know God, we learn to hate sin and love God.

Our attitude toward our fellow men becomes more wholesome and redemptive when we know the Lord. If we believe that God is critical and faultfinding, we will be. A study of history reveals that a nation's civilization is determined by its religion. People's concept of God determines their conduct and many of their customs. A true knowledge of God makes us Godlike. We read of the Sadducees of old, "Their ideas of God molded their own character. As in their view He had no interest in man, so they had little regard for one another."—*The Desire of Ages* (1940), p. 604.

Our prayer life becomes richer as we increase in the knowledge of God. We always find it much easier to commune with one we know. In every area of experience in Christian living there is joyful fellowship and growth when we know God. And the more of the fruits of this fellowship we manifest, the more we will "walk worthy of the Lord unto all pleasing" (Col. 1:10).

Let us pray that we may grow in grace and in knowledge of Him, and that we may be more fruitful in every good work.

FEBRUARY

Life in Christ *February 1*

The Fountain of Life

For with thee is the fountain of life: in thy light shall we see light. Ps. 36:9.

Have you ever read the parable of the "Men Who Made the River Flow?" "A good but unlearned man who had lived all his life in an arid region and had never seen a river set out to explore the world. In the course of his travels, he came to a river on the bank of which was a mill. Entering the mill, he was puzzled by the wheels, shafts, pulleys and belts, all of them in motion. 'Why do they go round?' he wondered. He looked out and saw the great water wheel turning and the water in violent motion. Then it dawned on him. 'The little wheels turn the big shaft that turns the great wheel in the water, and thus, the river is made to flow!'

"Having made this wonderful discovery, the thought came to him: 'What if the machinery should stop and the river cease flowing! What a terrible calamity that would be, for I have heard that rivers are most useful to mankind.'

"Just then, a floating branch became entangled with the water wheel, and the machinery slackened. 'There! It's stopping now! How fortunate that I came!' Seizing a belt, he pulled lustily and continued pulling; the wheels kept turning, and the river continued to flow.

"It was hard work, and he became very tired. But before he was completely exhausted, some of his friends entered the door. They, too, had decided to travel. When the situation was explained to them, and they understood how important it was to keep the wheels turning in order that the river might not stop, they took hold in good will and, by turns, pulled the belts, kept the wheels going and prevented the river from stopping."—*The Prism.*

How much we are like the men who made the river flow. Our text today reminds us that life has its source in Christ.

Life in Christ *February 2*

Fountains Versus Broken Cisterns

For my people have committed two evils; they have forsaken me the fountain of living waters, and hewed them out cisterns, broken cisterns, that can hold no water. Jer. 2:13.

What a contrast! On the one hand is a cool bubbling spring, ever ready to quench the thirst of the weary traveler. On the other hand is a broken cistern. Any water in it is gradually leaking out. Often one lifts the cover to quench his thirst and finds only cobwebs. Can you imagine forsaking the spring for the leaky cistern? Yet that is what many do in life today when they turn away from Him who is the fountain of life to seek satisfaction at the world's broken cisterns.

Many human hearts are like broken cisterns, ever needing repairing and refilling. Never happy within themselves, they find life empty and dry when someone else stops making them happy. They are always needing spiritual help. During a revival service, a camp meeting, or a week of prayer they thrill with new emotions. But after a while this inspiration, too, runs out, and they are discouraged—"broken cisterns, that can hold no water."

Human hearts need not be like broken cisterns. To the woman of Samaria, Jesus said, "Whosoever drinketh of this water shall thirst again: but whosoever drinketh of the water that I shall give him shall never thirst; but the water that I shall give him shall be in him a well of water springing up into everlasting life" (John 4:13, 14).

On another occasion Jesus said, "If any man thirst, let him come unto me, and drink. He that believeth on me, as the scripture hath said, out of his belly shall flow rivers of living water" (John 7:37, 38). This river of living water refers to the Holy Spirit, which all who believe on Jesus receive (see verse 39).

Are you like a broken cistern? Look to Christ, the Fountain of living water, and become a blessing to others—yourself a fountain of living water. With David you then can say, "My cup runneth over" (Ps. 23:5).

Life in Christ
February 3

IN HIM WAS LIFE

In him was life; and the life was the light of men. John 1:4.

In a certain country the government sends some people to certain mines, where they spend the rest of their lives, never again coming up to the light. Children are born there, and live there for years knowing no brighter world than the one the torchlighted tunnels afford. Life without Christ in this world of sin is like that. The lights of the non-Christian religions of the world are but dim candlelights in comparison with the sunlight of Christianity.

Think what it would mean to one of the children born in the mines referred to, to be brought out of his damp, dark, narrow confines into the fresh air, the bright sun, the beautiful fields and wide landscapes of the upper world. Coming in touch with Jesus Christ for the first time is like that.

Our text today tells us that the *life* is the light of men. That which lifts men out of darkness into light is a wonderful life.

"I'd rather see a sermon than hear one any day;
I'd rather one should walk with me than merely tell the way.
The eye's a better pupil and more willing than the ear,
Fine counsel is confusing, but example's always clear;
And the best of all the preachers are the men who live their creeds,
For to see good put in action is what everybody needs.

. . . . .

"When I see a deed of kindness, I am eager to be kind.
When a weaker brother stumbles and a strong man stays behind
Just to see if he can help him, then the wish grows strong in me
To become as big and thoughtful as I know that friend to be.
And all travelers can witness that the best of guides to-day
Is not the one who tells them, but the one who shows the way."

—"Sermons We See," from the *Collected Verse* of Edgar A. Guest, copyright 1934, the Reilly & Lee Co., Chicago.

Life in Christ *February 4*

HE THAT HATH THE SON HATH LIFE

He that hath the Son hath life; and he that hath not the Son of God hath not life. 1 John 5:12.

If you have Jesus, you have life; and if you do not have Jesus, you do not have life. "He that hath the Son." What does it mean to *have* the Son? John tells us what he means in the next verse. He says, "These things have I written unto you that believe on the name of the Son of God; that ye may know that ye have eternal life, and that ye may believe on the name of the Son of God."

To have the Son is to believe on His name. To believe on His name means more than just a mental assent or an intellectual acceptance of the fact that Jesus is the Son of God, for the devils believe that and tremble. It means to believe and trust with all your heart.

The gift of eternal life God promises to all who accept His Son, and "whatever gift He promises, is in the promise itself. 'The seed is the word of God.' As surely as the oak is in the acorn, so surely is the gift of God in His promise. If we receive the promise, we have the gift."—*Education,* p. 253.

Note the statement, "As the oak is in the acorn." Have you ever taken apart a seed, such as a peanut or a bean, and noticed the little plant within? God's word—His promise—Jesus compared to the seed. Just as the plant is in the seed, so is the gift in the promise. If, then, you accept the promises of God—if you believe them with all your heart—you have the gifts He promised. The gift of eternal life is in His promise of eternal life. When we accept God's Word, we accept Him who is the Word, and in accepting Him we have life.

Now then, to have life means to have understanding, faith, hope, love, power to think and to do, power to overcome life's enemies, and power to meet the demands of the hour—it means to have satisfaction and joy in service. Our text points out that to have what really counts in life, we must believe in Jesus and accept His promises. In these promises we have the very gifts He offers.

Life in Christ   *February 5*

I Am the Life

Jesus saith unto him, I am the way, the truth, and the life: no man cometh unto the Father, but by me. **John 14:6.**

Our text was Jesus' answer to Thomas' question, "Lord, we know not whither thou goest; and how can we know the way?" Jesus might have answered something like this: "Well, Thomas, I am going back to heaven, where my Father is, and where I shall prepare the mansions I told you about, and the way for you to get there is to live right—keep the commandments, love God and your fellow men, keep praying, studying, and working for others—and I'll come back to get you."

Instead, He said, "*I* am the way. *I* am the truth. *I* am the life. No man cometh unto the Father but by *me.*" Here lies the secret. Salvation comes, not in knowing the way, understanding the truth, or trying to live the life, but from Him who said, "I am"—the Person.

On one occasion Jesus spoke words difficult to understand. He said, "Except ye eat the flesh of the Son of man, and drink his blood, ye have no life in you" (John 6:53). No one understood Him. "What kind of talk is this? Does He expect us to be cannibals?" Many of His disciples walked no more with Him. Jesus turned to the twelve and said, "Will ye also go away?" In Peter's reply we have the truth of our text revealed. Peter said, "Lord, to whom shall we go? thou hast the words of eternal life. And we believe and are sure that thou art that Christ, the Son of the living God" (John 6:68, 69). Note the words, "To *whom* shall we go?"

Paul, too, understood when he wrote, "I know whom I have believed, and am persuaded that he is able to keep that which I have committed unto him against that day" (2 Tim. 1:12). Paul didn't say, "I know what I have believed," but, "I know *whom* I have believed." Not *what,* but *whom.*

Truth apart from the Person lays no hold on the human heart. In Christ truth lives and saves. I may not understand all the deep things of God, but I can understand **Him** through Jesus.

Life in Christ   *February 6*

Present and Future

Verily I say unto you, There is no man that hath left house, or parents, or brethren, or wife, or children, for the kingdom of God's sake, who shall not receive manifold more in this present time, and in the world to come life everlasting. **Luke 18:29, 30.**

The Christian life is not just a "pie in the sky someday" philosophy. Religionists talk a great deal about the life hereafter. The expressions "everlasting life," "live for ever and ever," et cetera, are prominent in the teaching of Christianity. Especially do Seventh-day Adventists talk about the coming kingdom and the new earth. And this is right. However, if not careful, we shall think of the blessings of Christianity in terms of life hereafter and forget the life here and now. There is danger of having too much futurism in our Adventism. According to Jesus, the rewards of Christian living are many in this present life also.

Is not the only life worth continuing throughout eternity the life that is worth while now? Why prolong forever that which has no value?

To think of the rewards of Christianity as being given out in the far-distant future alone is to consider the Christian religion a merit system. Jesus did not say, "I have come to outline a system by which you can merit eternal life." He said, "I am come that you might have life now and eternally."

It is not a matter of choosing between life now or life hereafter; it is a matter of choosing whether you want to begin living now, with the assurance of continuing to live with ever-increasing satisfaction throughout eternity, or whether you want to lose out on both for a few hours of pseudo pleasure.

Today's text is the answer to Peter's question, "Lord, we have left everything. What shall we have, therefore?" Jesus made it plain that true Christians who have forsaken things most precious to the human heart—possessions and loved ones—for the sake of the kingdom, will find more of both, here on earth and in the hereafter.

All the Treasures of Wisdom and Knowledge

In whom are hid all the treasures of wisdom and knowledge. Col. 2:3.

Russell H. Conwell tells the story of an ancient Persian by the name of Al Hafed. He was a wealthy and contented man. In the course of events there came a priest of Buddha who talked by Al Hafed's fireside, of gold and silver and diamonds. A mine of diamonds would purchase a whole kingdom.

That night Al Hafed could not sleep. He considered himself a poor man. He wanted to find a diamond mine. "What do you want with diamonds?" asked the priest the next morning. "I wish to be rich and place my children on thrones through the influence of their wealth."

Al Hafed sold his farm at a forced price; collected his money, which had been at interest; left his family in the care of a neighbor; and was off to search for diamonds. He searched far and wide through Arabia, Egypt, Palestine, Spain, and elsewhere. At last, sad and disillusioned, poor Al Hafed threw himself into the sea.

One day Al Hafed's successor on the old farm saw a flash of light from a pebble in the white sands of the shallow stream where he watered his camels. He took it to the house and left it on the mantel. A few days later the same old priest who had instructed Al Hafed, came to visit the new owner of the farm. The moment he entered he recognized the stone as a diamond. The two rushed out into the garden, and lo, other gems more valuable and more beautiful than the first came to the surface as they shoveled the sand in the bottom of the stream. Thus were the ancient diamond mines of Golconda discovered. Had Al Hafed remained at home, had he dug in his own garden, instead of poverty, starvation, and death in a strange land he would have had acres of diamonds.

Close beside us is Jesus Christ, the source of all true wisdom and knowledge. Why should we search far and wide? Let's open our hearts to Him today and rejoice in our long-sought-for treasure.

Life in Christ *February 8*

GOD WITH US

Behold, a virgin shall be with child, and shall bring forth a son, and they shall call his name Emmanuel, which being interpreted is, God with us. **Matt. 1:23.**

"Mamma, where is God" asked a little girl of her mother one day. "Oh, He's up in heaven." "Then He can't see me when I'm in the house." "Well, yes, He can, dear, because—well—He is just everywhere," replied the mother as she continued, busily engaged in her work. This answer did not satisfy Mary, but seeing her mother too busy to talk, she set out to find God. She searched everywhere—from the cellar to the attic, in all the closets and out in the shed.

"Mamma, I can't find God. I've looked everywhere. You said He was everywhere. I can't find Him anywhere." This caused Mother to do some serious thinking. Though busy, she must answer this important question. "What shall I say now?" she thought.

"Well, Mary, I'll tell you. You see, it is like this. You can't see God, but He is everywhere. He is inside of you." Just here, the telephone rang and Mother was relieved.

Several days later a beautiful red apple was missing from the fruit bowl on the dining room table. Mother had specified that this was for company and not to be touched. Here, now, was a time to teach Mary a lesson. In the course of the conversation the idea that "nobody saw me" came out. "Oh, yes," replied Mother, "God did." "No, He didn't," said Mary. "I closed my eyes and He couldn't see out."

We smile, but Mary's quest for God is the quest down deep in every heart. "Where is God?" we ask. He is everywhere, but no one has seen Him. In order that you and I may learn to know Him, He came and lived among us in person. What a world of meaning in those words, "God with us." From Jesus they are most reassuring. We can hear His voice—"Lo, I am with you alway, even unto the end" (Matt. 29:20). Thus, we are not alone. The very God of the universe is with us through all our joys, sorrows, failures, and triumphs.

Life in Christ *February 9*

GOD THE SON

But unto the Son he saith, Thy throne, O God, is for ever and ever: a sceptre of righteousness is the sceptre of thy kingdom. **Heb. 1:8.**

"How can Jesus be God when there is but one God?" Sir Ahmed of Turkey once asked Dr. Ussher, a Christian missionary. Dr. Ussher put his hand into a ray of light shining through a window and asked, "Your Excellency, what is this?" "Why, that is the sun," he replied. "Is this the sun, or is that it up there in the sky?" "There is no difference; it is all the one light." "Well, is that the sun that we see, or is there a body back of it that no man has seen, but the light declares it?" "Yes, I suppose there is a body that we know through the light." "Is there one sun, or two? Which is the sun?" "One sun, they are inseparable."

"Now," said Dr. Ussher, "when I put my hand in the light, I feel something; what is it?" "It is the sun." "Yes, it is a power that goes down into the blackness and death of the earth, takes hold of the life in the seed, and brings up the beautiful grass and flowers and trees. What is it?" "It is the sun. Without the sun, there is no life." "Your Excellency, is there one sun, or three suns?" "One sun." "Which is the sun— the light, the body, or the power?" "It is all one and inseparable."

"Well, Your Excellency, if you have no difficulty in recognizing a trinity in the sun with three things so distinct as the light, the body, and the power, why should you have difficulty in recognizing a trinity in the Godhead? God loved man and wished to manifest Himself to him. The manifestation of Himself He calls His Son. We Christians do not worship three gods, but one God: God the Father, 'whom no man hath seen at any time'; God the Son, who said, 'He that hath seen me hath seen the Father'; and God the Spirit, the power or influence that comes from the Father and the Son into your heart and mine and teaches us what He wants us to be and do—all one inseparable God."

We know there are three personal beings, but their relationship to one another in their dealings with man is nicely expressed here.

Life in Christ *February 10*

WE KNOW GOD THE FATHER THROUGH CHRIST

If ye had known me, ye should have known my Father also: and from henceforth ye know him, and have seen him. **John 14:7.**

It is not enough to know that there is a God, and that God rules. We need to know what *kind* of God exists and rules. In nature we see that He is a powerful God, as evidenced in wind and storm, in lightning and in earthquake, in the tremendous power of myriads of suns. We see that He is a God of wisdom, as evidenced in the fitness and balance of things, in design and purpose manifest everywhere. That He is a lover of the beautiful is obvious as revealed in birds and flowers, in sunset and afterglow, in rainbow and snowflake.

However, that He is a God of love and mercy, a loving heavenly Father, is clearly revealed only in Jesus Christ, for He was "God . . . manifest in the flesh"; the "express image" of His Father's person.

When Philip heard Jesus say the words of our text he said, "Lord, shew us the Father, and it sufficeth us." Jesus replied, "Have I been so long time with you, and yet hast thou not known me, Philip? he that hath seen me hath seen the Father; and how sayest thou then, Shew us the Father?" (John 14:9).

Is God, then, just a power pervading the universe? No, He is a loving personality. How do I know? Look at Jesus. See how the people were attracted by His wonderful personality. God is like that.

Yes, but isn't God too busy controlling an immense universe to be concerned about such a little speck as I? No, He is concerned; He knows all about you and your needs, and what is more, He loves you. How do I know? Look at Jesus. See Him approach the Pool of Bethesda, and knowing all about the impotent man, say to him personally, "Wilt thou be made whole?" That is what God is like.

But shouldn't I be afraid of Him? Will He not condemn me? No, look again at Jesus and see the little children blessed by Him, and hear Him say to the woman taken in sin, "Neither do I condemn thee: go, and sin no more" (John 8:11). That is what God is like.

Life in Christ   *February 11*

THE GLORY OF GOD IN THE FACE OF JESUS

*For **God**, who commanded the light to shine out of darkness, hath shined in our hearts, to give the light of the knowledge of the glory of God in the face of Jesus Christ.* 2 **Cor.** 4:6.

It is for persons, living persons, not abstract ideas, that the human heart longs. We are all like the little girl who, when put to bed, was told by her mother to put her arm around her doll and go to sleep. To this the girl replied, "I don't want to. I want to put my arms around somebody real."

The story is told of another little girl who was afraid to be left alone in the dark when her mother kissed her good night. To quiet her fears, her mother reminded her, "But dear, God is with you." "I know," said the child, "but I want somebody with a face."

Somebody real, somebody with a face. This the human heart needs, and this need Jesus supplies, for He reveals to us the glorious truth that God is real—a God with a face. As Browning puts it in David's song to Saul:

" ' 'Tis the weakness in strength, that I cry for! my flesh, that I seek
In the Godhead! I seek and I find it. O Saul, it shall be
A Face like my face that receives thee; a Man like to me,
Thou shalt love and be loved by, for ever; a Hand like this hand
Shall throw open the gates of new life to thee! See the Christ stand!' "

According to our text the light of the knowledge of the glory of God is seen in the face of Jesus, and this light shines out of darkness, illuminating our hearts. By "the glory of God" is meant His character. When Moses said, "Shew me thy glory," God granted his request by revealing His character. (See Exodus 33:18, 19; 34:6, 7.) In the face of Jesus, then, we behold the true character of God. This light—this knowledge—quiets our fears and calms our troubled spirits in the darkness of the world of sin. Nothing is so soul satisfying as a knowledge of God as revealed in Jesus.

Life in Christ *February 12*

ONE WITH GOD

That they all may be one; as thou, Father, art in me, and I in thee, that they also may be one in us: that the world may believe that thou hast sent me. John 17:21.

Jesus taught that man can be one with God. How can this be? The editor of *Advance* presents the following:

"A bar of iron infused with fire: like that can be the relation of man to God.

"It grips one, that figure. The more one thinks of it the more significant it seems. When you introduce a piece of iron into the fire, the fire enters into that piece of iron. When you keep yourself consciously immerged in the environing life and spirit of God, the life and spirit of God find their way into you. . . .

"The bar of iron does not cease to be itself when fusion with the fire takes place. It is still a bar of iron. But it is filled with qualities that it did not have before. Until it met the fire, it was cold and hard and resistant and inert; now it is ductile and shapable, and filled with a new kind of power; and whatsoever thing it touches, to that thing it passes on some portion of the fire.

"It is a glorious figure. Man and God—like that! A man, an individual man, even you or I, so permeated with the life and spirit of God that out from the human flesh shines somewhat of the power of the love of God; out through the human instrument goes somewhat of the attractiveness of God; and by means of the individual human life is passed on somewhat of the very life of God.

"The early English mystics, in the vivid language which now sounds quaint and picturesque to our ears, talked about being 'oned' with God. And that was the idea. Not 'oned' with God in the sense of being swallowed up in Him, as the religions of the East would have it; but 'oned' with God as the iron is 'oned' with the fire, so that while it is still iron it stands for new qualities and represents new elements."

May God grant us this experience today.

Life in Christ   *February 13*

REDEMPTION THROUGH HIS BLOOD

In whom we have redemption through his blood, the forgiveness of sins, according to the riches of his grace. **Eph. 1:7.**

Dr. Ussher's illustration of redemption is so fitting in connection with our text today. He said to Sir Ahmed of Turkey, one day, in discussing the pardoning of sin: "Your Excellency, I will call you the king; you have a son who is a friend of mine and loves me; I am in prison for a debt which I cannot pay. Your son comes to you and says, 'Father, my friend is in prison for debt; can you not pardon and release him?' You reply, 'My son, I, too, love him and do not want him to be in prison, but I cannot pardon him, for if I did, I would be wronging the whole people. I must treat all alike.' 'Well, Father, will you let me pay his debt and he go free?' 'Yes, my son, if he will accept it, I will not only let you pay the debt, but I will participate with you.'

"The son, without waiting to ask whether I accept or not, goes at once to the proper office and pays the debt, and it is marked on the books that my debt is paid. He receives a receipt, upon which is the government seal, stating that my debt is paid, and now I am free. But I do not know it. Then he comes to the prison with the receipt and says, 'Rise, Brother, you are free. Your debt is paid. I have paid it.'

"I may take one of three courses. I may say, 'No, I will not accept it; I will not be under obligation to anyone'; I may sit moping, with head in my hands, and say, 'I wish it were so. But I cannot believe it'; or I may fall at his feet and say, 'I thank you. I have nothing to give in return, but I shall endeavor by my life to show my thanks!' Either of the first two would be unworthy of me, and ungrateful. The third course would be the only way.

"This is as I understand Christianity. God is king. Jesus Christ, His Son, paid my debt and yours, too; yours just as much as mine. I believe it, and know I am free; if you will believe it, it will mean to you what it does to me."

Life in Christ   *February 14*

CHRIST LIFTED UP FOR US

As Moses lifted up the serpent in the wilderness, even so must the Son of man be lifted up: that whosoever believeth in him should not perish, but have eternal life. **John 3:14, 15.**

In the wilderness of Arabah, we are told, there is still a mottled snake with fiery red spots, whose bite is fatal in a few hours. The body swells with a burning rash; the tongue is parched with thirst. Those bitten writhe in agony until death brings relief. This was probably the pest that suddenly appeared in the camp of Israel.

As the children of Israel journeyed they became "much discouraged because of the way" (Num. 21:4-9). They complained about everything, and spoke against Moses and against God. This is typical of discouraged men and women. They criticize leadership, the food, and even God. Yet the Lord had miraculously led them "through that great and terrible wilderness, wherein were fiery serpents, and scorpions, and drought" (Deut. 8:15).

They separated themselves from God, and the Lord could do nought but withdraw His protection that they might see the results of such a course. It was then that the serpents bit the people. This was probably the season when these serpents were most numerous and active.

That "old serpent, called the Devil, and Satan," always strikes when we are discouraged, and sin has the same effect as the bite of a fiery serpent. It inflames every evil passion and leads only to death. It is incurable by man.

Now, what was the remedy for Israel? "If a serpent had bitten any man, when he beheld the serpent of brass, he lived" (Num. 21:9). Beholding Christ, who was "made to be sin for us," "in the likeness of sinful flesh," always brings new life. Why a serpent to represent Christ? The serpent of brass was made in the form of the fiery serpents, but it was perfectly harmless. So Christ was made in the form of our human nature, "yet without sin." What a wonderful Saviour is ours! When bitten by the serpent of sin, we may look to Him and live.

Life in Christ *February 15*

The Drawing Power of the Cross

And I, if I be lifted up from the earth, will draw all men unto me. John 12:32.

The great motive powers of the soul are faith, hope, and love.

"Avoiding complicated . . . reasoning, the messengers of the cross dwelt upon the attributes of the Creator of the world, the Supreme Ruler of the universe. Their hearts aglow with the love of God and of His Son, they appealed to the heathen to behold the infinite sacrifice made in man's behalf. They knew that if those who had long been groping in the darkness of heathenism, could but see the light streaming from Calvary's cross, they would be drawn to the Redeemer."—*The Acts of the Apostles,* pp. 248, 249.

The drawing power of the cross of Christ lies in the manifestation of love revealed there. There is no power more dynamic in the human heart than that of love. In the crucifixion we see, not the angry God who demands a sacrifice, but a loving God who is Himself the sacrifice.

On the cross we hear the words, "Father, forgive them; for they know not what they do" (Luke 23:34). We are drawn to a spirit like that.

On the cross we see what a terrible thing sin is. We see what sin does to men—what selfishness does to the human heart. We see our selfishness in contrast with the unselfishness of the Christ, and long to be like Him. Repelled by the disease, we are drawn to the remedy.

An infidel who doubted Christ's statement, because not all men are being drawn to Christ, was asked by a Christian for a definition of gravity. "That power which draws all things to the center of the earth," he replied. Pointing to a ball suspended over the sidewalk, the Christian asked, "Why is not that ball drawn to the center of the earth?" "Well, can't you see the chain holding it?" "Yes, sir, and the only reason some men are not being drawn to Christ is that there are too many chains holding them." God grant that no chains of earth keep us from being drawn to Him.

Life in Christ *February 16*

None Other Name

Neither is there salvation in any other: for there is none other name under heaven given among men, whereby we must be saved. **Acts 4:12.**

A few people were collected around a blind man who had seated himself on the bridge over a canal in the city of London. He was reading from an embossed Bible. A man on his way home from the city was led by curiosity to the edge of the group. Just then the poor man, who was reading in the fourth chapter of Acts, lost his place, and while trying to find it with his finger, kept repeating the last clause he had read, "None other name, none other name, none other name." Some of the people smiled at the blind man's embarrassment, but the man who had recently joined himself to the group went on his way thinking deeply.

He had lately become convinced that he was a sinner, and had been trying in many ways to obtain peace of mind. He made new resolutions, altered his habits, and took part in religious exercises, but all were ineffectual to relieve his conscience of its load. The words of the blind man kept ringing in his ears all that evening and the next day. All at once it dawned upon his consciousness: "I see it all now. I have been trying to be saved by my own works, my repentance, my prayers, my reformation alone. It is Jesus alone can save; for there is 'none other name, none other name, none other name, under heaven given among men, whereby we must be saved.'"

There is power in the name of Jesus. There are great names in history who have stirred the hearts of men: Alexander, Caesar, Napoleon, Lindbergh, MacArthur, and others. They, however, pass with the tide. They just seem to "fade away and die." But not so the name of Jesus. His name stands for the same, yesterday, today, and forever. Men have life through His name. And someday, "at the name of Jesus every knee" shall bow.

God grant that we may be among those who shall rejoice in His name.

Life in Christ *February* 17

OUR ADVOCATE

My little children, these things write I unto you, that ye sin not. And if any man sin, we have an advocate with the Father, Jesus Christ the righteous. 1 John 2:1.

In the light of jurisprudence, with the supreme court of the universe in mind, our text today presents a beautiful picture. Since we are facing judgment, it is of particular interest to us all. To think of appearing in an earthly court is, for most people, somewhat frightening, and it is with fear and trembling that some think of the judgment bar of God.

In Jesus Christ we need not fear. He is our Advocate, and the Judge at the bench is our Father. They both love us more than words can tell. If, in facing trial, you knew that your brother, whom you love and in whom you have confidence, were to be your attorney, and you knew also that your father, whom you respect and understand, were to be the judge, could you not rest your case in their hands with peace of mind? You could, if all were well between the three of you. This is your privilege today, provided you let your Elder Brother have your case.

The story is told of a woman whose husband died, leaving a large estate. The will, however, was contested, and it was necessary to go through the regular legal proceedings to settle the matter. A local attorney who knew the husband offered to take the case.

The woman, not willing to pay the attorney's fees, kept putting off making a decision, until she became aware of the fact that she was about to lose the whole estate. She rushed to the attorney's office to accept his former offer. "I'm sorry," he said, "but I have been appointed judge in this case since I talked to you. It is too late now."

Someday, if we do not accept the offer of our Saviour to be our advocate, it will be too late for us. However, in committing our case to Him and to our heavenly Father, we need have no fear. What peace of mind can be ours! What wonderful security for the soul this wonderful truth affords!

Life in Christ   *February 18*

OUR ABLE AND LIVING INTERCESSOR

Wherefore he is able also to save them to the uttermost that come unto God by him, seeing he ever liveth to make intercession for them. Heb. 7:25.

"The Redeemer, with a heart of unalterable love, . . . pleads his . . . blood in the sinner's behalf. The wounded hands, the pierced side, the marred feet, plead . . . for fallen man."—*Testimonies*, vol. 4, p. 124.

A beautiful picture is presented to us of the intercession of Christ in our behalf. We see Jesus pleading, "Father, My blood, My blood, My blood!" And then we see an exceeding bright light come from God, who sits upon the great white throne, and encircle Jesus. His pleading is accepted and His request is granted. (See *Early Writings*, p. 38.)

Satan would have us misunderstand this picture. He would like to have us think of our heavenly Father as a severe tyrant, who is angry with sinners and who would like to destroy them. It would then be just too bad for us were it not for a loving Saviour, who steps in between and pleads in our behalf and changes the attitude of God toward us. Oh, how our heavenly Father has been misrepresented! This picture Jesus corrects. He tells us that the Father Himself loves us. In fact, He so loves us that He gave His only Son for us.

In Christ, who came to reveal the Father, we see a loving God in whose government mercy and justice have kissed each other, and whose justice is rooted in love. Christ's pleading in our behalf must be understood in the light of jurisprudence. We see here a mature and understanding Attorney standing before the Judge—a mature and understanding Judge—pleading our case. This is no begging to change the attitude of the Judge, but this is a loving presentation of the fact that here is a sinner who has accepted the sacrifice in his behalf and is entitled to justification and acquittal. Nothing brings more joy and gladness to the hearts of both the Attorney and the Judge than to be able to grant pardon to every human soul.

Life in Christ *February 19*

OUR GREAT HIGH PRIEST

Seeing then that we have a great high priest, that is passed into the heavens, Jesus the Son of God, let us hold fast our profession. **Heb. 4:14.**

"*A great high priest!*" Just how great is He? Paul tells us in the verses and chapters that precede our text. First of all, He is the Son of God. "Unto the Son he saith, Thy throne, O God, is for ever and ever: a sceptre of righteousness is the sceptre of thy kingdom" (Heb. 1:8). He is the Creator and Upholder of all things, "by whom also he made the worlds," who upholds "all things by the word of his power" (vs. 2, 3). He is greater than angels, for "to which of the angels said he at any time, Sit on my right hand, until I make thine enemies thy footstool?" (v. 13). He is greater than the power of death and the devil, for He came "that through death he might destroy him that had the power of death, that is, the devil" (ch. 2:14).

He is greater than Moses, for He "was counted worthy of more glory than Moses, inasmuch as he who hath builded the house hath more honour than the house" (ch. 3:3).

This Great One was made a partaker of flesh and blood, "for verily he took not on him the nature of angels; but he took on him the seed of Abraham," and "in all things it behoved him to be made like unto his brethren, that he might be a merciful and faithful high priest" (ch. 2:16, 17).

This Great One, who was crowned with glory and honor, is passed into the heavens. There He is today, seated "on the right hand of the Majesty on high" (ch. 1:3). He it is who invites us to come and find help in time of need.

What more could we desire? The thought of His greatness may at first frighten us, but when we realize that He is our brother, and that "he is not ashamed to call them {us} brethren" (ch. 2:11), surely we can boldly approach the throne of grace to obtain mercy and to "find grace to help in time of need" (ch. 4:16).

Life in Christ   *February 20*

An Understanding High Priest

For we have not an high priest which cannot be touched with the feeling of our infirmities; but was in all points tempted like as we are, yet without sin. Heb. 4:15.

"No, I wouldn't go to him for help. He just wouldn't understand." "Oh, yes, he would." "How do you know?" "He went through the same experience. He knows what it is like, and he knows what to do. What's more, he cares."

You would go to such a counselor for help in time of need, wouldn't you? Just such a "Wonderful Counselor" is Jesus. He was tempted in all points like as we are. He understands.

He was accused of cowardice for refusing to unite with His loved ones in some forbidden act. He was pronounced narrow and straitlaced. He came unto His own and His own received Him not. He was misunderstood, misrepresented, and mistreated—in His own home and away from home. His work was criticized, His words were misconstrued, and most of His deeds of kindness were unappreciated. Most of His followers followed Him for what they could get out of Him, and when they saw it was not to their advantage to follow Him, they left Him. His mission was misinterpreted, His teachings were misapplied, and His statements were misquoted. One of His own betrayed Him, another denied Him, a third doubted Him, and all the rest fled and left Him when He needed help most. Men accused Him falsely, lied about Him, and made fun of Him. They whipped Him, spat in His face, and reviled Him. Finally, they crucified Him.

  "God understands your sorrow; He sees the falling tear;
  And whispers, 'I am with thee'; Then falter not, nor fear.
  God understands your weakness; He knows the tempter's pow'r;
  And He will walk beside you, However dark the hour.
  He understands your longing, Your deepest grief He shares;
  Then let Him bear your burden, He understands and cares."
                                            —Oswald J. Smith

Life in Christ *February 21*

COME BOLDLY AND FIND HELP

Let us therefore come boldly unto the throne of grace, that we may obtain mercy, and find grace to help in time of need. Heb. 4:16.

Since our heavenly Father has revealed Himself in Jesus, let us notice how He introduces Himself to men and women in need, as recorded in the messages to the seven churches of Revelation, and thus discover how He can help us in time of need.

To the first church of the first century He reveals Himself as walking in their midst and holding the seven stars in His right hand. He wants them to know that the church on earth is His chief concern and that He controls its leadership. This assurance was just what they needed as they went forth to proclaim His gospel to the pagan world.

To the men and women facing martyrdom He said He was "the first and the last, which was dead, and is alive" (Rev. 2:8). In other words, "I know the end from the beginning, and I've been through what you are going through. Trust me. Be faithful unto death, and I will give you a crown of life."

To those living in a time when false teachings and false practices were creeping into the church, and the traditions of men seemed to take precedence over the Word of God, Jesus introduced Himself as "he which hath the sharp sword with two edges" (Rev. 2:12). This is none other than the Word of God.

To men and women living in a time when darkness covered the earth and error sat enthroned He said, in substance, "I have eyes like a flame of fire and feet like fine brass. I can see through it all. I can see you in the darkness, and I am strong enough to carry you through."

To a church spiritually dead He is ready to make the Holy Spirit available. For those facing disappointment He has the key, and for those facing judgment He is the faithful and true witness. In other words, He is just the Saviour His people need. If He were to introduce Himself to you today, He would do so in terms of your needs. Let us come boldly today, and find that help so graciously made available.

Life in Christ — *February 22*

Our Wisdom and Redemption

But of him are ye in Christ Jesus, who of God is made unto us wisdom, and righteousness, and sanctification, and redemption. 1 Cor. 1:30.

Strange wording—this text of ours today. What did Paul mean, "of him are ye in Christ Jesus"? And why did he say that Jesus "is made unto us wisdom, and righteousness, and sanctification, and redemption"? Why didn't he say Christ "gives us" these things?

First, notice the reading in the Revised Standard Version: "He is the source of your life in Christ Jesus." This makes more plain the expression, "of him are ye in Christ Jesus." However, why is Jesus "made" our wisdom, et cetera?

There are four great terms here: wisdom, righteousness, sanctification, and redemption. These God does not present to man, as it were, wrapped up in a package. These represent experience and growth. Like character, which must be developed, they cannot be *given*.

Look at the term "wisdom." Teachers may give you knowledge, but real wisdom comes only from personal experience. Since the fear of the Lord is the beginning of wisdom, only in fellowship with Christ can we experience that growth which makes us wise unto salvation.

Righteousness, sanctification, and redemption come by faith, which, again, can be experienced only through fellowship with Christ. Sanctification is the work of a lifetime of this fellowship. Redemption means more than a home in heaven someday. "To restore in man the image of his Maker, to bring him back to the perfection in which he was created, to promote the development of body, mind, and soul, that the divine purpose in his creation might be realized,—this was to be the work of redemption. This is the object of education, the great object of life."—*Education,* pp. 15, 16. Redemption, although a free gift, is a privilege; it is fellowship with Christ, who will accomplish in us this wonderful restoration.

Let us thank God today for this privilege of fellowship with the Master, who *is* our wisdom, our redemption.

LIFE IN CHRIST

I am crucified with Christ: nevertheless I live; yet not I, but Christ liveth in me: and the life which I now live in the flesh I live by the faith of the Son of God, who loved me, and gave himself for me. **Gal. 2:20.**

Back in the seventeenth century there lived a man who was known as Brother Lawrence. His real name was Nicholas Herman, of Lorraine. One day, at eighteen, he was looking at a dry and leafless tree. As he thought about the change the coming spring would bring, there was stirred within him a new concept of the power and presence of God. He was converted, and from that time on he grew in the knowledge and love of God, endeavoring constantly to walk as in His presence. After serving as a footman and soldier, he was admitted as a lay brother among the barefooted Carmelites at Paris. He later became known as Brother Lawrence. Those who knew him considered him an outstanding Christian.

The secret of his success was his constantly practicing the presence of God. From his conversations and letters it is found that when he began his business he said to God, "Oh, my God, since Thou art with me, and I must now, in obedience to Thy commands, apply my mind to these outward things, I beseech Thee to grant me the grace to continue in Thy presence; and to this end do Thou prosper me with Thy assistance, receive all my works and possess all my affections."

As he proceeded in his work he continued his familiar conversation with his Maker. When finished, he examined himself to see how he had discharged his duty; if he found it well, he returned thanks to God; if otherwise, he asked pardon, and without being discouraged, adjusted his thinking and continued his exercise of the presence of God as if he had never deviated from it. "Thus," said he, "by rising after my falls, and by frequently renewed acts of faith and love, I am come to a state wherein it would be as difficult for me not to think of God as it was at first to accustom myself to it."

Life in Christ *February 24*

His Words Our Life

It is the spirit that quickeneth; the flesh profiteth nothing: the words that I speak unto you, they are spirit, and they are life. John 6:63.

Life in Christ is not just a theory. It must be a personal experience. Christ must be as real to us as is the food we eat.

It was a great day—that day when Jesus fed the five thousand. Many followed Him only for the miracles He performed, but many others were hungering and thirsting for soul satisfaction. To them He said, "I am the living bread which came down from heaven: if any man eat of this bread, he shall live for ever. . . . Verily, verily, I say unto you, Except ye eat the flesh of the Son of man, and drink his blood, ye have no life in you. Whoso eateth my flesh, and drinketh my blood, hath eternal life; and I will raise him up at the last day" (John 6:51-54).

What did Jesus mean—eat His flesh and drink His blood? The answer and explanation is nicely put in *The Desire of Ages,* pages 389-391.

"To eat the flesh and drink the blood of Christ is to receive Him as a personal Saviour, believing that He forgives our sins, and that we are complete in Him. . . . The life of Christ that gives life to the world is in His word. . . . As our physical life is sustained by food, so our spiritual life is sustained by the word of God. And every soul is to receive life from God's word for himself. As we must eat for ourselves in order to receive nourishment, so we must receive the word for ourselves. . . . In His promises and warnings, Jesus means me. God so loved the world, that He gave His only-begotten Son, that *I,* by believing in Him, might not perish, but have everlasting life. The experiences related in God's word are to be *my* experiences. . . . As faith thus receives and assimilates the principles of truth, they become a part of the being and the motive power of the life. . . . This is what it means to live 'by every word that proceedeth out of the mouth of God.' This is eating the bread that comes down from heaven."

Life in Christ *February 25*

The Lord Our Righteousness

In his days Judah shall be saved, and Israel shall dwell safely: and this is his name whereby he shall be called, The Lord our righteousness. **Jer. 23:6.**

There is coming a day when Jesus "shall reign and prosper, and shall execute judgment and justice in the earth" (Jer. 23:5). In that day, according to our text for today, His name shall be called "The Lord our righteousness." What does this mean? Why will He be so called?

Suppose two men meet in that day, and one says to the other, "Well, Brother A, how did you get here?" Do you suppose Brother A will reply, "Oh, I'll tell you, I struggled and worked and fought. I denied myself all the pleasures of earth. I did a lot of missionary work. I resisted temptation like a good one, and by persevering and enduring hardship all along the way, I finally made it." Will this be his testimony? By no means. Brother A will reply, "Friend, it is only because He loved me so. It is only because He was so kind, so patient, so long-suffering. He put up with my selfishness, my littleness, my meanness, and gave me life and guidance until I learned to know Him. And when I gave Him my heart, He gave me forgiveness. He strengthened me. He never forsook me. It is only because of His goodness and His righteousness that I am here."

And Brother B will reply, "That's how it is that I am here." All the redeemed will give the same testimony, and then all will sing His praise. It is His righteousness—His victory, His long-suffering, His patience, His love, His forgiveness, His goodness, His life and death— that saves us. We are "filled with all unrighteousness" (Rom. 1:29); "there is none righteous, no, not one" (ch. 3:10). Our righteousness is as "filthy rags" (Isa. 64:6). Every thought and motive is selfish. But in Christ all is changed. The filthy garments are taken away, and we can stand, clothed in His righteousness—garments pure and white.

Life in Christ *February 26*

THE HOPE OF GLORY

To whom God would make known what is the riches of the glory of this mystery among the Gentiles; which is Christ in you, the hope of glory. Col. 1:27.

There are two great mysteries in this world. One is the mystery of iniquity and the other the mystery of godliness. One we shall probably never solve, but the other we shall study throughout the ages of eternity, and it will be made more and more manifest, to our increasing wonder, joy, and satisfaction. Our text today speaks of this wonderful mystery, which, according to the verse preceding it, "hath been hid from ages and from generations, but now is made manifest to his saints." It is a glorious mystery—a glorious truth.

"Christ in you." We sing, "Let Jesus come into your heart," and, "Into my heart; into my heart; come into my heart, Lord Jesus." How can this be? How can one person get into another person's heart? If you think about it, this is happening every day. Isn't it interesting to watch two young people work their way into each other's heart?

A young couple met for the first time in an Ingathering singing band. As they walked along together, singing the hymns and gospel songs, chatting together between times, something began to happen. She occupied more and more of his thoughts, and for some mysterious reason he became more and more the subject of her conversation. They began to get into each other's heart. You can't explain this, but perhaps you have experienced it. Through fellowship it came about.

So it is in fellowship with Christ, in communion with the Saviour, that He comes into our heart. Just before His crucifixion, Jesus said to His disciples, "Abide in me, and I in you." "Herein is my Father glorified, that ye bear much fruit; so shall ye be my disciples. As the Father hath loved me, so have I loved you: continue ye in my love." "Ye are my friends" (John 15:4, 8, 9, 14).

This friendship with the Master is the hope of glory, the secret of successful Christian living. Let Jesus come into your heart today.

Life in Christ *February 27*

The Hope of Glory

Looking for that blessed hope, and the glorious appearing of the great God and our Saviour Jesus Christ. Titus 2:13.

What would life be like without hope? Take all dreams of hope for the future out of life, and what is left? To live creatively one must have hope for the future, with some assurance of the certainty of that hope. In the second coming of Christ modern youth has a hope.

Dan Gilbert, in his book *Thinking Youth's Greatest Need,* describes the alternative for modern youth as follows:

"He can go the way of the world, drugging himself with the deadening pleasures of a jazz age. He can seek escape in dissipation. He can smother himself in debauchery, blinding himself to the terrifying and horrifying things which seem to be in store for the world. He can flee from the future by stupefying himself in the present. Or, he can take the other course.

"He can live each moment in the exaltation of the thought that Christ will soon return. He can face the blankness and blackness of the future with serenity and courage. He need not rush into it—he need not flee from it. He can live this moment, with a sense of its supreme importance. He can face the terrors of dictatorship, of war, of worldly chaos—he can hold his head aloft, unabashed by what is before him. For he knows that out of impending chaos—Christ will come.

"This is the faith which youth needs, which youth requires, which the modern age demands. . . . With this faith, there is a future in a futureless world. There is security in the midst of insecurity. There is comfort in the midst of chaos. There is light in the midst of darkness. There is purpose in the midst of purposelessness. There is fulfillment in the midst of frustration. There is salvation in the midst of destruction."—Pages 153, 154.

With the glorious appearing of Jesus Christ will come everything worth while that young and old have ever hoped for.

Life in Christ *February 28*

HOPE BOTH SURE AND STEADFAST

Which hope we have as an anchor of the soul, both sure and stedfast, and which entereth into that within the veil. Heb. 6:19.

Can a person be sure of life eternal? Is there genuine assurance of the certainty of the Christian hope? The insecurity that comes from uncertainty is not conducive to peace of mind. But the promises in God's Word regarding peace of mind are clear and specific. Here are a few: "Great peace have they which love thy law" (Ps. 119:165). "Thou wilt keep him in perfect peace, whose mind is stayed on thee: because he trusteth in thee" (Isa. 26:3). "Peace I leave with you, my peace I give unto you: not as the world giveth, give I unto you. Let not your heart be troubled, neither let it be afraid" (John 14:27).

These promises would have no meaning if one could not be sure. But we can be sure. The plan of redemption was not an afterthought or an experiment. It was all thought through before the foundations of the world were laid, and that by a God who accomplishes His purposes (see Eph. 1). The assurance comes through Jesus Christ. *In Him* we are "blessed . . . with all spiritual blessings" (v. 3). We are *"accepted in the beloved"* (v. 6). *"In whom* also we have obtained an inheritance" (v. 11). *In Christ* we are predestinated to be adopted into the family of God (v. 5).

"For as in Adam all die, even so *in Christ* shall all be made alive" (1 Cor. 15:22). It was predetermined by God that all who continue in sin shall die, "for the wages of sin is death," but all who accept Christ will receive the gift of eternal life (Rom. 6:23). "Moreover whom he did predestinate, them he also called" (ch. 8:30). Now, if we are lost, it will be "because when I called, ye did not answer; when I spake, ye did not hear; but did evil before mine eyes, and did choose that wherein I delighted not" (Isa. 65:12). If we are lost it will be because we deliberately choose to be. In Christ we can be sure of life eternal. This hope we have, which is both sure and steadfast.

MARCH

Life and True Values March 1

A True Sense of Values

That ye may approve things that are excellent; that ye may be sincere and without offence till the day of Christ. Phil. 1:10.

In a legend of Old Saxony it is said that on a certain hill there grew a magic flower that had the power to bring a large reward to its finder. Whoever found it would also find a treasure house on the side of the hill, the door of which could be unlocked by the flower.

One day a shepherd boy found the magic flower, and in turn found the door to the treasure house. Immediately he entered. On long tables that ran the length of the room lay treasures of unsurpassed beauty. On the walls, too, they were, and some were hanging from the ceiling. At the far end of the room, upon a stool, sat a little old elf.

Remembering that all these treasures were his, the boy filled his pockets, and then his blouse, and finally his cap with sparkling gems. As he approached the door to leave, the little man spoke in kindly tones, saying, "Take what you want, my boy, but don't forget the best."

He thought he had taken the best, but he went back, carefully unloaded his collection, and repeated the process. As he was about to leave, again the old man gave this same advice.

Again he emptied and refilled his pockets, blouse, and cap, but as he was leaving, the voice called, this time most insistently, "Take what you want, my boy, but don't forget the best."

Soon after leaving, he noticed that what had been so heavy had become very light. Examination revealed only dry, worthless leaves.

You wonder what the boy should have taken with him. Could it be that he was so enamored by the glitter of gems that he didn't think about getting acquainted with the keeper? Just think what would have happened had the boy invited the keeper home with him. Access to all the treasures would have been his. And in counsel with him, he would have known how to choose the best. Could this be a lesson for us today?

Life and True Values — March 2

OF MORE VALUE THAN MANY SPARROWS

Fear ye not therefore, ye are of more value than many sparrows. Matt. 10:31.

Life's real values are personal—not material. Paul tells us in 1 Corinthians 13 that three things abide, namely, faith, hope, and love; and the greatest of these is love. These three do not exist apart from persons.

The Christian religion emphasizes the sacredness and supreme value of the individual. In all of God's wonderful creation there is nothing that can take the place of a person. Adam was surrounded by beauty and variety unsurpassed—unmarred by sin. Everything testified to the goodness of God, and was placed at man's disposal for his happiness. But nothing completely satisfied the heart of man. Then God created lovely Eve and presented her to Adam. A person was needed.

That God is interested in individuals and considers each of great value is demonstrated clearly in the life and ministry of Jesus. He was always interested in persons. Each little child was an object of His love, and some of His most precious revelations of truth were made to single souls, such as Nicodemus and the woman of Samaria at the well. He made long trips just to help individuals, such as the Syrophoenician woman and the two demoniacs of Gadara. His concern for the rich young ruler and the man at the Pool of Bethesda further illustrated this truth. Perhaps the experience of the thief on the cross furnishes us the finest evidence of His concern for persons. That Christ was concerned for a penitent thief in His hour of agony is amazing.

And to think that Jesus would have died for one lost soul! Down deep in every human heart is the need to be of value. This God has implanted. Often when one is discouraged and depressed, the thought is expressed, "Oh, I'm no good. I don't amount to anything, anyway." This is but the whispering of the enemy. Said Jesus, "Fear ye not, therefore, ye are of more value than many sparrows."

Life and True Values — March 3

OF MORE VALUE THAN FINE GOLD

I will make a man more precious than fine gold; even a man than the golden wedge of Ophir. Isa. 13:12.

What is there about a human being that makes him so valuable? It cannot be his body, as wonderful as that is. An analysis shows very clearly that man's material worth is very insignificant. Some have estimated that the chemical elements and compounds in the average human body are worth about a dollar, or perhaps two dollars, with prices as they are today. There are some seventeen different elements found in the human body, we are told: oxygen, carbon, hydrogen, nitrogen, sulfur, phosphorus, chlorine, fluorine, silicon, sodium, potassium, lithium, calcium, magnesium, iron, manganese, and iodine. One scientist, analyzing the human body from a chemical standpoint says it is composed of about ten gallons of water, enough fat to make seven cakes of soap, enough carbon for several gross of lead pencils, enough phosphorus to make about two thousand match heads, enough iron to make one nail, enough lime to whitewash a small chicken coop, and enough sulfur to rid one small dog of fleas.

And all of these chemical elements, in their raw state, would be worth very little, whether you are a genius or a moron, a financier or a pauper, a village idiot or an Einstein.

A man is of value, then, not in terms of the chemical elements that make up his body, nor in terms of his possessions. These count only as they affect his relationship to God and to his fellow man. A man is of value in terms of his knowledge, his tastes, his attitudes, his motives, his ambitions, his sense of values, his character, and his purposes. We are told in *Counsels to Parents and Teachers,* page 406, "The value of the human agent is estimated according to the capacity of the heart to know and understand God."

Looking at ourselves from this point of view, we can see that we are "more precious than fine gold," and that we can increase in value by God's grace. Let us pray that this may be our experience today.

A Crown of Glory—A Royal Diadem

Thou shalt also be a crown of glory in the hand of the Lord, and a royal diadem in the hand of thy God. Isa. 62:3.

A crown is the symbol of position, authority, distinction, and power. A royal diadem is a king's symbol of supreme authority. These are usually elaborate objects, some reaching the estimated value of approximately a million dollars. The British Imperial State Crown, for example, made for Queen Victoria in 1838, contains, we are told, 2,783 diamonds, 277 pearls, 17 sapphires, 11 emeralds, and 5 rubies. It is said that some of these gems were worn by Edward the Confessor and Queen Elizabeth.

According to our text today God's people, those redeemed from the earth, are to be "a royal diadem in the hand of thy God." God intends that we shall stand as symbols of His authority and power. God's power and authority have been challenged; His character has been misrepresented. Note the following statement: "The earth was dark through misapprehension of God. That the gloomy shadows might be lightened, that the world might be brought back to God, Satan's deceptive power was to be broken. This could not be done by force. The exercise of force is contrary to the principles of God's government; He desires only the service of love; and love cannot be commanded; it cannot be won by force or authority. Only by love is love awakened. To know God is to love Him; His character must be manifested in contrast to the character of Satan. This work only one Being in all the universe could do. Only He who knew the height and depth of the love of God could make it known."—*The Desire of Ages,* p. 22.

For this reason Jesus came to this world to reveal the true character of God to angels and to men. He has appointed His followers to carry on that work for Him. We are to be the symbols of the power of love, trophies of the grace of God. Thus, we shall be to Him a crown of glory.

Life and True Values *March 5*

One Lost Sheep

What man of you, having an hundred sheep, if he lose one of them, doth not leave the ninety and nine in the wilderness, and go after that which is lost, until he find it? Luke 15:4.

No parable of Jesus emphasizes the value of a human soul more vividly than the parable of the lost sheep. The value of that sheep to the shepherd is indicated by the fact that he left the ninety and nine in the wilderness to rescue it. We sing, "There were ninety and nine that safely lay in the shelter of the fold." In Luke's Gospel, however, the ninety and nine are left in the wilderness. If the shepherd had been lost in his search for one sheep, the ninety and nine would also have been lost, for they would have been without a shepherd, at the mercy of enemies of the wilderness.

This truth can best be understood when we realize that our little world is the lesson book of the universe, very important to both angels and men. It was here on this planet that Christ came to demonstrate the love of God in contrast with the selfishness of Satan. Had Christ been unsuccessful in His earthly life, had He failed in one particular, Satan's accusations would have been proved true. Satan could have said, "God requires of man that which He Himself cannot do." If Christ had been lost, all would have been lost. The whole universe, therefore, is involved. All heaven is interested and concerned. Isn't it strange how unconcerned are we who are most directly involved?

>"Safe were the ninety and nine in the fold,
>   Safe, though the night was stormy and cold;
>   But said the shepherd, when counting them o'er,
>   'One sheep is missing: There should be one more!'
>
>"The shepherd went out to search for his sheep,
>   And all thro' the night on the rocky steep
>   He sought till he found him, with love-bands he bound him,
>   And I was that one lost sheep."   —E. Toral Seat

Life and True Values March 6

THE WORLD VERSUS A SOUL

For what shall it profit a man, if he shall gain the whole world, and lose his own soul? Or what shall a man give in exchange for his soul? **Mark 8:36, 37.**

We always like to evaluate in terms of profit. The gain or loss is the most important aspect of any financial report. For our consideration today here is a report of nine of the world's most successful financiers. In 1923 a very important meeting was held in Chicago. Attending this meeting were the presidents of the largest independent steel company, the largest gas company, the largest utility company; the greatest wheat speculator; a member of the President's Cabinet; the greatest "bear" in Wall Street; the president of New York Stock Exchange; the head of the world's greatest monopoly; and the president of the bank of international settlements.

We must admit that this was a gathering of a group of the world's most successful money-makers. Twenty-five years later, of this group Charles Schwab had lived on borrowed money for five years before dying bankrupt; Howard Hobson was insane; Samuel Insull had died a fugitive from justice and penniless in a foreign land; Arthur Cuttin had died abroad, insolvent; Alfred Fall was pardoned from prison so he could die at home; Jesse Livermore died a suicide; Richard Whitney was released from Sing Sing Penitentiary; Ivor Kruger died a suicide, and so did Leon Frazer. What did they gain?

Our text today says, ". . . if he shall gain the whole world." Note the word "if." The men who do not consider the value of their soul lose both the world and their soul. (Those whose soul is saved gain both.) Was not the world promised to Abraham and to his seed? And do we not read, "If ye be Christ's, then are ye Abraham's seed, and heirs according to the promise"? Did not Jesus say, "Blessed are the meek: for they shall inherit the earth"?

No wonder Paul exclaimed, "But what things were gain to me, those I counted loss for Christ" (Phil. 3:7).

Life and True Values *March 7*

ONE OF THESE LITTLE ONES

Take heed that ye despise not one of these little ones; for I say unto you, That in heaven their angels do always behold the face of my Father which is in heaven. Matt. 18:10.

A man's sense of values is pretty well revealed in his attitude toward children, and generally a man gets an entirely new sense of values with the birth of his own first-born child. It was when Enoch begat a son that he began in a new way to walk with God.

Watch a young woman tenderly care for her little one. Notice how everything centers on that baby's welfare. God has placed that concern in every mother's heart; and unless it is seared by selfishness, it grows as the child grows. And why? Because a soul is so valuable in God's sight that He wants everything possible done to bring it up to be of real value to Him throughout eternity. That being true, "Despise not one of these little ones."

The context of the words of our text of today indicates that Jesus was referring also to new converts—babes in Christ. These too are precious in God's sight. There is great joy in heaven when a sinner repents and is born again. Special attention should also be given these, and great care should be exercised not to offend them. Those new in the faith are often weak and are in need of help, not criticism; encouragement, not censure. A stumbling brother should not be despised, but uplifted in fellowship and prayer. All heaven is interested in him.

The first time you bring someone else to Christ and you see that individual rejoice in sins forgiven and in the hope of eternal life, your own soul thrills through and through, and you begin to understand the joy of our Lord. "Ye are our ... joy," said Paul. Life's true values are always those connected with God's great family in heaven and in earth and with their welfare. May we never lose sight of the value of a human soul, including our own.

Life and True Values March 8

CALL NO MAN COMMON

And he said unto them, Ye know how that it is an unlawful thing for a man that is a Jew to keep company, or come unto one of another nation; but God hath shewed me that I should not call any man common or unclean. Acts 10:28.

There is a wealth of possibilities in even the most unpromising soul. Man has in him the making of a demon or of a son of God.

In a museum one can see the likeness of one of Babylon's kings, and right over his face is imprinted the footprint of a dog. Evidently the dog trod on the king's image while it lay in a soft pliable state, defacing it and almost obliterating it. How symbolic this is of so many for whom the marks of sin obscure the image of God. But in spite of all this, by the grace of God, this image can be renewed. Fierce cannibals, bearing the footprint of satanic savagery on their faces, have been restored, and you can see reflected there the image of the Divine. As the sculptor sees the angel in the shapeless block of marble, so the Lord sees His image in every man.

A ragged man, broken in body and spirit, racked by delirium tremens, was walking in Worcester, Massachusetts, one Sunday evening on his way to the river. He had so utterly ruined his life that, heartsick and desperate, he could think of only one way out—suicide. Suddenly a hand was laid on his shoulder and a few kind words were spoken to him. He was invited to go to church and later to sign the temperance pledge. This he did, and there followed a terrific battle with his appetite. For six days and nights he stayed in a wretched garret. When he returned to his work, weak, but conqueror, he was laughed at by his employer, but again a kind word, a friendly handshake, and an expression of confidence kept him from despair. This was the beginning of the wonderful life of service he was to render for God on two continents, for this was John B. Gough, the great temperance lecturer, whose life and work blessed thousands.

Call no man common. Every soul is valuable in the sight of God.

Life and True Values *March 9*

THAT THOU MAYEST BE RICH

I counsel thee to buy of me gold tried in the fire, that thou mayest be rich; and white raiment, that thou mayest be clothed, and that the shame of thy nakedness do not appear; and anoint thine eyes with eyesalve, that thou mayest see. Rev. 3:18.

Everyone would like to be rich. The desire for riches is implanted in every human heart. We sing, "My Father is rich in houses and lands; He holdeth the wealth of the world in His hands!" God *is* rich. He wants His children to be, but we are prone to think of riches in terms of things material only. The qualities of faith and love, the robe of Christ's righteousness, and clear spiritual vision are the things that really enrich our lives and bring true joy and happiness. That's why He counsels us to buy these of Him.

What good are material things if we have no faith in God or in our fellow men? How much happiness does money bring if we cannot love or be loved? Money can never buy love. All the wealth of the world is of no value without the righteousness of Christ, for without His righteousness we will perish with our wealth when this present world is re-created. Material riches can be obliterated in a moment by an atomic bomb, and storm and flood can sweep away our possessions, but they cannot rob us of our faith and love and spiritual discernment if we are clothed with the righteousness of Christ.

These true riches we secure from Christ. He said, "I counsel thee to buy of *me*." He did not say we must develop faith and love that will stand the test of fire before we can have fellowship with Him. We are to obtain these from Him. They are already tested. That was demonstrated on Calvary. Instead of prerequisites to fellowship with Christ, these riches are a by-product of that fellowship. Jesus stands at the door and knocks. He wants to come in. When we let Him in He brings with Him true riches. When we take Him into our fellowship, our lives are enriched and ennobled, and though poor in worldly goods, we will be rich in things that count in life here and hereafter.

Life and True Values   *March 10*

THINGS SEEN VERSUS THINGS NOT SEEN

While we look not at the things which are seen, but at the things which are not seen: for the things which are seen are temporal; but the things which are not seen are eternal. 2 Cor. 4:18.

Did you ever stop to think that there is more in this universe that we cannot see than there is that we do see? The human eye sees actually very little. Take the great and marvelous heavenly universe above us, with its suns and systems and galaxies. There was a time when we could see only about two thousand stars. Today through the telescope we can see literally millions, and still there are more. And what do we see? We see only in general outline, we do not see in detail. Even on Mars, our closest neighbor, we see what seem to be fields and canals, but very little is manifest clearly. Looking through a telescope of any size convinces us that there is far more above us than can be seen even with the aid of the most powerful instruments.

Look, too, at the universe beneath us—the infinitesimal—the universe we see through a microscope. Lo, and behold, there opens before our eyes another universe, equally as amazing as the one we see through the telescope.

Sometimes we are prone to think that the things we see are all there are, and this definitely affects our sense of values. Let us not be deceived. The things that are seen, that is, the material things, comprise only the structure of the universe in which mortal beings live and move. Obviously, what a machine is for is more important than the machine itself. The things that are seen exist for things that are much more important, many of which are not seen, but which are nevertheless real. Among the things not seen are the spiritual. Such beings as the Godhead and angels are invisible to the human eye, as also are such things as attitudes and motives. Though they reveal themselves in acts, they are the realities in the universe that are of eternal value. That's why our text says, "The things which are seen are temporal; but the things which are not seen are eternal."

Life and True Values   *March 11*

NOT IN POSSESSIONS

And he said unto them, Take heed, and beware of covetousness: for a man's life consisteth not in the abundance of the things which he possesseth. **Luke 12:15.**

Covetousness is based on a perverted desire for possession, with its roots in selfishness. A selfish heart is never satisfied. A boy is very happy with his new glassy marble until he sees another boy with an agate. A little girl is thrilled with her new rag doll until she sees the new plastic-skin doll cradled in the arms of her little neighbor. George is happy with his first secondhand bike until he sees his cousin with a brand-new one. And this attitude is not limited to the younger ones. Mr. A is happy and satisfied with his raise in salary until he learns that Mr. B received twice the amount of increase. When covetousness predominates our thinking, we evaluate things in terms of the amount of our possessions as compared with those of others. And when in this world we see all the inequalities in the distribution of wealth, some having so much more than others, we are dissatisfied. Envy, jealousy, and hatred follow, and all result in increased blindness to life's true values.

That Jesus was right when He said, "A man's life consisteth not in the abundance of the things which he possesseth," is clearly demonstrated when one becomes ill. Many a man would give all his material possessions for a new stomach or a new heart. Some have offered all they have in terms of material things for love, which they discover cannot be purchased with these. Our possessions in themselves are not evil, they can be a great blessing. It's not so much what one possesses, as what possesses him, that counts. If a man is possessed by love, all his possessions will be under control.

Obadiah tells us, "The house of Jacob shall possess their possessions" (v. 17). If a man would truly possess his possessions, and not be a slave to them, he must become a slave of Christ, if you please. Then Christ sets him free and he is restored to his dominion, possessor of, not a slave to, his possessions.

NOT BY BREAD ALONE

But he answered and said, It is written, man shall not live by bread alone, but by every word that proceedeth out of the mouth of God. Matt. 4:4.

One of the saddest texts in all the Bible is John 6:49: "Your fathers did eat manna in the wilderness, and are dead." There they were, eating angels' food, witnessing wonderful miracles and marvelous deliverances, traveling with Jesus Christ Himself as their guide, and yet completely insensible to the import of it all. They could have been inspired and prepared and strengthened to do a great work for God, and yet all was so ineffectual, so far as they were concerned, because they concentrated entirely too much on "bread alone."

David tells us they "lusted exceedingly in the wilderness, and tempted God in the desert. And he gave them their request; but sent leanness into their soul" (Ps. 106:14, 15). Leanness of soul always follows concentration upon bread alone. Fullness of bread with an abundance of idleness helped cause the iniquity of Sodom.

Too much bread and sickness go hand in hand, and often when bread is scarce, men and women can think more clearly and have better health. And it is on beds of sickness that we often learn that bread is not enough. We recognize then the value of a word from Him who is the source of our life.

It is only by God's sustaining power that we live at all. Even the energy and strength derived from a piece of bread is His. "In Him we live, and move, and have our being." The same creative power that is in the food we eat, is the power that restores us to health and strength when we are ill. That same power is in His Word. As we partake of it we grow in spiritual strength. It is possible, however, for us to read the Word of God and gain very little from it, because of the spirit in which we read it. Let us not, like our fathers in the wilderness, eat manna from heaven without sensing its import, but like Jeremiah of old, let us exclaim, "Thy words were found, and I did eat them."

Life and True Values — March 13

HARD FOR A RICH MAN

Jesus . . . saith unto them, Children, how hard is it for them that trust in riches to enter into the kingdom of God! Mark 10:24.

When Jesus said to the rich young ruler, "Sell that thou hast, and give to the poor, . . . and follow me" (Matt. 19:21), the young man went away grieved. Jesus too was grieved, for the young man had tremendous possibilities. He might have taken Judas' place among the twelve, for Jesus' invitation to him was the same as to Peter and Matthew and the others. Jesus did not ask every rich man to sell all he had. Here was an unusual opportunity for a young man, and he failed to grasp it, "for he had great possessions."

You see, riches have a tendency to give one a false sense of superiority, and it is this false sense of superiority, not their riches, that keeps men out of the kingdom. This is true whatever the riches may be—intellect, beauty, physical strength, skill, or superior talent in any line. The most brilliant student has a tendency to feel superior to his fellow schoolmates, as does the most beautiful girl, and the best athlete. If they do feel superior, they find themselves ostracized from the group. It is not their intellect, or their beauty, or their strength or skill that keeps them from being accepted; it is their pride and superiority complex that nobody enjoys. So it is in the kingdom of God.

Riches can be a source of wonderful blessing. Occasionally you hear someone misquote the Bible by saying, "Money is the root of all evil." Instead, the Bible says, "For the love of money is the root of all evil" (1 Tim. 6:10). Money is neither good nor evil in itself. It is how we relate ourselves to it and how it is used that make the difference.

Had the rich young ruler sold his possessions and stopped at that point, he would not have been happy then, either. Jesus further invited him to follow Him. How rich the young man would have been had he followed his Master! Following Jesus keeps one's perspective clear and enables him to use his riches to glorify God.

Life and True Values March 14

HIDDEN TREASURE

Again, the kingdom of heaven is like unto treasure hid in a field; the which when a man hath found, he hideth, and for joy thereof goeth and selleth all that he hath, and buyeth that field. **Matt. 13:44.**

This parable emphasizes that those things pertaining to the kingdom of heaven constitute real treasure worth investing everything we have to secure. It points out, too, that there is as much joy in discovering and securing the reality of the kingdom of heaven as there is in finding earthly treasure.

We are told in *Christ's Object Lessons*, page 104, that "the field containing the treasure represents the Holy Scriptures. And the gospel is the treasure. The earth itself is not so interlaced with golden veins and filled with precious things as is the word of God." Why is this treasure so hidden? Why are the Holy Scriptures so hard to understand? Does God conceal truth from man?

No, the truths in the Bible are veiled or hidden because of man's limitations. Language is only human and therefore inadequate. Words, particularly translated words, have different meanings to different people. We are deceived by preconceived opinions. We cannot comprehend the deep things of God any more than a child who is just learning his multiplication tables is able to understand calculus. The way of truth is progressive. We would not want it otherwise.

Occasionally Jesus enables men to catch glimpses of truth, to awaken within them the realization of its value. "He [Jesus] takes them to the threshold of the Infinite, flushed with the indescribable glory of God, and shows them the treasure there."—*Ibid.*, p. 106. Then He wants them to get rid of hindrances and dig, as a miner digs, to obtain more glorious riches. "Search, O search the precious Bible with hungry hearts. Explore God's word as the miner explores the earth to find veins of gold. Never give up the search until you have ascertained your relation to God and His will in regard to you."—*Ibid.*, p. 111.

Life and True Values   *March 15*

The Pearl of Great Price

Again, the kingdom of heaven is like unto a merchant man, seeking goodly pearls: who, when he had found one pearl of great price, went and sold all that he had, and bought it. Matt. 13:45, 46.

Christ is the pearl of great price, pure, white, flawless, and complete. "All that can satisfy the needs and longings of the human soul, for this world and for the world to come, is found in Christ. Our Redeemer is the pearl so precious that in comparison all things else may be accounted loss."—*Christ's Object Lessons,* p. 115.

How is this true? He is the source of our life—in Him we live, and move, and have our being. In Him we have redemption through His blood, even the forgiveness of our sins. And in Him are hid all the treasures of wisdom and knowledge.

"What is truth?" Jesus answers, "I am the truth."

"How can we know the way?" Jesus answers, "I am the way."

"Where do we come from?" The answer is, "In the image of God created he him."

"Why are we here?" Jesus answers, "As thou hast sent me into the world, even so have I also sent them into the world. . . . Neither pray I for these alone, but for them also which shall believe on me through their word; that they all may be one; as thou, Father, art in me, and I in thee, that they also may be one in us: that the world may believe that thou hast sent me."

"Where are we going?" Jesus answers, "I will come again, and receive you unto myself; that where I am, there ye may be also."

Not only is Christ the pearl of great price for us to obtain, but we are pearls of great price, to redeem which He paid His all. To think that we are of such value to Him as to warrant His sacrificing everything—risking His all—to ransom us, is a thought that overwhelms. If we human beings are worth that much to our Lord, why should we not recognize our true value as pearls of great price, and give our all to secure for ourselves and others the kingdom of heaven?

Life and True Values   *March 16*

THE RICHES OF GOD'S WORD

I have rejoiced in the way of thy testimonies, as much as in all riches. **Ps. 119:14.**

Life's true riches are found in abundance in God's Word. Here not only the wealth of the ages but also the wealth of eternity is stored. That which is of greatest value in it and that which brings the deepest joy is its revelation of the living Christ. Wherever this Word has gone men's lives have been transformed.

Eugene Nida, in his book *God's Word in Man's Language*, tells the following story: During World War II a young Belgian parachutist who was dropped into his country to work with the underground movement against the Germans was captured by the Gestapo and placed in solitary confinement. In the cell next to his was a Belgian pastor, likewise accused of espionage. These men discovered that they could communicate with each other by tapping the Morse code on the intervening wall. On one occasion the parachutist tapped, "It is hell to be alone with one's self." To this the pastor replied, "It is heaven to be alone with one's Lord." Sensing the parachutist's deep spiritual need, the pastor arranged with members of his congregation on the outside to send a Bible to this young man; but it was not merely a Bible that came into this man's cell. Jesus Christ came into his life and transformed him there in his solitary confinement. So much so that on his way to his execution he tapped out slowly to the Belgian pastor, who was later released, "I am going out to life and not to death."

The riches of God's Word can make heaven out of a lonely cell and bring life in the face of death. It is no wonder that all through the 119th psalm we find David expressing his appreciation of the testimonies.

Note a few of his statements: Verse 2, "Blessed are they that keep his testimonies." Verse 24, "Thy testimonies also are my delight and my counsellors." Verse 99, "I have more understanding than all my teachers: for thy testimonies are my meditation."

Life and True Values March 17

The Riches of God's Love

But God, who is rich in mercy, for his great love wherewith he loved us, even when we were dead in sins, hath quickened us together with Christ, (by grace are ye saved;) Eph. 2:4, 5.

There are no riches that can compare with the riches of God's love and mercy in Christ Jesus. They are beyond our comprehension. Particularly does His love seem so amazing when we realize that He loves us even though we do not love Him. Our text today brings to our attention the fact that even when we were dead in sins, God, because He loved us so, wanted to save us and give us new life together with Christ.

We are reminded of Paul's words in Romans 5:7, 8, "For scarcely for a righteous man will one die: yet peradventure for a good man some would even dare to die. But God commendeth his love toward us in that, while we were yet sinners, Christ died for us."

"The treasures of earth are not mine,
    I hold not its silver and gold;
But a treasure far greater is mine;
    I have riches of value untold.

"The treasures of earth must all fail,
    Its riches and honor decay,
But the riches of love that are mine,
    Even death cannot take them away.

. . . . .

"Come, take of the riches of Christ,
    Exhaustless and free is the store;
Of its wonderful fullness receive,
    Till you hunger and thirst nevermore."

—H. B. Hartzler

Life and True Values *March 18*

THE RICHES OF GOD'S GRACE

In whom we have redemption through his blood, the forgiveness of sins, according to the riches of his grace. **Eph. 1:7.**

Our text today brings to light the riches of God's grace, the riches of redemption and forgiveness of sins. God's grace and His love go hand in hand. Think for a moment of the riches of forgiveness. Perhaps we can better appreciate these riches in the light of the parable of the prodigal son "turned upside down."

Martin Jerod Kerr, in his book *Our Trespasses,* tells the story of the prodigal in a way to shock us into an appreciation of the true wonder of the parable as Jesus actually gave it. He tells the story very much like the one in the Bible until the point where the young man turns homeward. Then he goes on, "He had wondered whether by some coincidence his father might happen to be looking out of a window and see him coming and run out to meet him, but no one came. At last he reached the front door. He knocked, but there was no answer. Hearing noise that was going on inside, he knocked again, and louder. After a long wait and more knocking, he heard the bolts being drawn, and at last the door was opened. His father stood in the entrance peering out into the night. 'Father,' he cried, 'it's your son. I've made an awful mess of things, I'm afraid. I know it's all my fault, but honestly I'll try to do better if you will only let me come back. Will you take me back? Just as one of your servants?' His father looked at him strangely, 'My son? I have only one son, and he is inside with me.' And as the boy turned away, he could hear behind him the noise of music and voices."

What if Jesus had given the parable that way? Ah, but He didn't. He not only pictured the love of God as a forgiving heavenly Father but demonstrated that love again and again. The climax of that demonstration was the dramatic scene of the crucifixion when He cried out, "Father, forgive them; for they know not what they do" (Luke 23:34). Here we have revealed the riches of God's grace in Christ.

Life and True Values March 19

The Value of Influence

For none of us liveth to himself, and no man dieth to himself. Rom. 14:7.

Everett W. Lord, dean of the College of Business Administration of Boston University, once said, "The hours we invest in ourselves are worth a minimum of ten dollars apiece whether they be in college or out of college. There is no doubt on that point. Hard, unsentimental statistics prove it. But the hours or minutes we invest in other people have a worth beyond calculation. They reach out into unseen lives through ever-widening circles of influence touching the borders of eternity."

In *Christ's Object Lessons,* page 339, we read: "The life of Christ was an ever-widening, shoreless influence, an influence that bound Him to God and to the whole human family. Through Christ, God has invested man with an influence that makes it impossible for him to live to himself. Individually we are connected with our fellow men, a part of God's great whole, and we stand under mutual obligations. No man can be independent of his fellow men; for the well-being of each affects others. It is God's purpose that each shall feel himself necessary to others' welfare, and seek to promote their happiness."

Think, for example, of the influence of Mary's act of love in breaking the alabaster box of ointment upon her Saviour's feet. What a rich harvest of healing influence has flooded the world as a result of that one unselfish, thoughtful act!

"A little spring had lost its way among the grass and fern;
A passing stranger scooped a well where weary ones might turn.
He walled it in and hung with care a ladle on its brink;
He thought not of the deed he did, but judged that toil might drink.
He passed again, and, lo, the well by summers never dried,
Had cooled ten thousand parched tongues and saved a life beside."

—*Author Unknown*

Life and True Values March 20

FIRST THINGS FIRST

But seek ye first the kingdom of God, and his righteousness; and all these things shall be added unto you. **Matt. 6:33.**

Living is a matter of making choices. What a man is at the end of his life is the sum total of all his decisions. It is important, then, that he choose wisely. There are some decisions that take priority, upon which all others depend. You must first decide where you are going before you can determine the route to take. A man must decide what he wants to do before he buys his tools. If a man wants to be a surgeon or a minister, he will choose his college course accordingly.

The three most important decisions young people make have to do with their relationship to God, their choice of a lifework, and their choice of a life companion. Of these three the first takes priority, for the character of one's lifework as well as that of one's life companion will be determined by one's relation to God. It is also well to choose one's lifework before choosing a life companion, because the kind of wife a man has makes a big difference to him in his profession. Too many do not take this into consideration, and they find later their choice of a life companion interfering with their career as well as with their relationship to God.

"Choose you this day whom ye will serve" (Joshua 24:15). Around this choice all others revolve. Sometimes choosing to serve God seems to jeopardize the supplying of food and clothing and shelter. This happens in a world that has turned its back on God, but our heavenly Father knows our needs, and these will be cared for. His promises are sure. "All these things shall be added unto you." Notice, too, we are to seek not only the kingdom of God but also His righteousness. Too many Christians seek the kingdom with all its blessings and rewards, and forget His righteousness. Once we seek and find the righteousness of Christ, all the blessings and rewards of the kingdom follow. Every other choice will be made in that light, and glorious will be the results in the life. Let us make first things first, today.

Life and True Values March 21

A GOOD NAME AND LOVING FAVOR

A good name is rather to be chosen than great riches, and loving favour rather than silver and gold. Prov. 22:1.

A good name. What is in a name? In the business world the brand name of a piece of merchandise is always of importance. One would rather pay a little more to get merchandise with the good name than to pay less and not be sure. Certain names stand for certain qualities. So it is with men.

Men name their dogs Nero, but their sons Paul. And why? Nero stands for infamy and horror. Paul stands for Christian character. It is the character suggested by the name that makes the difference. A good name and loving favor go hand in hand. Should we through bribery, shrewd bargaining, maneuvering, and trickery destroy them? Should we through cheating, misrepresentation, or even lack of dependability lose both? Would it not be better to lose a little silver and gold to make for good relationships? Often silver and gold blind us to the needs of others. A certain wealthy man who had lost sight of God received a call from his former pastor. The pastor asked him to look through the window and to tell what he saw. The man replied that he saw people walking by on the sidewalk below. The pastor then asked him to look into a mirror and state what he saw. Obviously, the rich man saw only himself. The pastor then said, "When you looked through the window glass, you saw people, but as soon as a little silver was added to plain glass, you saw nothing but yourself." So it is, sometimes, with men who once knew God and were compassionate with their fellow men. They have often allowed silver and gold to obscure the face of God and the needs of their fellow men.

What shall one do who has unfortunately inherited a bad name? The only procedure is to so live as to lift the reputation of that name by a life in association with a name that is above every name. Jesus Christ can change your name. He was able to change Jacob to Israel. He can do the same for you and for me.

Life and True Values March 22

BEFORE HONOR IS HUMILITY

The fear of the Lord is the instruction of wisdom; and before honour is humility. **Prov. 15:33.**

More important than to *receive* honor is to *deserve* it, and he is most deserving of honor who humbly serves most. There are people who are more interested in the crown than they are in the cross. There have been great men in the world who have fallen far short of being the help they might have been, simply because they were more interested in position and honor than in humble service and in doing what was right.

According to Henry Ward Beecher, such a man was Daniel Webster, of American history fame. After outlining the many ways in which Webster towered above his fellows, Beecher goes on to say, "He sacrificed them all for the bubble of the Presidency. He sold himself for it, and he sold himself at such a price that he was not esteemed worth anything by the men who bought him, and they threw him off and his heart broke and he died counting his whole life to have been a total failure." According to Beecher, here was a man who would give up his clear views of right in order to curry favor for position and honor.

Quite different from this was the attitude of Henry Clay. Having felt called upon to define his position on the subject of slavery, and having carefully prepared his argument, Clay read it to Colonel Preston, at the same time asking his opinion of it. "I quite agree with you in your views, Mr. Clay," replied the latter, "but I think it would be better for you to leave out such and such parts. The expression of such opinions, I feel, will injure your prospects for the Presidency in my part of the country." "Am I right, Sir?" asked Clay. "I think you are." "Then, sir," said Clay with decision, "I shall say every word of it and compromise not one jot or tittle. I would rather be right than President."

We need more men who would rather humbly serve in the fear of the Lord than sit in the places of worldly honor. These will be honored at last, for "he that humbleth himself shall be exalted."

Life and True Values March 23

OBEDIENCE BETTER THAN SACRIFICE

Behold, to obey is better than sacrifice, and to hearken than the fat of rams. 1 Sam. 15:22.

It was a great day of victory for Saul. At least he thought so. But somehow his judgment had become so perverted that he could disobey God and still think he was obeying God. Strange, isn't it? Temporary success always blinds selfish men. Wonderful things had been accomplished that day. The enemies were destroyed, and the armies of Israel had experienced a great victory. God had given specific instructions to spare nothing. Saul and the people, however, spared Agag and the best of the sheep and oxen and lambs. As Saul returned and met Samuel, he said, "Blessed be thou of the Lord: I have performed the commandment of the Lord." So blinded was Saul that he could disregard God's command and yet joyfully exclaim, "I have performed the commandment of the Lord." Samuel questioned the noise of sheep and oxen. Saul replied, "Oh, these we've kept for sacrifice." It was then that Samuel said, "Behold, to obey is better than sacrifice."

Saul had missed the purpose of the sacrificial system altogether. He had confused the symbols with what they symbolized, and thought they were an end in themselves. We, too, may miss the significance of our acts of worship. We may confuse the form with the content.

God is more interested in obedience and service motivated by love than He is in a multitude of forms and ceremonies or great sacrifices. In fact, sacrifices without obedience are obnoxious to Him. Listen to His appeal through Isaiah the prophet: "To what purpose is the multitude of your sacrifices unto me? saith the Lord: I am full of the burnt offerings of rams, and the fat of fed beasts; and I delight not in the blood of bullocks, or of lambs, or of he goats." "Wash you, make you clean; put away the evil of your doings from before mine eyes; cease to do evil; learn to do well" (Isa. 1:11, 16, 17).

Even in worship we should keep our sense of values clear. May God help us to learn the value of obedience through love today.

Life and True Values March 24

CHOOSE THE NARROW WAY

Because strait is the gate, and narrow is the way, which leadeth unto life, and few there be that find it. **Matt. 7:14.**

Before us stretch two ways, the broad way and the narrow way. We must choose. The wise choice is the narrow way. Why?

The word "narrow" carries with it a connotation that is rather damaging. We think of a man as narrow who has a narrow point of view. With self as the center and his own grasp as a radius, he draws around himself a circumference that makes a very small circle, within which he lives and moves. Jesus is not talking about this kind of narrowness. He says, "Narrow is the *way*," not "Narrow is the *man*." You will find the big man in the narrow way, and the little man in the broad way. The broad-minded men walk the narrow way, while the narrow-minded men travel the broad way.

This is true because only the narrow way is the successful way. Men achieve success only by stern, severe discipline. All creativity comes within narrow limits. The chemist and the physicist must walk the narrow way. The more progress a man would make in the field of research, the smaller must be his area of concentration.

This principle lies at the basis of all the fine arts. The arts are called fine because of the narrowness of the limitations that they impose. Musicians must walk the narrow way. They cannot be flat or sharp. Artists must work in harmony with the laws of perspective and color. In the fine art of living, it is the narrow way that leads to the abundant life. A life channeled into narrow lines of constructive activity is the happy life.

Occasionally someone says to a young man or woman, "Don't be so narrow-minded." He implies that to be true to moral laws is to be narrow; to be broad-minded one must be free to do as he pleases. Actually, the individual who thinks only of immediate desires is narrow.

Whereas the person who thinks in terms of eternal values is the broad-minded one.

Life and True Values March 25

A RECOGNITION OF SPIRITUAL NEED

Blessed are the poor in spirit: for their's is the kingdom of heaven. Matt. 5:3.

Life's greatest values are right attitudes. Jesus was more concerned with attitudes than with good works of ritual, rules or regulations. He was anxious about relationships, for a right relationship with God and our fellow man is the essence of Christian living. And that which counts most in relationships is attitudes. These reach down deep into the heart. A man is what his attitudes reveal him to be.

In the Beatitudes of the Sermon on the Mount Jesus talks about the attitudes that bless humanity, attitudes that are fundamental in Christian growth and welfare. First He says, "Blessed are the poor in spirit." This sounds strange. Have you ever seen a person who manifested a very poor spirit in a given situation? Does Jesus pronounce a blessing upon such? Obviously not. What he actually says is this: "Blessed are those who recognize their spiritual poverty." Goodspeed translates it: "Blessed are those who feel their spiritual need."

Sad is the condition of an individual who desperately needs a physician but doesn't know it, will not recognize his need. There isn't very much a physician can do for such a one. We remember the Pharisee who prayed with himself, "God, I thank thee, that I am not as other men are" (Luke 18:11). Not much could be done for him. But the publican recognized his great need, and he went home justified. Jesus could do more for publicans and harlots who felt their need than He could for self-righteous Pharisees. The blessing in this attitude, this recognition of need, lies not only in its placing a man where he can be helped and taught but also in its placing him in a position of having something definite to work toward. Before him lie wonderful opportunities for growth and spiritual achievement. This is stimulating. "Their's is the kingdom of heaven," said Jesus. The use of the present tense here is interesting. A man who has this attitude makes room for the Holy Spirit, and he has the kingdom of heaven within.

Life and True Values March 26

A CAPACITY FOR TRUE SORROW

Blessed are they that mourn: for they shall be comforted. **Matt. 5:4.**

Here's a strange statement. To the superficial observer it seems that Jesus is saying, "Happy are they who are sad." Is He putting a premium upon the sad and the gloomy? No. We are told in *The Ministry of Healing:* "It is a positive duty to resist melancholy, discontented thoughts, and feelings—as much a duty as it is to pray. If we are heaven-bound, how can we go as a band of mourners, groaning and complaining all along the way to our Father's house?"—Page 251.

Such is not the kind of mourning Jesus blesses in this beatitude. There is a sorrow that brings deep-seated joy. When one becomes aware of his spiritual poverty, he is saddened by what he finds in himself, and he begins to see sin in a different light. He is filled with a sorrow that works repentance. He will always be conforted.

This attitude involves our relation to others—entering into their sorrows and sharing their heartaches and burdens. The capacity to be sympathetic is Christlike. Occasionally we hear of a person who boasts of not shedding a tear for years. Such a one should really be ashamed of his insensitive heart, which cannot sympathize with another's woe. The true Christian will be sad when he sees others throw their lives away in sin.

Jesus was a man of sorrows and acquainted with grief; however, His greatest sorrow was not His own personal pain, but the sufferings of others in sin. The weight of a sin-burdened world broke His heart. He said to the women who followed His cross, "Weep not for me, but weep for yourselves" (Luke 23:28). Jesus bore our griefs and carried our sorrows that He might redeem us from sin, which causes heartache and sorrow. As His followers, when we learn to love as He loved, we will also learn to share another's burden, and in sharing, there is comfort and joy. The word "comforted" means "strengthened by being with." There is strength, joy, and satisfaction in the fellowship of suffering.

Life and True Values │ March 27

HUMILITY AND SELF-CONTROL

Blessed are the meek: for they shall inherit the earth. **Matt.** 5:5.

Meekness is too often associated with weakness. We think of a meek little lamb as one that is unable to stand up for its rights and therefore becomes the prey of more courageous wolves, that take advantage of it. This is far from what Jesus had in mind. Meekness is not weakness, but strength—strength of self-control coupled with humility.

A missionary once asked some native children to explain what Jesus meant when He said, "Blessed are the meek." One little fellow replied, "A meek man is a man who can give soft answers to rough questions." He was right. It takes more of the grace of God to give soft answers to rough questions than to conquer a city. The wise man tells us in Proverbs 16:32, "He that is slow to anger is better than the mighty; and he that ruleth his spirit than he that taketh a city."

Moses is said to be an example of true meekness. Of him we read in Numbers 12:3, "Now the man Moses was very meek, above all the men which were upon the face of the earth." There was nothing weak about Moses. What a wonderful spirit he manifested, however, that day when he pleaded for Israel, and said, "Lord, forgive their sin, and, if not, blot me, I pray thee, out of thy book which thou hast written." Here is a mark of true greatness.

Meekness at its best, in all its wonder and strength and beauty, you see demonstrated by the Master Himself as you follow Him from Gethsemane to Calvary. When He was reviled, He reviled not again. Self-control and humility have their roots in unselfishness, which is the fruit of the love of God in the heart. We can see why this wonderful quality precedes the first two. Most retaliation is prompted by wounded pride, or selfishness. The recognition of our own spiritual poverty, together with a sympathetic, understanding heart, makes one humble before God, who gives strength of self-control. May God grant us His spirit that we may manifest that attitude of meekness today.

Life and True Values　　　　　　　　　　　　　　　　March 28

A Longing for Righteousness

Blessed are they which do hunger and thirst after righteousness: for they shall be filled. **Matt. 5:6.**

Two young people were discussing the matter of Christian living, when one said to the other words to this effect: "It is not that I especially enjoy being a Christian, but there is no other way. There is no question but that Christianity is true. According to all the prophecies we are living in the last days. Soon Jesus will come, and I don't want to be lost. If only I hadn't heard about these things, then I wouldn't have to live them, but since I have, and since I don't want to burn, well, here goes, I'll do my best." This attitude implies that righteousness is something forced upon one, something to be avoided if possible, something that does not bring true joy and happiness.

Jesus spoke of righteousness as being highly desirable, satisfying, necessary to life and happiness, attractive. What a difference! What if you heard someone say, "Oh, I wish I didn't have to eat, but I don't want to die. So here goes." What would you think? It would obviously be an indication of ill health. As a normal appetite is a good indication of physical health, the desire for righteousness is a good indication of spiritual health. When people lose their desire to worship, pray, or read the Bible, it is a sign of danger.

Outward conformity to rules and regulations without a change of heart, a longing desire within, brings no joy, and such religion is worth nothing. A man's true tastes and his desires are a pretty good test of his character. If we analyze our tastes, we will discover that they have become perverted. This is what sin has done to the human race. Jesus wants to purify and ennoble these. We should pray as did David, "Create in me a clean heart, O God; and renew a right spirit within me" (Ps. 51:10).

Once we catch a glimpse of the life He offers, we discover within us a longing for His righteousness. As we nourish that longing, like eating good food, we delight in it more and more.

Life and True Values March 29

SYMPATHY AND MERCY

Blessed are the merciful: for they shall obtain mercy. Matt. 5:7.

Apion, who was called Plistonices, in the fifth book of his *Wonders of Egypt,* describes an amazing experience that he saw with his own eyes in the city of Rome in the days of Julius Caesar. In the great circus, he says, a battle with wild beasts on a grand scale was being exhibited to the people. There was brought in the slave of a cruel exconsul of Northern Africa. The slave's name was Androclus. When the lion saw him from a distance, says Apion, he stopped short, as if in amazement, then approached the man slowly, quietly, and began to lick his feet and hands. Androclus, while submitting to the caresses of so fierce a beast, regained his lost courage and gradually turned his eyes to look at the lion. Then, says Apion further, man and lion exchanged joyful greetings, as though they recognized each other. This being truly astonishing, the people broke out into mighty shouts. Julius Caesar called Androclus to him and inquired the reason for his being spared.

It was then that Androclus related a strange and surprising story. He said that after fleeing from his cruel master he had hidden in a cave in a lonely desert. A lion with one paw lame and bleeding had entered, making known by groaning the torturing pain of his wound. At first sight Androclus was afraid, but the lion held up his paw, and he saw a huge splinter imbedded in the sole of the foot. This he removed, and then he dressed the wound as best he could. The lion lay down to rest. It was years later that the slave and the lion met on that famous day in the circus. Because Androclus had been merciful to the lion he now obtained mercy from the lion. "Blessed are the merciful: for they shall obtain mercy."

Life and True Values *March 30*

PURITY OF HEART

Blessed are the pure in heart: for they shall see God. Matt. 5:8.

Purity of heart involves purity of thought and purity of motive. Impure words and actions come from impure thoughts. "Out of the abundance of the heart the mouth speaketh. A good man out of the good treasure of the heart bringeth forth good things: and an evil man out of the evil treasure bringeth forth evil things" (Matt. 12:34, 35). Polluted springs cannot give forth fresh, clear, clean water. We need, therefore, the Holy Spirit to purify the springs, and to bring every thought into captivity to Him.

Not only are clean thoughts to be cherished, but pure motives are to prompt every action. It is motive that gives character to an act. It is not so much what we do that counts as why we do it. When we truthfully examine our motives, it is surprising how many ulterior ones prompt even some of our seemingly noble acts and deeds. Is it possible that we are kind and courteous to a rich man in order to win his favor? Is it possible we give more when others are watching than we do when no one sees? Is it possible that we take certain positions to be well thought of rather than to serve? Because of selfish motives, have we taken an unfair advantage of a weaker brother? Just how honest are we at heart in all our dealings and reports? Have we ever by silence given the wrong impression? Have we told the truth about another that would better have been left untold, simply to lower that one in the eyes of someone whose respect we wanted? Have we hoped that we would be better thought of in comparison? These are searching questions.

Clean hands and a pure heart give strength and security. "My strength is as the strength of ten, because my heart is pure."

Let us pray today, "Lord, take my heart; for I cannot give it. It is Thy property. Keep it pure, for I cannot keep it for Thee. . . . Mold me, fashion me, raise me into a pure and holy atmosphere, where the rich current of Thy love can flow through my soul."—*Christ's Object Lessons*, p. 159.

Life and True Values
March 31

Peace and Good Will

Blessed are the peacemakers: for they shall be called the children of God. Matt. 5:9.

Living in a world of sin, sick with strife and trouble, we do not need to look far to find the place where the peacemaker is needed. Troublemakers are everywhere. Jesus wants us to be peacemakers. Altogether too many are not at peace with God, with themselves, or with their fellow men. Like Saul of Tarsus, they are constantly kicking against their consciences and taking it out on others. Many a man, struggling against giving his heart to the Lord, takes it out on his family or fellow workmen on the job. Often at home a vicious cycle begins. The man gets angry with his wife. She, in turn, scolds Junior. Junior goes outside and kicks the dog. The dog is irritated and chases the cat. The cat comes running into the house through an open door, with the dog after her. This disturbs the man reading his paper. He shouts at his wife. The wife shouts at Junior. Junior screams at the dog, and the dog barks at the cat, and around and around they go.

Whence come all these conflicts? Mostly from the lack of the Prince of Peace in the life. When Christ is lacking within, there is missing the unifying power of the Holy Spirit in a man's life. Selfishness, insecurity, together with misunderstanding, lead a man into conflict with himself, with others, and with God.

A troublemaker is a man who is at war with all three. He cannot be content to fight his own battle. He must involve everybody else. The peacemaker, on the other hand, has found peace with God in his own soul through Jesus Christ and His forgiveness. Experiencing this joy, he seeks to help others find their peace with God and thus with themselves. Then it is surprising how peace with fellow men follows.

APRIL

Life Through Faith　　　　　　　　　　　　　　　　　　　　*April 1*

WE LIVE BY FAITH

Now the just shall live by faith: but if any man draw back, my soul shall have no pleasure in him. Heb. 10:38.

"That's the trouble with Christianity! You must have faith in so much you can't see and can't understand!" So speak those who find it hard to accept certain phases of Christianity. Strange how this suddenly becomes a problem in the field of religion, when every day we live by faith in things and men much less certain than God.

Is not faith the key to success in any worth-while endeavor? Take research, for example. How much time and energy would a man expend in scientific experiments if he did not have faith in the laws of nature? How much money would a scientist invest in a project pertaining to electronics, if he did not have faith in the laws of electricity?

In the field of business there would be no progress without faith. Some years ago, lots for homes were selling for $150 each in a certain area around La Sierra College. Five years later they sold for $1,000 apiece. Suppose we had been in the real-estate business, and Mr. James, who owned a number of the lots referred to, had said to us, "Look, friends, I'll sell you these lots at $150. Five years from now they will sell for $1,000." And suppose we had reasoned thus: "No, we'll wait and see. It must be proved first, then we'll invest." How much would we have profited by such a procedure?

Every day we live by faith. We have faith in our public utilities, in the milkman, in the seeds we sow. How many friends would you have if you had no faith in human beings? The just live by faith—faith in God, faith in themselves, and faith in their fellow men.

Faith is the key to knowledge, the key to fellowship, the key to success in business, to success in every endeavor involving the laws of nature and our relation to men and women about us. Why should it not be the key in our relation to God? It is.

Life Through Faith *April 2*

Faith Defined

Now faith is the substance of things hoped for, the evidence of things not seen. Heb. 11:1.

If asked to define faith, most of us would quote our text for today; but if an accurate census could be taken of every man's understanding of what faith really is, there would probably be a great variety of concepts, ranging from some profound philosophy of life down to that of the small schoolboy who said, "Faith is believin' somethin' you know ain't so."

What is faith? First, let us remember that to define is to circumscribe. To define faith in terms of a formula is to limit it. Faith has many aspects. This month we shall consider some of them.

Let us read our text for today from Weymouth's translation. "Now faith is a confident assurance of that for which we hope, a conviction of the reality of things which we do not see." Today let us think of faith as that confident assurance that comes from fellowship with Christ. The person who lives by faith, lives with a conviction of the reality of fellowship with Christ, who said, "Lo, I am with you alway, even unto the end." Some things can be experienced but not explained. Faith is one of these. Think of it as a relationship that is dynamic, which deepens our convictions and increases our sense of the reality of the spiritual.

Thus faith is not merely an attitude of mind with a psychological effect, it is an assurance that grows through fellowship. Faith is not a mystical, magical power that can be mustered up or prayed down to work great miracles. If it were, then the greater the power to work miracles, the greater the faith. Faith would be measured by miracle-working power, but many great men of faith never worked a single miracle in the superficial sense of the term. The power of faith is the power that comes from fellowship with the Divine. Neither is faith an insurance against calamity. Many faithful men suffered martyrdom, but it was fellowship with Christ and His sufferings that gave them courage. May God grant us that fellowship with the Master today.

Life Through Faith   *April 3*

THE EYE OF FAITH

These all died in faith, not having received the promises, but having seen them afar off, and were persuaded of them, and embraced them, and confessed that they were strangers and pilgrims on the earth. Heb. 11:13.

Faith is not blind. One aspect of faith is clear spiritual vision. Let us call this the "eye" of faith. Our text today declares that the great men of faith "all died in faith, not having received the promises, but having *seen* them." Abraham *"looked* for a city which hath foundations, whose builder and maker is God" (v. 10). Moses "endured, as *seeing* him who is invisible" (v. 27).

Through the eye of faith we see. We see the reality of the spiritual world—the reality of God, of Jesus Christ, of angel ministry, and of heaven, where they are preparing a place for us.

The eye of faith gives true perspective. A young sailor climbs a tall mast for the first time. He looks down and sees the rolling billows far below, and is paralyzed with fear. An old-timer shouts, "Look up, sailor; fix your vision on a star." He does, and is steadied by the gaze and enabled to do his work. You see, it is the view of the distant that steadies against the whirl of the present. Through the eye of faith we look back over the past and see the guiding hand of God in the affairs of men. Through the telescope of prophecy we look into the future and see the triumph of righteousness in the establishment of the kingdom of God. This gives us courage and strength today.

When passing through the valley of the shadow and through troubled waters, by the eye of faith we can see one like unto the Son of man by our side. We are not discouraged by the darkness of a trying hour, nor overwhelmed by the glitter and brilliance of a momentary temptation, because through the eye of faith we can view the present in the light of eternity. This gives us a true sense of values.

As we pray today for increased faith, let us think of it in terms of increased insights and spiritual vision.

Life Through Faith *April 4*

THE HAND OF FAITH

For in Jesus Christ neither circumcision availeth any thing, nor uncircumcision; but faith which worketh by love. **Gal. 5:6.**

There is in faith the element of insight and vision. But vision without action accomplishes nothing. Skillful action in harmony with a great vision is what produces results. Of what value is a new insight if we do not act in harmony with it? Today we are reminded that the faith that "availeth any thing" is the faith that works—"faith which worketh by love." "Faith without works is dead" (James 2:26).

This is true in all fields of endeavor. How much does an architect accomplish if he only dreams of a new design for a bridge or a building? Unless he puts his ideas on paper and plans carefully every detail, and then in cooperation with his engineers and craftsmen of various talents acts accordingly, his dream perishes with him.

A business executive studies the complex details of a large concern and thinks through a more efficient plan of operation. Unless he is able to effect a reorganization and work his plan, what good is it?

The same is true in the field of fine arts. That which makes an artist great, whether he be a poet, a painter, a sculptor, or a musician, is his unusual ability to express his creation on paper, on canvas, in stone, or through some musical instrument. The greater the vision and the more skillful the action in harmony with it, the greater the contribution. Without the action, the vision dies with the artist.

In no field is this more true than in the field of human relations. How successful would a young man be in courting a young woman if he never expressed the love he had in his heart? What good would be your confidence and faith in a physician if in time of need you never called him? You may have ever so much faith and confidence in an attorney; but when you are in need of legal advice, if you neither ask for counsel nor follow it, your faith availeth nothing.

As in every area of life, so it is in our relation to Jesus Christ. Only "faith which worketh by love" counts.

Life Through Faith April 5

THE SHIELD OF FAITH

Above all, taking the shield of faith, wherewith ye shall be able to quench all the fiery darts of the wicked. Eph. 6:16.

A diamond perfectly cut and polished has many facets. Each reflects the light, and together they sparkle in wondrous beauty. From different points of view, a diamond presents a glory that distinguishes it from all other gems. Faith is like that. It, too, has many facets. One is insight—the eye of faith. Another is works—the hand of faith. Faith has in it also the element of belief and trust.

Let us notice this aspect of faith as it is brought to view in the expression "the shield of faith." Our text presents the picture of an ancient warrior going forth to meet the enemy, protected by his shield. Paul points out that we are to face our spiritual enemies, "taking the shield of faith, with which" we "can quench all the flaming darts of the evil one" (R.S.V.).

Satan always strikes at the weakest spot. For his arrows he uses words of discouragement and criticism, doubt and condemnation, as well as calamities and adverse circumstances of all kinds. Temptations and deceptions of many varieties are hurled at us from every angle. These arrows are to be met by faith—which makes them all of no avail.

Note the following statement: "The Father's presence encircled Christ, and nothing befell Him but that which infinite love permitted for the blessing of the world. Here was His source of comfort, and it is for us. He who is imbued with the Spirit of Christ abides in Christ. Whatever comes to him comes from the Saviour, who surrounds him with His presence. Nothing can touch him except by the Lord's permission. All our sufferings and sorrows, all our temptations and trials, all our sadness and griefs, all our persecutions and privations, in short, all things work together for our good."—*The Ministry of Healing,* p. 489.

What a wonderful shield! Let us cultivate the consciousness of His presence with us today.

Life Through Faith *April 6*

TRUST GOD, NOT YOUR IDEAS FOR GOD

Trust in the Lord with all thine heart; and lean not unto thine own understanding. Prov. 3:5.

Isn't it strange that the wise man should say, "Lean not unto thine own understanding"? One would think he should have said, "Trust in the Lord, and use your head." Does God give man a mind and then counsel him not to use it? By no means. We are not to neglect the use of our reasoning powers, for we remember the words, "Come now, and let us reason together" (Isa. 1:18).

Our text today calls for a recognition of the limitations of human reason. There are many things in this vast universe in which we live that transcend reason. God wants us to know that in these areas we can trust Him. Our own understanding is so very limited that to lean upon it alone is to limit God in what He can and would like to do for us.

Take, for example, the widow in Old Testament times whose two sons were about to be taken as slaves in payment of the family debt. When Elisha was called he asked, "What hast thou in the house?" When told she had only a pot of oil, he gave instructions to borrow empty vessels of all the neighbors, not a few; and the widow was asked to pour the oil from its container into these. Of all the foolish things to do! What good would it do to pour what oil she had into the other containers? From the human point of view the best she could do would be to pour the oil from one pot to another, and the result would be a lot of greasy dishes to be washed and some of the oil she had had would be gone. Had she leaned on her own understanding in that hour she would not have received the blessing from the Lord, and she would have lost her sons. However, she had learned to trust in the Lord with all her heart, and to lean not unto her own understanding. Marvelous was the result. The vessels were all filled with oil. She went into the oil business and paid her debt.

God wants us to use our minds, but first He wants our hearts. Then He can bless us. Let us give Him our hearts today.

Life Through Faith   *April 7*

HE SHALL DIRECT THY PATHS

In all thy ways acknowledge him, and he shall direct thy paths. Prov. 3:6.

It is a wonderful thing to have the right kind of guide as we travel along life's pathway. We need one in whom we can have confidence, and we need to follow him if we expect to reach our destination. The Lord invites us to acknowledge Him in all our ways, and we are assured of His direction. "God never leads His children otherwise than they would choose to be led, if they could see the end from the beginning, and discern the glory of the purpose which they are fulfilling as coworkers with him."—*The Ministry of Healing,* p. 479.

There are times in human experience when we find it hard to believe that God is directing. However, God is able not only to make all things come out right in the future but also to use the things that are not good as agents, or steppingstones, to the fulfillment of higher purposes in the present as well.

Think of the experiences of Jacob and Joseph. How Jacob's heart must have ached when he saw the attitude of his sons toward Joseph and when he thought a wild beast had destroyed his favorite son! Was God directing in this? How terrible Joseph must have felt when he was cast into the pit and then taken out and sold into Egypt! Was this God's doing? What thoughts must have gone through his mind when he was cast into prison for doing what was right, standing true to principle, refusing to sin against God and Potiphar! How could God allow him to be thus mistreated when he had been true and loyal to Him?

As Jacob suffered because of the supposed loss of his son, he exclaimed, "All these things are against me." But in the end it was clearly revealed that God was directing. Not all that happens is God's doing, but "in everything God works for good with those who love him" (Rom. 8:28 R.S.V.).

Friend, if in all your ways you acknowledge God and, like Joseph, resolve to be loyal and true, God will direct your paths too.

Life Through Faith   *April 8*

FAITH AND FULL ASSURANCE

Let us draw near with a true heart in full assurance of faith, having our hearts sprinkled from an evil conscience, and our bodies washed with pure water. Heb. 10:22.

There are people whose conscience seems always to bother them no matter what they do. Others are troubled over past sins that were confessed and made right long ago. A voice seems to say, "You had better ask forgiveness again," or, "There must be something wrong or you wouldn't feel as you do."

Another group is troubled over past sins that can't be made right, and a voice says, "There is just no hope for you." Other disturbing voices say, "Nothing you do is just right, you might as well quit." "Maybe you aren't doing all you should." "You shouldn't rest, that's being lazy." "If you are having fun, it must be wrong."

An unhealthy conscience gives certain individuals no end of trouble over past unwise promises. "You can't break your promise now. You had better be true to your word and go ahead even if you know it is not right." Often there is trouble over little details, to the exclusion of the more important issues. This indicates an unhealthy conscience and the inability to distinguish between the voice of the Holy Spirit and the voice of Satan.

Wrong ideas about God and His requirements result in an unhealthy conscience, and Satan takes advantage of this. When you really learn to know your heavenly Father as a God of love, who understands, who does not expect the impossible, and who does not hold you responsible for that over which you have no control, you can rest assured that any voice contrary to the way of peace and joy and love is not His. "By their fruits ye shall know them" (Matt. 7:20). The voices that bring only anxiety and frustration are from Satan, not God. Faith in God brings peace of mind and heart. Let us draw near today with a true heart, in full assurance of faith. This is the remedy for an unhealthy conscience. This is the secret of a happy Christian life.

Life Through Faith *April 9*

JUSTIFIED BY FAITH

Therefore we conclude that a man is justified by faith without the deeds of the law. Rom. 3:28.

When we think of faith in terms of fellowship and trust, justification by faith takes on new meaning. Christian living is a matter of a satisfying personal love relationship with God and our fellow men, in a great controversy. In this controversy sin separates men from God and from one another; and because of sin, forgiveness is necessary if a satisfying relationship is to be re-established.

Justification is the term applied to that act which takes care of past sins and reinstates us into the right relationship with God again (see Rom. 3:25). This involves forgiveness. Now, forgiveness is a transaction that takes place in the heart, and this is more important than the record of that transaction in heaven. Sometimes we are more concerned about the sin on the record than we are about the sin in our hearts. It is true that one sin left unconfessed on the record book of heaven will keep us out of heaven, but not because it is on the record. Rather, because it is in the heart.

Since forgiveness is a heart experience, we can understand that forgiveness can be experienced only in an atmosphere of love, fellowship, and faith.

No amount of good works, no careful future obedience or promises to obey, will take care of our past transgressions. Only the pardoning grace can set us free. This is why we are justified by faith without the deeds of the law. Justification, or forgiveness, is not merited by good works. How glad we can be that this is true. Faith and love alone can truly forgive, and faith and love are attitudes involving persons. There is no faith, love, and forgiveness apart from persons. The real person in whom we can have faith and whom we can love is the Lord Jesus Christ, who has faith in us and who loves us. In this atmosphere of love and fellowship, forgiveness—justification, if you please—is an understandable reality.

Life Through Faith *April 10*

BY GRACE THROUGH FAITH

For by grace are ye saved through faith; and that not of yourselves: it is the gift of God. Eph. 2:8.

Faith is not our Saviour; Jesus is. Salvation is the gift of God "in . . . kindness toward us through Christ Jesus" (Eph. 2:7). Salvation is not the result of faith which we can work hard to develop. Salvation comes only by grace, an attribute of God that operates in our behalf, through no merits of our own, but becomes effective in our lives through faith. Jesus offers it to us as a gift from His Father and makes possible our accepting it through fellowship with Himself.

Will Ripley, Jr., was sentenced to be shot July 8, 1863, for sleeping on guard. Abe Lincoln, President of the United States, listened to Will's younger brother, Dan, age fourteen, plead for his brother's life. Impressed with the lad's appeal, he pardoned Will and stayed the execution. Did Will earn this stay of execution? Did he merit pardon? By no means. It was only by the grace of the President that he was permitted to live. Was there any room for boasting then? No, only rejoicing and gratitude. So it is with our salvation from sin.

Suppose a friend should give you a new airplane that required two pilots, offer to teach you how to fly it, and volunteer to be your copilot to take you to your destination. Suppose that you should accept his offer, take his instruction, and begin your flight. You would make mistakes, but he would help you and make up for your deficiencies and lack of knowledge. Upon arriving at your destination, would you have whereof to boast? No, you would be there only because of your faith in your friend's graciousness. So with our salvation. It is offered us as a gift through Jesus Christ, made possible by the grace of God.

We, too, need a copilot, if you please. Jesus says, "Without me ye can do nothing" (John 15:5). He offers to be with us "even unto the end" of the journey. Let us have faith, let us believe what He says, accept His gift, invite Him to be our copilot, and keep in close touch with Him all along the way.

Life Through Faith   *April 11*

Through Faith We Understand

Through faith we understand that the worlds were framed by the word of God, so that things which are seen were not made of things which do appear. Heb. 11:3.

How can things seen be made out of things not seen? "By the word of the Lord were the heavens made; and all the host of them by the breath of his mouth." "For he spake, and it was done; he commanded, and it stood fast" (Ps. 33:6, 9).

In creating things material God was not indebted to pre-existing matter. This is hard for us to understand. When God tells us something beyond the reach of man's reason, it can be understood only by faith. We take Him at His word, and study and plan and act accordingly. As we do we increase in knowledge and understanding. Gradually we come to know more and more about the things that seem at first so difficult of comprehension.

It is easier for us today to understand our text than it was a few years ago. Matter was for centuries thought to be eternal. Now in an atomic bomb we see matter reduced to energy. On the basis of God's Word we understand that at creation matter was made from energy proceeding from God. In an atomic explosion, then, we have creation in reverse.

Faith is the key to knowledge. Each new discovery confirms the truth of God's Word, which in turn throws new light on each discovery.

It is also true that lack of faith is the cause of much misunderstanding. Think how true this is in the field of human relations. Through faith we understand our friends. When you have no faith in a person, it is easy to misunderstand him. It is easy to misinterpret his words and actions. But when you have confidence in an individual, you take him not so much for what he says as for what he means. What you read between the lines in a letter, for example, is dependent upon your attitude toward the one writing it. Faith that includes fellowship, love, and insight always brings understanding.

Life Through Faith   *April 12*

FAITH AND ACCEPTABLE WORSHIP

By faith Abel offered unto God a more excellent sacrifice than Cain, by which he obtained witness that he was righteous, God testifying of his gifts: and by it he being dead yet speaketh. Heb. 11:4.

Two outstanding young men came to worship before the Lord at the gate of the Garden of Eden. Both knew the truth of God for that time. Both erected altars according to specifications, and brought an offering unto the Lord. Both were sinners, and both acknowledged the claims of God to reverence and worship. The worship of only one, however, was acceptable; that of the other was not. What made the difference?

Faith made the difference. Cain cherished feelings of rebellion in his heart. He murmured against God. He questioned the divine justice in expelling his parents from Eden. He had no true feelings of repentance and no recognition of his need of a Saviour. Unbelief and rebellion caused him to lose the sense of God's presence, and worship became mere routine. Then one day when he decided to bring his own produce rather than purchase a lamb from his brother, his pride was hurt because God did not accept his offering. This he bitterly resented, and he began to harbor hatred in his heart.

Abel, on the other hand, saw and defended the justice of God in His dealings with Adam and Eve, and manifested a spirit of loyalty both to his parents and to his God. He gratefully accepted the provisions made for his salvation. He saw in the sacrifice of the lamb the wonderful love of God. His own act was an expression of his sorrow for his sin and a demonstration of his loyalty. He was accepted.

Worship is significant only when we understand the goodness and greatness of God, and have a sense of His personal presence. This comes by faith. In His presence we see ourselves as we really are, and we are led to fall at His feet and say, "God be merciful to me a sinner." As He assures us of His pardoning love, we are led to express our thanksgiving for His goodness and to dedicate our lives to His service.

By Faith We Walk With God

By faith Enoch was translated that he should not see death; and was not found, because God had translated him: for before his translation he had this testimony, that he pleased God. Heb. 11:5.

Abel was murdered and Enoch was translated. Both were men of faith. Strange, isn't it? Yet in this there is wonderful consolation. Tragedy is not necessarily a sign of lack of faith. So often in human experience when sorrow comes or when our prayers are not answered as we hoped they would be, we wonder whether these experiences are due to lack of faith. They may be the result of lack of faith, but not necessarily so. It is not what happens to us that shows our faith, but how we react to what happens and how we relate ourselves to the Lord.

Enoch's experience was recorded for our encouragement. The fact that he pleased God and was translated shows that it is possible for us to do so. We are told that Enoch walked with God (Gen. 5). This he learned to do particularly after he begat a son. When he became a father himself he gained a new insight into the heart of God. He probably reasoned thus: "If God feels about me as I do about my son, I'll try to be a better son." Through this experience he understood more fully the father-son relationship. Enoch received a new insight into the heart of God through a new human relationship.

How could Enoch walk with God? We are told: "Pray in your closet; and as you go about your daily labor, let your heart be often uplifted to God. It was thus that Enoch walked with God."—*Steps to Christ* (Pocket ed.), pp. 98, 99. Two cannot walk together unless they are agreed (Amos 3:3). When two men are in perfect harmony with each other they understand each other, and they enjoy communion and comradeship. This comes as a result of spending time together. God wants that kind of friendship with us. As we cultivate constantly the consciousness of His presence, as we talk with Him and listen to His voice in His Word and His works, we are drawn closer to Him. This is walking with God by faith.

Life Through Faith April 14

FAITH IN A PERSONAL GOD

But without faith it is impossible to please him: for he that cometh to God must believe that he is, and that he is a rewarder of them that diligently seek him. Heb. 11:6.

Many believe God exists but do not know what kind of God exists. Only a personal God—a God who loves, who is pleased with nothing less than to have men and women serve and love Him because they have faith and confidence in Him—can satisfy the deepest longing of the heart. We would not be satisfied with a God who is pleased with a group of robots or puppets doing His will because He demands and manipulates their response.

The Christian religion is a satisfying, personal love relationship with God that cannot be maintained without faith any more than any love relationship can be experienced without it. In love the most rewarding experience is that of companionship and response. Truly the Christian believes that God is a rewarder of them that diligently seek Him. Every Christian has been showered with blessings and gifts innumerable; but too many, like the prodigal son, take the Father's gifts and leave the Father. A good question for us to ask ourselves is, Which do we love most—God or His gifts?

Often we ask God for things material and physical. We serve Him hoping that these will be supplied; and when on occasion they are not, or they are even taken from us, we lose faith in God as a rewarder. The gifts without the giver bring no lasting satisfaction.

Two little girls were rejoicing in the fellowship of their father, who had just returned from a long trip. As always on such occasions, he brought something home for the children. This time he brought home a kitten. In the evening one of the girls was playing with the kitten, and was trying to make the other jealous because she had the kitten. The other thought a moment and then jumped into her daddy's lap and exclaimed, "I don't care. I have Daddy." God is pleased when we are more interested in Him than we are in His gifts.

Life Through Faith *April 15*

RIGHTEOUSNESS BY FAITH

By faith Noah, being warned of God of things not seen as yet, moved with fear, prepared an ark to the saving of his house; by the which he condemned the world, and became heir of the righteousness which is by faith. Heb. 11:7.

Several interesting statements are here made concerning Noah's faith. First, he believed even though the events foretold seemed impossible from a human point of view. He was warned by God concerning rain and a great flood. These were "things not seen as yet," but Noah had confidence in God and acted accordingly.

Then again, it is said that he "moved with fear." The word "fear" used here really means "he took heed." He acted, not merely because he was afraid, but because he had faith. Living by faith is not moving by fear as we generally think of the word, but by insight and trust in harmony with God. Faith acts intelligently in the light of revelation.

Notice, too, that it was by his acts that he condemned the world. Righteousness by faith is not righteousness by verbal condemnation. What the world needs is a life in harmony with God's will. Sinners are convinced more by sanctified lives than by sanctimonious words. Our attitude should be like that of Jesus, "Neither do I condemn thee: go, and sin no more" (John 8:11).

Noah became "heir of the righteousness which is by faith." An heir is one who inherits something. What one inherits he does not earn. It is generally what his father has earned and passed on to him. Characteristics are inherited as well as money and land. Faith in God brings rich rewards in both material and spiritual blessings. When a man so relates himself to God as the word *faith* implies, he inherits from his heavenly Father, not only better health, a keener mind, greater ability, and a home in the earth made new, but also the character of Jesus. He becomes like Him, reflecting His image and manifesting His character. This is the most valuable inheritance one can realize.

Life Through Faith April 16

Faith and Obedience

By faith Abraham, when he was called to go out into a place which he should after receive for an inheritance, obeyed; and he went out, not knowing whither he went, Heb. 11:8.

By faith Abraham obeyed. We don't like the word "obey" any more. Somehow the word connotes tyranny or slavery, because there are in this world of sin situations in which men and women obey only because they must. This is not the obedience that pleases God.

There are three kinds of obedience. First, there is the obedience of fear—obeying from fear of punishment. There is no joy in this kind of obedience, for it is not willingly given and brings no satisfaction to either the one who obeys or the one who is obeyed.

Then there is the obedience of duty—obedience because it is expected. Disobedience brings no success; therefore it pays to obey. Obedience is the *best policy*. Would it not be well if we had more men and women who obeyed because it was their duty? Yes, but if this is the only motive for obedience, there is lacking the real joy of living.

The third kind of obedience is the obedience of faith and love. This is the obedience that brings joy to the heart of God and man. When one has faith in God and loves Him, obedience becomes a pleasure. It is a real adventure to obey God, for He leads us often as He did Abraham—into places we know nothing about.

When we learn to obey as did Abraham, we are safe. A little girl and her daddy enjoyed walking along a railroad track. When the train would come, they would step aside, and watch it go by, and resume their walk, balancing themselves on the narrow rails. One day after a train had passed, they had hardly started to walk again when Daddy shouted, "Jane, lie down quickly." Without waiting to ask why, she fell flat immediately, and a second train they had not expected roared by. Had she not obeyed instantly she would have been killed. Jane had learned first to obey when Daddy spoke and then ask why later. That is the obedience of faith.

Life Through Faith   *April 17*

WOMEN OF FAITH

Through faith also Sara herself received strength to conceive seed, and was delivered of a child when she was past age, because she judged him faithful who had promised. **Heb. 11:11.**

We hear a great deal about men of faith. Today let us think about women of faith. In the first place many of these great men of faith owe their faith to God-fearing mothers. We hear about only a few. "It was Jochebed, the Hebrew mother, . . . strong in faith, . . . of whom was born Moses, the deliverer of Israel. It was Hannah, the woman of prayer and self-sacrifice and heavenly inspiration, who gave birth to Samuel. . . . It was Elisabeth the kinswoman and kindred spirit of Mary of Nazareth, who was the mother of the Saviour's herald."—*The Ministry of Healing,* p. 372.

Were it not for Sarah's faith, Abraham would probably not be known as the father of the faithful. How much would Barak have accomplished without the faith of Deborah? Yet Barak gets the credit as does Abraham. It doesn't seem fair, does it? Yet in the books of heaven the truth is recorded, and someday all will be revealed.

The story of Sarah's faith is most encouraging. We are led to think at times that the heroes of faith were more or less superhuman. There is something delightfully human and divine in Sarah's experience. In Genesis 18 we read of the promise made that Sarah would have a son. This seemed impossible because both Abraham and Sarah were too old. And Sarah laughed. "And the Lord said unto Abraham, Wherefore did Sarah laugh, saying, Shall I of a surety bear a child, which am old? Is any thing too hard for the Lord?" How truly human was Sarah, and how wonderfully loving and understanding was the Lord. Even though Sarah laughed at the promise at first and even lied, denying that she laughed, the Lord was kind, and as a result Sarah became the mother of the faithful, judging "him faithful who had promised."

This experience should encourage us when sometimes God's Word seems so impossible of fulfillment in our behalf.

Life Through Faith　　　　　　　　　　　　　　　　　　　　　　April 18

Faith Tested

By faith Abraham, when he was tried, offered up Isaac; and he that had received the promises offered up his only begotten son. Heb. 11:17.

Here was a real test of a man's faith. Abraham was asked to offer up his only son—the son who was to be the father of a great multitude. There are several things about this request that seem quite puzzling. How could Isaac, still unmarried, be the father of a great multitude if he were slain? Would not this be murder? Does God require human sacrifices? How did Abraham know this was the voice of God speaking to him? Could not this be the voice of Satan, seeking to thwart God's plan? Was not this a request contrary to the will of God?

In the first place Abraham knew this was the voice of God. He had heard that voice so often and had established such a relationship with his Lord that there was no mistake about it. Abraham's faith is revealed in the words spoken that third day when he said to the servants, "Abide ye here with the ass; and I and the lad will go yonder and worship, and come again to you" (Gen. 22:5). He did not know, of course, just how it would be possible for him to offer Isaac and both of them return, but he believed "that God was able to raise him up, even from the dead; from whence also he received him in a figure" (Heb. 11:19).

Just why would God put Abraham through such a test? Did God need to do this to find out whether Abraham was dependable? Did not God know Abraham's heart? Of course, God knew. However, God had certain lessons to teach. Through this experience Abraham would better understand how his heavenly Father felt in giving His only-begotten Son as a sacrifice on the cross. Also the universe saw a demonstration of how far the love of God in the heart of a man will go.

Tests of faith like this are not given to beginners. They are reserved for the mature, for far-reaching purposes, and no man is tested above that he is able. Sarah, we are told, was not notified; for it would prove to be too much for her. We can take courage from this.

FAITH AND HOPE

By faith Joseph, when he died, made mention of the departing of the children of Israel; and gave commandment concerning his bones. Heb. 11:22.

Hope for the future! This is needful for all who are alert and alive. "Hope springs eternal in the human breast," Pope said. Particularly do young people live in hope. Hope for the future with some assurance of the certainty of that hope is a basic human need. Take the element of anticipation out of life, and what is left? Very little.

Hope deals with things "not seen as yet," and is therefore closely allied with faith. One does not hope for that in which he has absolutely no faith. The Christian, however, has a hope that is sure and steadfast. It is based on the promises of God, which never fail. And God has given us so many evidences of the certainty of His promises that we have a real basis for the faith which is "the assurance of things hoped for" (Heb. 11:1, R.S.V.).

Take Joseph's experience, for example. He was well acquainted with the promises to Abraham, his great-grandfather. Many times he had opportunity to doubt these and become discouraged, not only during dark days, but during days of prosperity as well. Why should he and his people be concerned with the Promised Land? Were they not comfortable in Egypt, and were they not favored with the best of the land? Was not he, Joseph, next to Pharaoh? What more could they want?

Joseph's faith, however, did not allow his hope to grow dim. By faith he could see beyond the temporary present to the eternal future. He remembered all the evidence of God's guidance; and though he realized he must die before the fulfillment of his hopes, he "gave commandment concerning his bones" as an evidence of his faith in the blessed hope.

There is danger that we in this generation allow the Advent hope to grow dim. Let us, as did Joseph, hope in faith.

Life Through Faith *April 20*

Faith and Courage

By faith Moses, when he was born, was hid three months of his parents, because they saw he was a proper child; and they were not afraid of the king's commandment. Heb. 11:23.

It took a great deal of courage on the part of Amram and Jochebed, the parents of Moses, to defy the king's commandment. The commandment had been given that every male child was to be cast into the river. This was a move on the part of Satan to defeat the purpose of God. He knew that it was time for a deliverer to be raised up among the Israelites; and he thought to destroy him at birth. Right at the time the decree was in full force Moses was born. Amram and Jochebed were not afraid, because they had faith.

We need courage! One may have a genuine desire to be a good Christian; he may really want to be of service to God and man; he may have great dreams of the future, of great accomplishments for good; he may from the bottom of his heart long for purity and righteousness; but if he has no courage, all else is of no avail. It takes courage to realize our ideals and to give force to our convictions.

We, too, live in a day when Satan is seeking to destroy the people of God. More than any other generation, we need courage. Faith gives courage. Thinking of faith in terms of belief, there are certain beliefs that give us courage. First there is belief in the purpose and providence of God. He can and does accomplish His purposes. Then there is belief in ourselves—a belief born of God's belief in us. Again our belief in ourselves and that of others in us, give us courage and inspire us to carry on at times when we might otherwise give up. And finally, belief in the promise "I am with you" makes our courage complete.

"Anywhere with Jesus I can safely go,
Anywhere He leads me in this world below;
Anywhere without Him, dearest joys would fade;
Anywhere with Jesus I am not afraid."

—Jessie H. Brown

Life Through Faith   *April 21*

FAITH AND ENDURANCE

By faith he forsook Egypt, not fearing the wrath of the king: for he endured, as seeing him who is invisible. Heb. 11:27.

The experience of Moses in Egypt gives us courage to endure and teaches us not to become discouraged even though we may make a mistake. "By faith he [Moses] forsook Egypt, not fearing the wrath of the king." When we read the record in Exodus 2:14, 15 we find what seems to be a different story. When Moses was reminded of his killing the Egyptian, an act of which he thought no one knew, he "feared, and said, Surely this thing is known." And he had reason to fear, for when Pharaoh heard it he sought to slay Moses, so Moses fled.

In the light of this record Paul still says, "By faith he forsook Egypt, not fearing the wrath of the king: for he endured, as seeing him who is invisible." How can this be? The wonderful truth is that a man's life is measured, not by one mistake, but by the over-all character of his life. This one rash act on the part of Moses was used by God to make possible a preparation for his work. Moses was not ready. He needed the wilderness training. When Moses fled, he did not lose his faith in God, though he had opportunity to do so. He could have given up. All along he had been instructed that he was to be Israel's deliverer. Now in endeavoring to deliver one Israelite, he failed. Surely God had forsaken him, or he had been led to wrong conclusions. However, he did not reason thus. Earlier in Moses' life God had overruled and used the very decree condemning the Hebrew children to death, for the shaping of circumstances to make possible the training and education of the future leader of His people. Here God used Pharaoh's intention to destroy Moses as a means of placing him in a position to receive the final phase of his training for his lifework. And though Moses made a grave mistake, his life was not a failure. This should give us courage not to give up when we make a mistake, but to grasp the hand of God by faith and hold on. Moses endured as "seeing him who is invisible." This is the secret of successful endurance.

FAITH AND OBSTACLES

By faith they passed through the Red sea as by dry land: which the Egyptians assaying to do were drowned. **Heb. 11:29.**

Often in life, particularly in carrying on some worth-while endeavor or in making progress in the battle against evil, we come face to face with seemingly insurmountable obstacles. In the exodus from Egypt, Israel came face to face with the Red Sea. The Egyptians were in pursuit, and it was a tense moment in an impossible situation, from a human point of view. There seemed to be no escape. The people were weary and terrified. They trembled and murmured. "Thus the angel of God appeared to their deluded minds as the harbinger of disaster."—*Patriarchs and Prophets*, p. 284. Why had Moses brought them out into the wilderness to die?

How truly human was their experience! Yet in spite of their fears and complainings, "by faith they passed through the Red sea as by dry land: which the Egyptians assaying to do were drowned." Here again we see that faith is not necessarily the absence of fear in a given dangerous situation. This experience also reveals the fact that in some circumstances even men of faith see things wrong and see the wrong things; and when weary and terrified, they are baffled and tremble in certain tense moments. This should be a source of encouragement to us.

The wonderful truth for our consideration today is that faith in God overcomes obstacles and enables us to do at God's bidding what would drown mere human endeavor apart from God; for the Egyptians were drowned, whereas the people of God went through as on dry land. The same manifestation that was to the Egyptians darkness and despair was to the Israelites light and deliverance.

The following words of Moses to Israel and of the Lord to Moses that day are still applicable to us as we face insurmountable obstacles in Christian life and service today. "Fear ye not, stand still, and see the salvation of the Lord, which he will shew to you to day." "Speak unto the children of Israel, that they go forward" (Ex. 14:13-15).

Life Through Faith   *April 23*

FAITH AS A GRAIN OF MUSTARD SEED

And the Lord said, If ye had faith as a grain of mustard seed, ye might say unto this sycamine tree, Be thou plucked up by the root, and be thou planted in the sea; and it should obey you. Luke 17:6.

These words of Jesus were in reply to the request of the disciples when they said, "Lord, increase our faith." They made this request after hearing Jesus say, "If he [thy brother] trespass against thee seven times in a day, and seven times in a day turn again to thee, saying, I repent; thou shalt forgive him." Here is a difficult life situation. If a brother should trespass against us seven times a day, we would find it most difficult to forgive. From a human point of view alone it would be as impossible to uproot the deep resentment within our hearts caused by such conduct as it is to uproot a tree and plant it in the sea. Jesus tells us this can be done through faith.

Faith is not a formula, or a theory, but a living, growing thing implanted within every heart. The Creator has implanted within seeds living germs, and He has provided soil, water, sunshine, and air for their growth. As the seeds lay hold upon these they sprout and grow. Just so He who made man has implanted within him this living germ we call faith. He has also provided for its growth certain elements. Let us consider a few of these: First, there is the Word of God—the bread of life that nourishes us. Then there is prayer. In communion with God our faith is strengthened.

Opportunities for worship are also given us. Worship includes opening our hearts and minds to the influence of the Holy Spirit. Sacred music plays an important part in worship. Hymns and gospel songs lift us heavenward. As we share our faith with others and see them rejoice in the Lord, our own faith becomes stronger.

Through faith the seemingly impossible is accomplished. Mountains of difficulty are removed and trees deeply rooted are plucked up. Such faith can be ours.

Life Through Faith *April 24*

Faith Cometh by Hearing

So then faith cometh by hearing, and hearing by the word of God. Rom. 10:17.

"'Have faith! Have faith!' That's all you say! How can a fellow have faith in something he can't understand and that doesn't even make sense?"

"I just don't have faith in anything, any more! It seems that nothing is dependable, and one is asked to believe so much that he can't see."

"If faith is so important to Christian living, how can I get faith?"

Statements and questions such as these have been expressed by many through the years. Simply to say, "Have faith, brother, have faith!" does not produce men and women of great faith.

God tells us where faith comes from and how it is developed. It comes from hearing the Word of the Lord. Bible reading with open mind and heart will result in increased faith in God, and for a number of reasons. It increases our spiritual vision, and gradually there unfolds before us God's wonderful plan of salvation, and the things we don't understand become more clear.

Bible reading increases the effectiveness of our decisions and actions by revealing to us the way that leads to life. Bible reading increases our trust in God. It is what enables us to see that God has never failed to fulfill His promises. As we see how God has guided in the affairs of men of old, we can more easily believe that He guides in our affairs.

Bible reading brings us into contact with Christ and with the world's truly great men—men of faith. In this personal fellowship we find faith and confidence growing within us. They follow as naturally as day follows the sunrise.

Let us take time today to hear the Word of the Lord. Listen for the still small voice as you read it yourself, or as you hear it read, and you will find your faith increasing, and peace of mind will result from the wonderful security it gives.

Life Through Faith　　　　　　　　　　　　　　　　　　　　*April 25*

HELP THOU MINE UNBELIEF

Jesus said unto him, If thou canst believe, all things are possible to him that believeth. And straightway the father of the child cried out, and said with tears, Lord, I believe; help thou mine unbelief. **Mark 9:23, 24.**

Some things are hard to believe because of our limited insight, and Satan takes advantage of this to cause us to lose faith. When faith is weak but the heart sincere, Jesus understands and helps. He does not condemn honest doubt. Often He works miracles to strengthen and establish our faith, but He wants us to live by faith, not miracles.

A certain man was unemployed. He picked up a few odd jobs here and there, but was barely able to provide the necessities of life in supporting his family. One day he heard a sermon on tithe. He listened to the promise: "Prove me now herewith, saith the Lord of hosts, if I will not open you the windows of heaven, and pour you out a blessing, that there shall not be room enough to receive it" (Mal. 3:10). He said, "I'd like to see the Lord pour out a blessing I couldn't receive!" It was quite a struggle for him to decide to pay tithe. He had a hard time believing God would require this of him. Under the influence of the Holy Spirit one night, he gave his heart to the Lord and resolved to return unto the Lord His own in tithe. The next Monday he received in the mail three letters offering him employment. He could accept only one. Here was a blessing there was not room enough to receive.

Some people are more troubled with doubt than others. Let those who are, take courage in the thought that honest inquiry leads to strong faith. God does not give a man a mind and then condemn him for using it. Job in his hour of trial, we are told, argued with God. There is something heart warming about this. It reveals an attribute of our heavenly Father, the knowledge of which strengthens our faith. Not that God stoops to argue, but He is willing to help us think things through if we are sincere, and He understands our immaturity.

Let us pray today, "Lord, I believe; help thou mine unbelief."

GREAT FAITH

Then Jesus answered and said unto her, O woman, great is thy faith: be it unto thee even as thou wilt. And her daughter was made whole from that very hour. Matt. 15:28.

On several occasions Jesus said to His disciples, "O ye of little faith." But it was to the Syrophoenician woman that He said, "O woman, great is thy faith." Jesus, with His disciples, was in the territory of Tyre and Sidon. A woman of Canaan came to Him and cried out, "Have mercy on me, O Lord, thou son of David; my daughter is grievously vexed with a devil." However, He answered her not a word. She was persistent. The disciples besought Jesus to send her away. When she heard His reply to the disciples, she came and worshiped Jesus, saying, "Lord, help me." Jesus responded to the woman in a very strange way. To the superficial observer it doesn't even sound like Jesus. He answered her plea with these words, "It is not meet to take the children's bread, and to cast it to dogs." To this she replied, "Truth, Lord: yet the dogs eat of the crumbs which fall from their masters' table." It was then that Jesus spake the words of our text today.

The greatness of her faith is revealed not only in her persistence but also in her words. First, she called Jesus the Son of David. This implies that she knew something about Him and that she was familiar with the Scriptures concerning His ancestry. She made it plain to Jesus that she considered Him the Lord and Master of the Gentiles as well as of the Jews and that He was her Lord and Master. Her insight and attitude stand out in sharp contrast with that of the disciples.

The disciples had been with Jesus for months. This woman no doubt met Him that day for the first time, and yet one glimpse of the Master's love, with openhearted, sincere desire, did more for her than months of following with selfish desire for personal gain in an earthly kingdom had done for the disciples, who were blinded by prejudice.

Great faith is impossible apart from unprejudiced personal contact with the Master. Let us follow this simple woman's example.

Life Through Faith April 27

THAT THY FAITH FAIL NOT

But I have prayed for thee, that thy faith fail not: and when thou art converted, strengthen thy brethren. Luke 22:32.

"Simon, Simon, behold, Satan hath desired to have you, that he may sift you as wheat: but I have prayed for thee, that thy faith fail not." These words of Jesus to Peter just before he denied his Lord cause us to wonder whether Jesus' prayer was answered. Jesus prayed that Peter's "faith fail not," and that very night he denied his Lord with cursing and swearing.

What happened? Did not our heavenly Father hear the prayer of His Son? Oh, yes, He did, and in this account we have one of the most faith-strengthening experiences on record. The comforting thought is this: To fall is not to fail, necessarily. Peter fell that night, but his faith did not fail. As soon as he realized what he had done, he went out into the Garden of Gethsemane and there poured out his soul to God. This should give us courage when we under trial deny our Lord.

Satan often presses home the thought that we are failures—that there is just no hope for us. When such thoughts go through our minds, let us remember Peter's experience, and in deep repentance not lose faith, but claim God's promise of forgiveness.

Why did Peter fall that night? He was too self-confident and unaware of his inner weakness. He failed to watch and pray. He slept when he should have been seeking strength. Peter also chose the wrong crowd. He deliberately placed himself in a position to be tempted, and he lost out.

Jesus knew Peter's weakness and sought to prepare him for the ordeal. And when Peter did succumb, the memory of the Saviour's words, together with His look of love, sent him to Gethsemane brokenhearted.

Many of us, like Peter, are too self-confident and careless, and we go into a garden of Gethsemane after we fall, instead of spending time there beforehand.

Life Through Faith *April 28*

CAST NOT AWAY YOUR CONFIDENCE

Cast not away therefore your confidence, which hath great recompence of reward. **Heb. 10:35.**

A little fellow had just been to Sabbath school for the first time. There he had received a beautiful little card with a picture on it of an angel watching over two little children; underneath were the words "Have faith in God." His daddy had picked him up, and they were riding along. Suddenly a gust of wind swept through the car and out went his precious card. "O Daddy, stop!" he cried. "I've lost my faith in God."

We smile as we think of his cry, but how true it is in life. When a stormy wind sweeps away some precious possession, many lose their faith in God. In experiencing personal suffering and trial as well as in viewing perplexing world affairs, there are times when we wonder whether God is still on the throne. But remember, "As the wheel-like complications [in Ezekiel's vision of the wheels] were under the guidance of the hand beneath the wings of the cherubim, so the complicated play of human events is under divine control. Amidst the strife and tumult of nations, He that sitteth above the cherubim still guides the affairs of this earth."—*Prophets and Kings,* p. 536. And "often our plans fail, that God's plans for us may succeed."—*The Ministry of Healing,* p. 473. Cast not away, therefore, your faith in God. There is great recompense of reward.

The two verses following our text for today present good reasons for remaining faithful. "For ye have need of patience, that, after ye have done the will of God, ye might receive the promise. For yet a little while, and he that shall come will come, and will not tarry" (Heb. 10:36, 37).

Once Jesus asked this question, "When the Son of man cometh, shall he find faith on the earth?" (Luke 18:8). It is an unanswered question, because it must be answered personally. Will He find faith in your heart and mine?

HAVE FAITH IN GOD

And Jesus answering saith unto them, Have faith in God. **Mark 11:22.**

Sometimes God seems to do strange things. Jesus cursed a fig tree one day, and in the morning the disciples were amazed to find it withered. When they called this to the attention of Jesus, He "answering saith unto them, Have faith in God." They didn't understand it then, but later they did. Often we do not understand at the moment why God does what He does.

The story is told of a hermit who guided a traveler through a forest in Germany for three days. They spent the first night with a man who treated them royally. The next morning the hermit took with him a silver goblet. The second night they spent in a barn. They did not mind, for in the house there was drinking and carousing, and the householder was very rough. The next morning the hermit gave the silver goblet to their rude host.

Once more night fell, and they were rather reluctantly permitted to stay in a house in which a beautiful boy lived with his father. In the morning the boy accompanied them on their journey. When they came to a river the hermit urged the boy to cross the bridge with them. In the midst of the stream the hermit tripped the lad, and he fell in and drowned. This was too much for the traveler. He demanded an explanation of these strange actions on the part of one who was supposed to be a man of God. "I am doing as God does," said the hermit. "But now I am going to do as God does not do and tell you why. The silver goblet was a poison cup. Our first host's enemy gave it to him that he might drink from it and die. I took the cup to save his life. The second host is a very wicked man. His cup of iniquity is full. I gave the cup to him to end his life of sin. The father of this boy is a bandit. If the boy lived, he too would become a bandit. I took his life to save his soul."

While this story does not present a true picture of God, it does show how different things look when we understand all the factors.

Life Through Faith April 30

THE AUTHOR AND FINISHER OF OUR FAITH

Looking unto Jesus the author and finisher of our faith; who for the joy that was set before him endured the cross, despising the shame, and is set down at the right hand of the throne of God. Heb. 12:2.

There was once a young man who thought for a while he could live without religion and without faith. He would spend his life making money and a name for himself. John, we shall call him, was a talented fellow with a brilliant mind and a pleasing personality. He was a minister's son, who thought his father too old-fashioned and out of date. Modern science, in this young man's mind, had made his father's God a myth and religion unnecessary. As he grew older he found it necessary to adopt as his own some basic philosophy of life. He decided to study all the philosophers and pick that philosophy which appealed to him most. He enjoyed his study and marveled at the depth and beauty of a number of great men. The more he studied, the more he began to wonder who was right. There were so many different answers.

Finally he decided to study the biographies of the philosophers to see which one most satisfactorily lived his own philosophy. As he studied he became more and more convinced that there was only one philosopher who lived what he taught. That was Jesus.

Not only did Jesus live what He taught, but He alone can point to an empty tomb and say, "I was dead and am alive and have the key." After several years of study, John found his faith in his father's God being renewed, and through looking unto Jesus, he was converted. So wonderfully satisfying was his experience, and such a contrast did he see in his study between the religion of Jesus Christ and all the other world religions, that he decided to champion the cause of Christianity.

In Christ our faith has its beginning, and in Christ is our faith perfected. No wonder we are told, "It would be well for us to spend a thoughtful hour each day in contemplation of the life of Christ. . . . Beholding the beauty of His character, we shall be 'changed into the same image from glory to glory.'"—*The Desire of Ages,* p. 83.

MAY

Life Through Prayer   May 1

MEN OUGHT TO PRAY

And he spake a parable unto them to this end, that men ought always to pray, and not to faint. Luke 18:1.

In a certain city there was a judge who was more concerned with position and the feel of power than he was with service, a man who was gratified by allowing men and women in need to "ask and plead and entreat in vain."

There was a woman in that vicinity whose husband had died, and because of an adversary, she was about to lose all of her property. She pressed her case before this judge and was persistently repulsed. "The judge knew that her cause was righteous, and he could have relieved her at once, but he would not. He wanted to show his arbitrary power, and it gratified him to let her ask and plead and entreat in vain."—*Christ's Object Lessons,* p. 165. However, because of her persistence, he finally agreed to take care of her case, to save his reputation and to avoid giving publicity to his partial, one-sided judgment.

Jesus told this story to teach us that we ought to pray always and not give up. Why ought men to pray? First of all, men and women are in the position of this woman, who, because of an adversary, was about to lose everything. Man has lost his connection with God and has a real adversary—Satan. We cannot retrieve our lost fortunes alone.

To use other figures, we are pilgrims in a strange land, and we need instruction. We are soldiers in the land of the enemy, and we need contact with our captain. We are actors on a stage in which the great controversy between good and evil is being dramatized, and we need directions. We need guidance in order to know how to play our part well. We've been deceived and weakened by sin. We need to be enlightened and strengthened. Help comes through prayer. We need contact with the source of our life and power to carry on in the midst of adversaries. That's why men ought to pray.

Life Through Prayer May 2

GOD HEARS PRAYER

O thou that hearest prayer, unto thee shall all flesh come. Ps. 65:2.

Have you ever talked to someone, and asked questions, only to discover that he wasn't even listening? You remember how frustrated you were? There are people who do not pray because they feel that God is not listening.

In order for prayer to be satisfying and worth while we must establish certain beliefs. Unless prayer is grounded upon a sound foundation of belief, it is nothing more than wishful thinking. What are these beliefs? We believe that God is a personal being, a God of love, who cares about us and desires to help us. These facts were demonstrated when God was made flesh and dwelt among us in the person of Jesus Christ. Jesus was the express image of His Father's person. Thus we have evidence that God is a personal, living God and that it is rewarding to pray to Him. We believe that God knows what is best for our lives and that He understands. We believe that we are free moral agents, but that God has a plan for our lives and that He wants to guide us. We believe that not everything that happens is God's will but that nothing can happen to defeat His will. Though His plans may be thwarted, victory is certain if we cooperate with Him. We believe that what counts most is not what happens to us but how we react to what happens. We believe that the universe is both flexible and faithful to man and God. If we believe these things, we can understand how prayer can be necessary and effectual.

Yes, God always answers prayer—either Yes, or No, or Wait awhile. But prayer should not consist only of requests to be granted, denied, or postponed. Once we establish a friendship with God there are many prayers that do not need answering. We learn to share our experiences with Him and to listen to His words as true friends who love each other share experiences, seek counsel, and even enjoy the fellowship of silence. Once we believe in the kind of God Jesus revealed His Father to be, how different are our prayers!

Life Through Prayer

"LORD, TEACH US TO PRAY"

And it came to pass, that, as he was praying in a certain place, when he ceased, one of his disciples said unto him, Lord, teach us to pray, as John also taught his disciples. Luke 11:1.

As the disciples heard Jesus pray, as they noticed the effect upon His life, as they saw Him come from the secret place of prayer refreshed and strengthened, and then as they watched Him face life's problems with such wonderful poise, good judgment, love, and confidence, they realized that they needed what He had. So they said to Jesus, "Lord, teach us to pray."

The words "teach us" imply that the art of prayer is something we must learn. To pray is not merely to say words or to present a series of requests. Prayer is something far greater and deeper and more significant. It is something we learn to grow into.

Saying, "Teach me to pray" is like saying to a great musician, "Teach me to play the piano." It takes practice and experience. It's more like a child saying to his parent, "Teach me manners. Teach me to say Thank you. Teach me how to get along with others." The words "teach us" signify not merely the idea of rote-memory work, as teaching a child a memory verse to be repeated on the Sabbath day. They involve establishing a relationship, developing an understanding and various methods of communication. How to approach God, how to understand Him, how to open our hearts fully to His Holy Spirit—these are the things that count when it comes to praying. It is like saying, "Lord, teach us how to be better men and women, so that we will be better friends, better servants, better witnesses, better soldiers."

The worth-while things in life do not come in little packages, big formulas, or magic words. They are developed through experience. It is true that Jesus gave a model prayer, but in it are great principles that we need to learn as we live with them day by day. May God grant that we too may have within our hearts a desire to learn how to pray, how to be the kind of men and women who can pray.

Life Through Prayer   May 4

AFTER THIS MANNER PRAY YE

After this manner therefore pray ye: Our Father which art in heaven, Hallowed be thy name. **Matt. 6:9.**

What you believe about a person affects your relationship to that person. What you believe about God affects your relationship to God and, consequently, affects your prayer life.

One of the greatest burdens of Jesus was to reveal the fatherhood of God to man. In the Sermon on the Mount alone, the term "Father" as applied to God is used seventeen times. And after His resurrection, when Mary was about to touch Him, Jesus said unto her, "Touch me not; for I am not yet ascended to my Father: but go to my brethren, and say unto them, I ascend unto my Father, and your Father; and to my God, and your God" (John 20:17).

Jesus wants us to recognize Christianity as a matter of Father-son, Father-daughter relationships. Unfortunately, too many fathers are not what they ought to be; therefore, the concept of fatherhood is not always appreciated. There have also been so many misrepresentations of the character of God that our heavenly Father has been misunderstood. Jesus came to erase these and to reveal the true character of God to men. He wants us to know that our great God, our Creator, is our loving heavenly Father. Prayer becomes much more satisfying in this light. Once we understand this we can begin to understand how to pray, for we then become children in comradeship with our Father. Our prayers become, in addition to requests, conversations and communions as we share with Him all of life's experiences.

We are reminded that our Father is in heaven. Here Jesus emphasizes not the distance away but His position. Jeremiah tells us that "a glorious high throne from the beginning is the place of our sanctuary" (Jer. 17:12). It is a wonderful thing to know that our heavenly Father is in control of things. He sees the end from the beginning, and He is our refuge and strength. May this wonderful prayer become more meaningful to us each day.

"THY WILL BE DONE"

Thy kingdom come. Thy will be done in earth, as it is in heaven. Matt. 6:10.

As we study the model prayer, we find a proper order and sequence brought to light. First of all, "Our Father." Here is a relationship established. Second, "which art in heaven," the recognition of His greatness in awe. Then follow three prayers of adoration and surrender before we ever bring requests for our necessities before Him. This is the way it ought to be. We are interested in God's name and in His kingdom and in His will. His interests become our interests. These are the marks of mature prayers. If we would learn how to pray, let us learn to think more of God and His love, His character, and His interests. We should think more of His name than of ours.

When we pray, "Thy kingdom come," let us remember that the interests of His kingdom are our interests. We want that kingdom established in our own hearts, and in the hearts of others. We commit ourselves to help bring that about, so that His second kingdom may come when our Lord returns as King of kings and Lord of lords.

We are concerned, too, with His will, not just ours. Jesus prayed, "I delight to do thy will, O my God: yea, thy law is within my heart." God's will is expressed in His law, not in the spirit of legality, but in the spirit of love. The angels were surprised that there even *was* a law. Where love reigns, law is not necessary. Does a lover need a policeman to keep him from harming a loved one? Does a happily married couple need a divorce law to keep them from separating? No, it is the most natural thing in the world for them to want to stay together, to enjoy fellowship, and to seek each other's happiness. When we learn to love God we come to appreciate His goodness. We find our own wishes less and less prominent. His will dominates our thinking more and more. The praying man learns to distrust his own wisdom and to trust in the will of God, knowing that as he blends his will with God's, life and happiness follow.

Our Daily Bread

Give us this day our daily bread. Matt. 6:11.

> "There was once a little boy,
> His father named him Jimmy.
> He asked for every single toy;
> His playmates called him 'Gi' me.'"

If your prayers and mine were carefully analyzed, would they be found to consist mostly of requests, first, last, and all the way through? Would the angels perhaps be justified in calling you and me "Gi' me," like the boy in the jingle? It is perfectly proper to ask God for things, but note the position of the requests for personal needs in our model prayer. It is after we have recognized our relationship with our heavenly Father, and have shown our concern for His will, His glory, and His interests, that we may in confidence ask that our own needs be supplied. Only then can we pray in true perspective.

Even here we pray not for ourselves alone. Notice the request is "Give *us*." We are reminded that we are not alone in this world. Why should I have bread while my family is starving? What right have I to expect my needs to be supplied when conditions are such that no other man's needs are met? Trusting our heavenly Father to do what is best, let us as children wait, as it were, at the table to be served.

This request reveals our dependence upon God for all temporal and spiritual blessings. Too many of us are like the swine, who eat acorns but look not at the oak. We forget the source of our bread.

This request speaks of spiritual bread as well. Says Jesus, "I am the living bread." We partake of Christ through His Word. Many of us pray for our daily bread, and then do not eat what is set before us. Our need for food is a daily need. Past wonderful meals are not sufficient. We need each day to partake of food. Eat and live today.

Life Through Prayer May 7

Forgiveness

And forgive us our debts, as we forgive our debtors. Matt. 6:12.

Jack, a sheep dog, had run amuck one night and killed some of the sheep. Jack was Dan's best friend. Dan's father had Jack killed and buried before Dan came home from school, thinking this course the most merciful. In the wee hours of the next morning Dan decided to run away from home and join his brother in the Army. The Civil War was on.

Abe Lincoln was taking one of his early morning walks when he found Dan. "An' father shouldn't a killed 'im unbeknownst to me. I'll never forgive him that, never!" said Dan as he discussed the problem with Abe, not knowing who Abe was. "Quite right," said the President. "Don't you ever forgive him, Dan, or don't ever forget it—under one certain condition." "What's that?" asked the boy, a trifle puzzled. "Why, that you also never forget all the kind and just things that your father has done for you. How old are you, Dan?" "Fourteen, going on fifteen." "In fourteen years a father can pile up a lot of good deeds," said Lincoln, "but I suppose he's done a lot of mean ones to cancel 'em all off has he?" "No," admitted Dan. His frankness pleased the President, and they talked together as they walked along.

Lincoln told Dan there were twenty-four deserters wanting pardon. They had served their country well through the long years of the war. Surely all their good deeds were not blotted out by one mistake. He made a bargain with Dan. "You go home and forgive your dad, and I'll forgive these twenty-four men." The two shook hands, and the boy went home with a forgiving spirit in his heart as he thought about all the good things his dad had done for him, and the happiness that forgiveness would bring to the twenty-four men.

It takes much of the grace of God to forgive. That is why this particular request comes where it does in the Lord's Prayer.

DELIVERANCE

And lead us not into temptation, but deliver us from evil: for thine is the kingdom, and the power, and the glory, for ever. Amen. Matt. 6:13.

Why should we pray, "Lead us not into temptation"? Does God tempt men? No, we read in James 1:13 that God Himself tempteth no man. Temptation is enticement to sin, and this does not proceed from God, but from Satan and the evil of our own hearts. The word "temptation" also includes, however, the idea of test, or trial; and so when we pray we have the right to say, "Let us not succumb in the time of trial." The idea is, "Bring us not into trying experiences except to deliver us and teach us the lesson we need to learn. Give us strength to stand the test of this day. Keep us from being drawn away by the desires of our own evil hearts, and deliver us from the power of the evil one."

Let us realize, too, that with this prayer we have God's promise: "There hath no temptation taken you but such as is common to man: but God is faithful, who will not suffer you to be tempted above that ye are able; but will with the temptation also make a way to escape, that ye may be able to bear it" (1 Cor. 10:13). We should, however, walk in the way of righteousness and not deliberately place ourselves in the way of temptation. Someone has said, "If you don't want to do business with the devil, don't go window-shopping in his windows." This is good counsel. God does not tempt us, but He leads us through the land of the enemy and permits us to encounter obstacles and trials, using them to develop our characters. "Every temptation resisted, every trial bravely borne, gives us a new experience and advances us in the work of character building."—*The Mount of Blessing* (1956), p. 117.

The model prayer closes with the recognition that His is the kingdom, the power, the glory, forever. This keeps men from debasing self-worship and pride. It shows that we recognize in God our all in all—the kingdom is His, the power is His, the glory, or character, is His.

ASK, SEEK, KNOCK

Ask, and it shall be given you; seek, and ye shall find; knock, and it shall be opened unto you: for every one that asketh receiveth; and he that seeketh findeth; and to him that knocketh it shall be opened. Matt. 7:7, 8.

Does prayer change God's mind? If we ask, seek, and knock long enough, will we finally get God to do what He would not do otherwise? If not, why pray? If so, this implies a changeable God who can be persuaded or who will do what the most able, talented, or persistent demand that He do. Quite a problem, isn't it? No, "prayer is not to work any change in God; it is to bring us into harmony with God."—*Christ's Object Lessons*, p. 143.

However, because we pray, God can do some things that He could not do otherwise. How is this true? First of all, my praying puts me in touch with the Divine. If I stop praying, there is no more fellowship. It is in fellowship that changes are wrought. If I keep praying, I am at least in contact with God; and in time He can work the needed work of grace in my heart and do what He could not do otherwise. Hence, Jesus urges us to persevere in prayer.

It is also true that in the light of the great controversy between good and evil, God can do some things because we pray that He cannot do unless we ask Him. Should He do them without our asking, Satan would object; but because we ask, God can do what He could not do otherwise.

The mature Christian, however, doesn't want to change God's mind. He has learned that God's way is always best. He wants to know the mind of God, so his asking, his seeking, his knocking, show a perseverance in wanting to break through the human into the presence of the Divine that he might know God's plan and follow it.

Let us continue to ask, to seek, and to knock, for we know that we shall receive, we shall find, and there shall open for us many doors through which new light will shine.

Life Through Prayer May 10

Ask, Believing

And all things, whatsoever ye shall ask in prayer, believing, ye shall receive. **Matt. 21:22.**

This promise has been a discouraging one to many. They have asked for things, actually believing they would receive them, and they did not receive them.

There is the story of a woman who heard that Jesus had said, "Verily I say unto you, If ye have faith, and doubt not, . . . ye shall say unto this mountain, Be thou removed, and be thou cast into the sea; it shall be done" (Matt. 21:21). There was a mountain just back of her house which was in her way. If only that mountain could be removed. The more she thought about the statement of Jesus, the more she thought she would try it; so one night before going to bed, she said to that mountain, "Be thou removed into the sea." The next morning after she looked out of the window she said, "There's that mountain, just as I expected it would be."

Could we say that she did not have enough faith? Had she had more faith, would the mountain have been removed? No. To expect such an answer would be misinterpreting the promise of Jesus. To ask in prayer, believing, is to ask in harmony with the will of God. All requests will be granted if we take into consideration that which lies behind them and recognize that God has our needs in mind—which needs we may misunderstand. The woman in the story, for example, might have discovered that that was not what she wanted after all. For many possible reasons that mountain's remaining in place might have been the real answer to her prayer.

Mountains of difficulty can prove to be a blessing rather than a hindrance, and we can thank God for *not* granting our requests as often as we can thank Him for granting what we actually ask. If my faith is in my prayer rather than in God, it may be shaken at times; but if my faith is in God, then I can know that He will answer my prayer according to His wisdom and according to my need.

Life Through Prayer   *May 11*

YE ASK AMISS

Ye ask and receive not, because ye ask amiss, that ye may consume it upon your lusts. James 4:3.

"Please, Daddy, buy me that doll—please, Daddy!" begged a little girl one day in a store. "Why do you want that doll, Jane?"

"Oh, because she is so pretty and I just love her! Besides, she is prettier than Mary's doll, and Mary thinks she is so smart. If I had that doll, wouldn't Mary envy me! Please, Daddy, buy it now." We smile, but so often, though not expressed, our own requests in prayer are motivated similarly.

So often we ask that we may satisfy selfish desires. Samson of old saw a woman of the Philistines whom he wanted for his wife. He spoke to his parents saying, "Get her for me, for she pleaseth me well." Even though he did not get that particular girl, he did get one of the daughters of the Philistines, and we all remember the sadness that experience brought him. Sometimes we receive, even though we have asked amiss. God lets us have what we want that we might learn certain lessons. When granted such requests, we generally find the result is leanness of soul. This was the experience of the children of Israel when they were wandering in the wilderness. Often they thought about the food they had enjoyed back in Egypt, and the record says they "lusted exceedingly in the wilderness, and tempted God in the desert. And he gave them their request; but sent leanness into their soul" (Ps. 106:14, 15).

If you want an interesting revelation, make a list of all the requests you make of God. Keep these on file. Note very carefully, too, what you consider to be the real motives behind these requests—the real needs as you see them. Record faithfully the answers to these requests as you receive them. After a period of time you will be surprised how few prayers were really unanswered. You will discover, too, how childish some of those requests were and how impossible it would have been for any father of love to grant them.

Life Through Prayer   *May 12*

Ask for Wisdom

If any of you lack wisdom, let him ask of God, that giveth to all men liberally, and upbraideth not; and it shall be given him. James 1:5.

Every problem we face in life is a call to prayer. Whenever we come face to face with that which calls for wisdom and understanding, we have this counsel from heaven, "If any of you lack wisdom, let him ask of God." God is interested in all phases of life. He wants us to do His will and to understand it, and He expects us to reason things out.

A young prophet was considering some of the problems of his day, and he asked some questions of God. There were some problems he couldn't understand. He even questioned God's justice, and then He said, "I will stand upon my watch, and set me upon the tower, and will watch to see what he will say unto me, and what I shall answer when I am reproved" (Hab. 2:1). He expected to be upbraided for questioning God, but God didn't reprove Habakkuk. He went on to explain the problem.

If we lack wisdom, we can ask of God, and to us all He will give liberally and will not upbraid us or scold us or reprove us. In asking for wisdom, however, we must realize that we need to learn some things by experience rather than by explanation. Too many times we expect God to hand us a formula, to give us cut and dried answers to life's questions. These are not always available. When we pray let us ask for wisdom and understanding and realize that since some things can be learned only by experience, we must trust Him and believe that He will lead us through the experiences necessary to give us the wisdom we so definitely need. If we lack wisdom, let us study His counsel provided in the Bible and the Spirit of prophecy. Let us not expect God to work a miracle in instructing us when He has already given us clear and practical information in His Word. Unless we listen to instruction that He has given us, why should He give us more?

Life Through Prayer   *May 13*

Ask in Faith, Nothing Wavering

But let him ask in faith, nothing wavering. For he that wavereth is like a wave of the sea driven with the wind and tossed. James 1:6.

We are to pray in faith, nothing wavering—having no doubts. Note: "But he must ask in sincere faith without secret doubts as to whether he really wants God's help or not. The man who trusts God, but with inward reservations, is like a wave of the sea, carried forward by the wind one moment and driven back the next. That sort of man cannot hope to receive anything from God, and the life of a man of divided loyalty will reveal instability at every turn" (James 1:6-8, Phillips' translation).

What about doubt? Is there no hope for a man who has doubts in his mind? Many brilliant young men and women have been filled with doubts, and have gone through life frustrated, insecure, and unhappy. Are they lost?

There are two kinds of doubters. There is the individual who questions with a desire to ascertain truth, and there is the person who doubts as to whether he really wants God's help. He is the individual who is like a wave of the sea. Honestly searching after truth, having a sincere desire to know what is truth that one may live in harmony with it, is a prerequisite to sound faith.

If you have been struggling with doubts, take courage from the experiences of Thomas and Philip. Doubting Thomas would not believe that his Lord was risen until he could put his hand in His wounds. Philip was a sincere seeker for truth, but he was slow of heart to believe. "Yet Philip was a student in the school of Christ, and the divine Teacher bore patiently with his unbelief and dullness. When the Holy Spirit was poured out upon the disciples, Philip became a teacher after the divine order. He knew whereof he spoke, and he taught with an assurance that carried conviction to the hearers."—*The Desire of Ages*, p. 293.

Life Through Prayer *May 14*

God Heareth the Prayer of the Righteous

The Lord is far from the wicked: but he heareth the prayer of the righteous. **Prov. 15:29.**

There is only one prayer a wicked man can pray, and that is the prayer of the publican, "God be merciful to me a sinner" (Luke 18:13). And when he prays that prayer sincerely, he is no longer a wicked man, but at that moment is a justified man through Jesus Christ his Lord. The Pharisee, who seemed so righteous, "prayed with himself," not God. That which determines whether one is wicked or righteous when he prays is his attitude. One's attitude in prayer is determined by one's concept of himself and his own needs. The Pharisee trusted in himself, and he prayed thus with himself, "Lord, I, I, I." His was a self-centered prayer. What he needed was a true knowledge of himself. He needed to compare his life with the life of Christ, not with that of the publican who stood nearby. In that comparison he would not appear so righteous. The publican, on the other hand, was aware of his need. There was a deep longing for purification. *His* prayer, God heard. He went down justified. The prayer of the Pharisee was not heard. It was a mere repetition of words.

Our text today, however, does pose a problem in the light of human experience. If the Lord is far from the wicked, but heareth the prayer of the righteous, why is it that the wicked sometimes prosper and the righteous suffer? In this connection we must remember that physical and material prosperity or adversity are not related to moral worth. We must not evaluate our standing with God on the basis of *how much* we suffer, but on *how* we suffer. The prosperity of the wicked is only temporary, and in many cases only apparent. The suffering of the righteous is also only temporary, and is used by God as a furnace of affliction, as it were, to prove their temper and to determine whether they can be fashioned for His work. God suffers with them. He hears their prayer and stands by their side giving them strength to suffer triumphantly.

Life Through Prayer 　　　　　　　　　　　　　　　　　　　　　　　　May 15

Prayer No Substitute for Right Action

He that turneth away his ear from hearing the law, even his prayer shall be abomination. **Prov. 28:9.**

Prayer is no substitute for right action. After the great victory that God had gained for Israel at Jericho, the Israelites were self-confident. They began to lay plans for the conquest of Ai, and even Joshua proceeded without seeking counsel from God. In their conflict with the men of Ai, however, they were defeated. This was the first time they had met the Canaanites in actual battle, and this was just a little town; if defeated here, what would be the results in the greater conflicts before them! Joshua fell on his face and cried unto the Lord. The answer from Jehovah was, "Get thee up; wherefore liest thou thus upon thy face? Israel hath . . . transgressed my covenant which I commanded them" (Joshua 7:10, 11). It was a time for prompt and decided action, not for despair and lamentation.

Prayer never takes the place of right action. Occasionally in human experience we are tempted to pray to the Lord for help in situations that are contrary to His instructions. For example, consider a young woman who is about to marry an unbeliever. Definite instruction is given us, "Be ye not unequally yoked together with unbelievers" (2 Cor. 6:14). But because she loves him, and there seem to be so many things in his favor, she asks God for guidance. Obviously her prayer is valueless, because the Lord has given instructions that He expects her to follow.

This kind of prayer is an abomination unto the Lord. So would be the prayer of a shrewd businessman for success in a shady deal. However worthy the end may be, if the means are not in harmony with God's will, how can we pray for success? No; prayer is not a substitute for right action.

We must always remember to pray in harmony with God's will as we know it, and continually study to understand more fully what that will is.

Life Through Prayer May 16

Prayer for the Sick

And the prayer of faith shall save the sick, and the Lord shall raise him up; and if he have committed sins, they shall be forgiven him. James 5:15.

A little girl was exposed to chickenpox near the end of the school year. There was so much to look forward to—the school picnic, the closing exercises, and a trip to grandpa's farm. She looked forward to everything with keen anticipation, and she didn't want to get sick.

But she got the chickenpox. One morning she said to her mother, "Mamma, isn't Jesus stronger than Satan?" "Yes, dear," her mother replied. "Well, then, why did He let me get chickenpox?"

The experience of this little girl is symbolic of the experience of many adults. Hundreds of prayers have ascended to God *by* the sick, as well as *for* them, and in some instances it has seemed as though God didn't listen, or as though He had forgotten His promises, or was unmindful of the particular individual involved.

Why is this so? Perhaps God has some lesson to teach. There are some things more important than physical healing. The little girl needed to experience some inconsequential disappointments in her little life to strengthen her to meet greater ones to come. Many a man learns to know God while flat on his back in a hospital. Important decisions are often made during these periods when men and women are forced to lay aside their work. God is interested in making men whole spiritually as well as physically.

There are many reasons why God cannot immediately cancel out disease. Some diseases are the result of sin. While God forgives, God cannot always cancel the consequences immediately. When we pray for the sick let us pray that God's will may be done and that His purposes may be fulfilled in our lives and in the lives of those for whom we pray. When we do, we have the assurance of salvation and the assurance of the resurrection, which assurances are far more important than physical healing.

Life Through Prayer   May 17

EFFECTIVE PRAYER

Confess your faults one to another, and pray one for another, that ye may be healed. The effectual fervent prayer of a righteous man availeth much. James 5:16.

The effectiveness of prayer is due not so much to the choice of words as to the life of the man who prays. Here, for example, is a deacon who offers prayer practically every Sabbath, because there are very few men in the little church who are willing and able to do it. During the week he operates a garage in the little town nearby. During marble season boys become regular nuisances asking for ball bearings to use as marbles. "Steelies," the boys call them. One Friday a ragged little fellow comes in, and for some reason the man is not in good humor. A young woman passes by just in time to hear him scolding the little fellow with words that shock her. All this young woman can think about when he prays the next Sabbath is what she heard in his garage as she passed by the day before. It is not so much what a man says as what he is that makes prayer effectual. The kind of pray-er I am is more important than the kind of prayer I offer.

There is healing in the fellowship and atmosphere of prayer; hence, the counsel, "Confess your faults one to another, and pray one for another, that ye may be healed" (James 5:16). The physical effect of prayer is recognized by many physicians. They realize that in an attitude of prayer men are relaxed, and the forces of healing can operate more efficiently. There is nothing that so unites the hearts of men and brings about the correct atmosphere of mutual trust as a recognition of common needs. Barriers are broken down when we share our needs with one another. As we confess our faults one to another we are able to understand one another, and in fellowship approach our heavenly Father for help to overcome these faults. And when we are interested not only in our own salvation but also in that of others, that mutual concern for one another creates an atmosphere that enables God to do for us what He could not do otherwise.

Life Through Prayer May 18

PRAYER AND THE LAWS OF NATURE

Elias was a man subject to like passions as we are, and he prayed earnestly that it might not rain: and it rained not on the earth by the space of three years and six months. James 5:17.

Will God upset the laws of nature when we pray? Can we expect the Creator to change the weather simply because we ask Him?

Miracles in answer to prayer are often thought of as activities contrary to nature. This implies that the laws of nature are self-working and that God interferes as He sees fit. This is not correct.

"God does not annul His laws, but He is continually working through them, using them as His instruments. They are not self-working. God is perpetually at work in nature. She is His servant, directed as He pleases. . . . The hand of infinite power is perpetually at work guiding this planet. It is God's power momentarily exercised that keeps it in position in its rotation."—*Testimonies,* vol. 8, pp. 259, 260.

All the forces of nature are God's power in action. There is not that great difference between the natural and the supernatural that many suppose. For many the natural seems to be ascribed to ordinary causes, unconnected with the power of God. This is not true. All the marvelous powers of the universe are God's power continually at work. In God we live and move and have our being. Every breath, every throb of the heart, is continual evidence of the power of an ever-present God.

When working a miracle, then, God simply uses His servants, the powers of nature, in a way out of the ordinary. In what we call divine healing, He simply speeds up the healing process.

When we pray we are in touch with God, who is in perfect control of all the forces of nature. Whenever He sees best He uses them to His glory and our welfare. Nature is consistent because God is consistent. We would not want the universe otherwise. We can trust God when we pray, and rejoice in the assurance that all the forces of nature are under His control for the accomplishment of His great purposes.

Life Through Prayer May 19

"I Have Set the Lord Always Before Me"

I have set the Lord always before me: because he is at my right hand, I shall not be moved. Ps. 16:8.

A saintly colored maid was questioned about her method of prayer. "I ain't got no method," she replied. "While I wash de clothes, I asks de Lord to wash hearts whiter than snow; while I irons 'em I reminds Him of de troubles an' problems that need ironin' out. While I sweeps de flo' I just ask Him to sweep out faultfindin' from de hidden corners of ma heart, so He can bless, an' He always does."

This dear soul, like David, had learned the secret of setting the Lord always before her. This is the kind of prayer life that brings results. Our prayer life will be successful if we keep in an attitude of prayer. Thus we will pray morning, noon, and night. Especially in the morning will we seek the Lord, but all day long we will cultivate the consciousness of His presence. Ralph S. Cushman wrote:

> "I met God in the morning,
>   When my day was at its best,
> And His presence came like sunrise,
>   Like a glory in my breast.
>
> "All day long the presence lingered;
>   All day long He stayed with me;
> And we sailed in perfect calmness
>   O'er a very troubled sea.
>
>   .   .   .   .   .
>
> "So I think I know the secret
>   Learned from many a troubled way:
> You must seek Him in the morning
>   If you want Him through the day."
>
> —From *Spiritual Hilltops*. Copyright 1932, by Ralph S. Cushman. By permission of Abingdon Press.

Life Through Prayer   *May 20*

PRAY WHEN IN TROUBLE

And call upon me in the day of trouble: I will deliver thee, and thou shalt glorify me. Ps. 50:15.

God invites us to pray when in trouble. Repeatedly we find ourselves in difficulty. Every problem is a call to prayer. We should not pray only when in trouble, of course, but it is by no means wrong to cry unto God in time of need. Deliverance from trouble is not a once-and-for-all experience. We can expect trouble as long as we live in this world of sin and as long as Satan and his angels exist.

The children of Israel "cried unto the Lord in their trouble, and he delivered them out of their distresses." Four times is this verse repeated in the 107th psalm. You would think that they would have learned their lesson, but again and again they found themselves in trouble, only to cry unto the Lord, and again He delivered them. Aren't we like that? Should we not take courage and realize that we have a loving, kind, long-suffering heavenly Father, who wants us to call upon Him? He has promised deliverance, and He has also promised that the experience will not be in vain. He will use it for some good.

> "When we pray we open windows
> And we see a wider view.
> Flooded with the light of heaven,
> Life takes on a different hue.
> Unseen hands reach out to help us,
> And in manner wonderful,
> Peace steals on the restless spirit—
> Peace, profound, unspeakable.
> Strangely is the heart disburdened;
> Somewhere, Someone takes the load.
> We are touched by God's own finger
> And a blessing is bestowed."
>
> —PATIENCE STRONG

Life Through Prayer

GOD KNOWS OUR NEEDS

Be not ye therefore like unto them: for your Father knoweth what things ye have need of, before ye ask him. **Matt. 6:8.**

Have you ever wondered how God could answer conflicting prayers? In wartime, for example, sincere Christians on both sides of the battle line pray for victory. How can God give victory to both? Two sincere Christians can be praying—one prays that it will not rain, the other prays for rain. How can both be answered? In the same household a teen-ager's prayer may be absolutely the opposite of the prayer of the parents. How can God, who loves both, and who is concerned about the welfare of both, answer both prayers? We can see how God is face to face with many conflicting requests on the part of His children. How is He able to answer all of them?

First of all, God is more interested in the petitioner than in the petition. He loves both parties who pray conflicting prayers, and does not weigh one request against another. He does not decide which loves Him most, nor does He make the decision on the basis that one merits His blessing more than the other. No, God sees the need behind the petition. Our heavenly Father knows what things we need before we ask Him.

Our needs and our interpretation of our needs may be two different things. Our important needs are those that present no conflicts whatever as far as the prayers of others are concerned. God knows the need behind our petitions, and He can supply that need in any way He sees fit. When we realize this, we can say as we pray, "Lord, this is my need as I see it. Open mine eyes that I may see how to cooperate with Thee so that this need might be fulfilled." Then if we find that someone else has been praying in a way that seems to cause a conflict, we need never worry whose prayer God will answer; for God has a thousand ways of answering both prayers of which we know little or nothing.

We can rely on the promise in Philippians 4:19: "But my God shall supply all your need according to his riches in glory by Christ Jesus."

Life Through Prayer May 22

HE GIVES BETTER THAN WE ASK

If ye then, being evil, know how to give good gifts unto your children: how much more shall your heavenly Father give the Holy Spirit to them that ask him? Luke 11:13.

Someone has said there are four kinds of asking: First, there is asking to receive; this is the way we all begin. That is all we know. As children we ask to receive, but God wants us to "put away childish things" and grow up.

Second, we learn about asking to believe. As we grow, more and more questions arise in our minds, and we realize our need of faith. We want to know the meaning of life and the answers to certain great questions. We want to find something we can believe. Then we realize that even more than that is essential.

With the maturing process comes the realization that what we are is important, and so we learn the third kind of asking—asking to be. The mature prayer is not so much "Give me" as "Make me."

Then finally we learn about asking to give. When we ask to share, we become more Christlike. He lived to bless others. When we reach that state God can do more for us and we can be of greater value to Him.

In the words of Frances Ridley Havergal's hymn we have expressed the kind of prayer that is mature.

"Lord, speak to me, that I may speak in living echoes of Thy tone;
 As Thou hast sought, so let me seek Thy erring children lost and lone.

"O lead me, Lord, that I may lead the wandering and the wavering feet;
 O feed me, Lord, that I may feed Thy hungering ones with manna sweet.

"O strengthen me, that while I stand firm on the Rock, and strong in Thee,
 I may stretch out a loving hand to wrestlers with the troubled sea."

Life Through Prayer *May 23*

Pray for Guidance

For thou art my rock and my fortress; therefore for thy name's sake lead me, and guide me. Ps. 31:3.

Guidance is more valuable than things. In fact, on a journey a guide is even more valuable than a map. The more we journey through life, the more we recognize our need for a guide; and so it is only proper and fitting that we should pray, "Guide, O Lord, guide me."

We have the promise that the answer to that prayer will be, "I will instruct thee and teach thee in the way which thou shalt go: I will guide thee with mine eye" (Ps. 32:8).

Sometimes we are disappointed because we do not receive some outward guidance for which we long, and thus we are led to ask God for a sign. We remember how Gideon wanted to be sure of certain matters, and presented before the Lord some alternatives, definite external signs, on which to base his decision. The Lord, however, is more interested in inward guidance than He is in outward manifestations. Those who seek for external signs alone will not be persuaded "though one rose from the dead" (Luke 16:31).

What do we do when we ask for signs? First, we put the responsibility on God to make our decisions for us. This He does not always want to do. He wants us to develop our own God-given abilities. No mature earthly father wants to make all decisions for his son. Second, in asking for signs, we force the hand of God. We are saying, "Lord, You've got to tell me by eight o'clock tomorrow morning just what You want me to do." He will not be forced. Third, God does not confuse or reverse His guidance. Yet, many who ask for signs over and over again find that the answer is different at different times.

If we trust God, He will give us sufficient outward evidences of His guidance; but if He does not give us an outward sign immediately, He wants to guide us more maturely; and true guidance comes from within, not from without. Therefore, we need to pray for wisdom, for strength, and for good judgment, and trust Him to open the way as He sees fit.

Life Through Prayer   *May 24*

Prayer and Communion

Stand in awe, and sin not: commune with your own heart upon your bed, and be still. Ps. 4:4.

There was something about Jesus that was different. As the people looked upon Him, "they saw a face in which divine compassion was blended with conscious power."—*The Ministry of Healing*, p. 51. He would come forth from seasons of communication with His Father refreshed and surrounded with an atmosphere of light and peace. He had received a new endowment of both physical and mental strength, and His life breathed out a fragrance and manifested a divine power that reached men's hearts.

Wouldn't you like this to be true of you? It can be. Here is the secret: "All who are under the training of God need the quiet hour for communion with their own hearts, with nature, and with God. In them is to be revealed a life that is not in harmony with the world, its customs, or its practices; and they need to have a personal experience in obtaining a knowledge of the will of God. We must individually hear Him speaking to the heart. When every other voice is hushed, and in quietness we wait before Him, the silence of the soul makes more distinct the voice of God. He bids us, 'Be still, and know that I am God.' This is the effectual preparation for all labor for God. Amidst the hurrying throng, and the strain of life's intense activities, he who is thus refreshed, will be surrounded with an atmosphere of light and peace. He will receive a new endowment of both physical and mental strength. His life will breathe out a fragrance, and will reveal a divine power that will reach men's hearts."—*Ibid.*, p. 58.

Read it through twice today and let its beauty and wonder sink deep into your heart. Here is described the prayer life and its results in human experience that make for strength and happiness.

Life Through Prayer May 25

Prayer and Meditation

Let the words of my mouth, and the meditation of my heart, be acceptable in thy sight, O Lord, my strength, and my redeemer. Ps. 19:14.

Have you ever wondered how Jesus could spend all night in prayer? What did He talk about? Have you ever prayed all night? Have you ever prayed for one hour? What do you say after the first ten or fifteen minutes? After you have presented all your needs and have mentioned all your loved ones, friends, enemies, the missionaries you know, and have included all the problems of the world, with special mention of men of state in every nation, what do you do next?

These questions imply that prayer is a one-sided conversation on our part, most of which consists of petitions. Praying is much more. It includes meditation, letting God talk to us, thinking about what He has said and is saying. Have you ever been surprised how quickly the time has gone by when in conversation with a friend? So it is when we learn to pray in a larger sense.

Spiritual leaders are men who have learned the art of meditation. We read that "Isaac went out to meditate in the field at the eventide" (Gen. 24:63). And the Lord said to Joshua, "This book of the law shall not depart out of thy mouth; but thou shalt meditate therein day and night, that thou mayest observe to do according to all that is written therein: for then shalt thou make thy way prosperous, and then thou shalt have good success" (Joshua 1:8). David says, "His delight is in the law of the Lord; and in his law doth he meditate day and night" (Ps. 1:2). He speaks of his own experience thus: "I remember thee upon my bed, and meditate on thee in the night watches" (Ps. 63:6). "My eyes are awake before the watches of the night, that I may meditate upon thy promise" (Ps. 119:148, R.S.V.).

Talking to God, listening to His voice, and thinking about what He says—all this constitutes prayer. It is no wonder that Jesus could spend all night in prayer; He had so many things to think about, so much to receive from His heavenly Father.

Life Through Prayer May 26

THE SPIRIT HELPETH

Likewise the Spirit also helpeth our infirmities: for we know not what we should pray for as we ought: but the Spirit itself maketh intercession for us with groanings which cannot be uttered. Rom. 8:26.

J. B. Phillips translates our text today and the next verse as follows: "The Spirit of God not only maintains this hope within us, but helps us in our present limitations. For example, we do not know how to pray worthily as sons of God, but His Spirit within us is actually praying for us in those agonizing longings which never find words. And God Who knows the heart's secrets understands, of course, the Spirit's intention as He prays for those who love God."

It is wonderful to know that God understands. There are longings impossible to express in words. These the Holy Spirit translates into the language of heaven, and we are blessed accordingly. We think of the simple faith of the little fellow who was on his knees saying the alphabet. When asked why he was reciting his letters on his knees, he replied, "I don't know how to pray, but I know Jesus can take these letters and make the right words out of them."

The Lord knows our hearts and accepts every sincere prayer. There was Jimmy. Every day he would go into the church, kneel awhile, and then run along on his way. The pastor asked him one day, "Jimmy, what do you say when you are on your knees in there?" "Well, Mister," replied Jimmy, a bit embarrassed, "I don't know how to pray, but I simply say, 'Jesus, it's Jimmy.'" One day Jimmy didn't show up as usual, nor the next day. Three days went by. The pastor wondered, "Where is Jimmy?" The next day when Jimmy didn't show up at the church, he went to find him. Up and down the narrow streets and alleys he went asking for Jimmy. Finally he found him sick in bed. He was very sick. His lips were moving. The pastor bent over him and put his ear very close to catch the words, "Jesus, it's Jimmy. Jesus, it's Jimmy." With these words on his lips, Jimmy died. As the pastor walked away, he thought, "The next words Jimmy will hear are, 'Jimmy, it's Jesus.'"

Life Through Prayer May 27

Pray in Jesus' Name

Verily, verily, I say unto you, Whatsoever ye shall ask the Father in my name, he will give it you. John 16:23.

To pray in the name of Jesus means more than merely adding the words "We ask it all in Jesus' name" to the end of our prayers. "It is to pray in the mind and spirit of Jesus while we believe His promises, rely upon His grace, and work His works."—*Steps to Christ* (Pocket ed.), p. 101. "It means that we are to accept His character, manifest His spirit, and work His works."—*The Desire of Ages* (1940), p. 668. Prayer is not just saying words. It is not simply the tongue that prays, but the whole man. Our spirit, our actions, our attitudes, all speak. A sense of helplessness pleads for help more eloquently than carefully phrased sentences with a selfish motive.

In the light of the Father-Son relationship of God and Jesus, this expression "to pray in the name of Jesus" takes on new meaning too. For example, two boys, Jim and George, were buddies in the service. They had been together in a number of battles and had become fast friends. One day Jim was severely wounded. George took care of him as best he could, but Jim died. As he was dying he said, "George, when and if you get home, tell Dad I did my best; tell him of all the good times we've had together." It was almost a year before George had a chance to see Jim's dad. During that year Jim's father had grown bitter. In his sorrow he shut himself away from all social contacts. Rarely would he admit anyone into his home. When George returned he went to look up Jim's father. He knocked at the door; there was no answer. He knocked again and again. Finally the door opened a little and a voice grumbled, "What do you want?" "Mr. Walters, I'm George Rogers. I knew your son. I was with him when he died." The door opened. "What's that you say? You knew my son! Come right in."

If a human father in the name of his son will admit a stranger, how much more will our loving heavenly Father in the name of His Son Jesus admit a child of His—you or me.

Life Through Prayer May 28

WATCH AND PRAY

Take ye heed, watch and pray: for ye know not when the time is. Mark 13:33.

"Keep your eyes open; keep on the alert" (Phillips). Prayer is not to take the place of the fullest use of all our powers. We are told to watch and pray. We are to combine intelligent observation with our devotions. "The Lord God of heaven will not supply the deficiencies that result from mental and spiritual indolence."—*Fundamentals of Christian Education,* p. 374. Too many people think of prayer as a substitute for effort. This is not the case. We are told to watch.

Watch what? Be on the alert for what? First of all, we need to watch God's opening providences. It is very possible for God to open a door and for us not to see it because we have been watching the wrong things. Perhaps we have been looking at ourselves, perhaps we have been grieving over wounded pride, and cannot see God's opening providences. Let's watch for these.

Then let's watch for the needs of others. Often the needs of another are opportunities for us. Therefore let us be on the alert to see openings for service. Let us watch, also, our own tendencies and weaknesses. Many a person has been spared an inglorious defeat in temptation because he has watched his own weaknesses and thus has kept from placing himself on the enemy's territory. We should watch, too, for the deceptions of the enemy. Subtle they are; he will deceive, if possible, the very elect in these great days in which we live. Let us be aware of Satan's schemes, and let us keep our eyes open to the signs of the times and watch the developments that fulfill prophecies. We are told that eternal vigilance is the price of liberty. Eternal vigilance is also the price of readiness. This is doubly true, since we do not know the time when He cometh; lest coming suddenly He find us sleeping. "In such an hour as ye think not the Son of man cometh" (Matt. 24:44). "And what I say unto you," Jesus said, "I say unto all, Watch" (Mark 13:37).

Life Through Prayer May 29

Pray for Others

Moreover as for me, God forbid that I should sin against the Lord in ceasing to pray for you: but I will teach you the good and the right way. 1 Sam. 12:23.

It is easy for our prayers to become self-centered requests for personal benefits alone. God wants us to become unselfish. He wants to take us out of our little narrow circles into a world of service for others, and throughout the Scriptures we are taught to pray for others. Intercessory prayer must not be omitted from our worship.

We are told to pray for God's people, to pray for the peace of Jerusalem, and to pray for all men, including kings. The apostle Paul prayed continually for his converts and asked them to pray for him. It was when Job prayed for his friends that his captivity was turned (Job 42:10).

Jesus prayed for His friends. In that wonderful prayer recorded in John 17 He prayed for His disciples; and then He added, verse 20, "Neither pray I for these alone, but for them also which shall believe on me through their word." Here Jesus prayed for you and for me, as yet unborn.

As we pray for one another, God can accomplish for us and through us what He could not otherwise. Samuel said, "God forbid that I should sin against the Lord in ceasing to pray for you." He considered it a sin not to pray for Israel even though they had rejected him as their leader and wanted a king. They were still God's people. God wanted Samuel to continue to plead in their behalf, for God could do some things for Israel because Samuel prayed that He could not do otherwise. We cannot fully understand this; but this must be true or there would be no need for intercessory prayer. God does everything He can to save all.

Remember, too, we must combine activity with our prayers. It is not enough just to pray for a man. We should do everything in our power to help him.

Life Through Prayer   May 30

PRAY IN CHURCH

Even them will I bring to my holy mountain, and make them joyful in my house of prayer: . . . for mine house shall be called an house of prayer for all people. Isa. 56:7.

The church has various uses, but God says it is to be first and foremost a house of prayer for all people. This is the designated place of prayer, where God meets with His own. Of course, prayer is acceptable anywhere and at any time. There is no place where we cannot hold communion with God, but God would have us dedicate a place of prayer and meet together for the hour of prayer. None should be excluded, all should be welcomed. In Christian experience those who forsake not "the assembling of themselves together," who attend the prayer service in the middle of the week as well as the Sabbath services, are most likely to be the ones who are strong spiritually.

In church we worship, we pray and listen, we pray and meditate, we pray and sing. The church is not an end in itself, not simply an organization to which we should belong, not merely something we should get people to join, not something that will ensure for us a home in the kingdom simply because we have our name on its roster. The church, I repeat, is not an end in itself, but a place of prayer, a place of worship, a place of communion, a place where we talk to God and listen to His Word. We have the promise that where two or three are gathered together, there Jesus will be in their midst. Let us claim that promise.

Students of human nature are finding today the therapeutic value of the fellowship of prayer. Not only is one lifted heavenward and strengthened physically and spiritually in private, individual prayer, but marvelous blessings are received by experiencing "togetherness" in group prayer, where men and women unite their hearts in a common interest for a common purpose. Combine the sharing of experiences with the benefits of prayer and you have a force, a power, and an experience for good that is unsurpassed in this world of sin.

Life Through Prayer May 31

Pray With Thanksgiving

Be careful for nothing; but in every thing by prayer and supplication with thanksgiving let your requests be made known unto God. Phil. 4:6.

Is there enough of thanksgiving in your prayers? Perhaps one reason why thanksgiving does not form a larger part of our praying is that we are not thankful at heart. It is the attitude of thanksgiving that produces words of thanksgiving. One must *be* thankful in order to *give* thanks sincerely, and to be thankful one must feel in his heart appreciation and gratitude.

The man who sees nothing for which to be thankful is blind. There are a number of factors that blind us—attitudes of mind that destroy the spirit of gratitude and thanksgiving. One of the most common is self-centeredness. The self-centered person considers all blessings as due him. "I had it coming to me," he says. "Why should I thank him; he's getting paid for it, isn't he?" Such a person is never thankful, because he feels he deserves more than he gets or because someone else has more. This shows itself in self-pity.

Another gratitude-destroying factor is a false sense of values. We are prone to evaluate life in terms of physical and material prosperity. Consequently, we feel we have nothing for which to be thankful if we have little of this world's goods or if we are failing in health.

Seeing everything in terms of the immediate present only—a lack of perspective—often causes one to complain rather than to give thanks. However, if we could view present experiences in terms of tomorrow and the over-all picture, we might be extremely grateful. Often when we look back at what seemed very unpleasant, we are glad events turned out as they did.

The self-centered person, the person with a false sense of values and a lack of perspective, is the overanxious person. Our text today begins, "Be careful for nothing." It simply means not to be overanxious.

JUNE

Life and Love   *June 1*

THE GREATEST OF THESE IS LOVE

And now abideth faith, hope, charity, these three; but the greatest of these is charity. 1 Cor. 13:13.

Life and love are inseparable in human experience. "In this life we have three great lasting qualities: faith, hope, and love; but the greatest of them is love" (Phillips' translation).

Life without love is like a fireplace without the fire. It is cold and hard and black. All is dark and chilly; put a fire in it, and suddenly there is light and color and warmth. In its glow one envisions memories of the past and dreams of the future. Such is life with love.

Life without love is like a well without water. It is empty. Nought but mockery awaits one who comes to quench his thirst; but let that well become a fountain, and it overflows—bringing life and health and joy to all, satisfying the deep longings of the heart. Such is life with love.

Life without love is like a violin without strings. It is dead. There is no song, no music, nothing through which a man might pour out his soul; but add the strings, and the skilled master musician can bring forth melodies and harmonies that stir the hearts of men. Such is life with love.

"Love is a precious gift, which we receive from Jesus." "Human love should draw its closest bonds from divine love. Only where Christ reigns can there be deep, true, unselfish affection."—*The Ministry of Healing,* p. 358.

One physician has said, "Without love, we lose the will to live. Our mental and physical vitality is impaired, our resistance is lowered, and we succumb to illnesses that often prove fatal. We may escape actual death, but what remains is a meager and barren existence, emotionally so impoverished that we can only be called half alive."—SMILEY BLANTON, *Love or Perish,* p. 4. (Simon and Schuster.)

Life and Love *June 2*

Empty Words Without Love

Though I speak with the tongues of men and of angels, and have not charity, I am become as sounding brass, or a tinkling cymbal. 1 Cor. 13:1.

Words have power to stir men. P. M. Roget has said, "False logic disguised under spacious phraseology too often gains the assent of the unthinking multitude spreading far and wide the seeds of prejudice and error. A misapplied or misunderstood term is often enough to give rise to fierce and unending disputes. A misnomer has turned the tide of popular opinion. An artful watchword spoken in a tense situation has kindled the flame of deadly warfare and changed the destiny of an empire."

It is "out of the abundance of the heart [that] the mouth speaketh." If love fills the heart, the words do wonders; if there is no love there, they can do no good and they may do much harm.

"Nineteen hundred years ago
  The Prince of Peace foretold
That someday love would supersede
  The rule of force and gold.

"Sixty generations gone!—
  Yet love is just a creed.
When will the nations learn to trust
  Love's way in word and deed?

"When will men sacrifice for love
  As for revenge and hate?
How long must history record,
  'Too little love, too late' "?

Life and Love   *June 3*

WISDOM AND KNOWLEDGE WITHOUT LOVE

And though I have the gift of prophecy, and understand all mysteries, and all knowledge; and though I have all faith, so that I could remove mountains, and have not charity, I am nothing. 1 Cor. 13:2.

Understanding and knowledge and faith all seem very important to us, and they are. But without love they count for nothing. It would seem that had we understanding and knowledge, we could do right; had we faith so that we could move mountains, all would be well. However, love supersedes all. In this connection we think of that good old hymn we love so well:

"At first I prayed for light: could I but see the way,
How gladly, swiftly would I walk to everlasting day!
And next I prayed for strength: that I might tread the road
With firm, unfaltering feet, and win the heaven's serene abode.
And then I asked for faith: could I but trust my God,
I'd live infolded in His peace, though foes were all abroad.
But now I pray for love: deep love to God and man;
A living love that will not fail, however dark His plan.
And light and strength and faith are opening everywhere!
God waited patiently until I prayed the larger prayer."

Wisdom and knowledge without love can be dangerous, because they may be used for destructive ends and thus counteract the purpose for which God has given us intelligence. You recall it was the partaking of the fruit of the tree of the knowledge of good and evil that brought all the sin and woe upon this world. This was true because knowledge apart from God, without love, is the source of all evil.

Knowledge without a purpose is valueless. It is love that gives purpose and meaning to our knowledge. What good is it to know without love? Have you ever known a person who seemingly knew everything but was very unlovely personally? For the true Christian, wisdom, knowledge, and faith are combined with love, and are constructive.

Life and Love   *June 4*

PHILANTHROPY WITHOUT LOVE

And though I bestow all my goods to feed the poor, and though I give my body to be burned, and have not charity, it profiteth me nothing. 1 Cor. 13:3.

Is not selling one's possessions and giving to the poor a commendable procedure that should merit favor? Jesus once asked the rich young ruler to do just that, but he went away sorrowful, for he had great possessions. Had he done as Jesus invited him to do, would he not have profited thereby? It is no small matter to part with one's possessions. Why should not this be acceptable? Not only does Paul say that this does not count without love, but what is more, even to suffer bodily pain, perhaps to the point of martyrdom, is of no avail. Touch a man's possessions, and you touch his life line. Touch a man's body, and you go a step further. Many a man is willing to give up his possessions to be free from pain. Satan first took away Job's possessions, then he touched Job's body with boils, and still Job was faithful. We marvel at his loyalty.

Paul says it is possible to do all this for nothing—without love. And why? One may endure all the trials of Job from a selfish motive. One may sell all his possessions and give to the poor to be thought of as a great philanthropist, to be seen of men, to become famous in this way. Martyrdom may be an acceptable way to die and escape from reality, but it may not merit divine favor. Walking through the fire can bring the praise and admiration of one's fellow men, but only those acts motivated by love count.

"There are those who . . . are not moved by any deep sense of the love of Christ, but they seek to perform the duties of the Christian life as that which God requires of them in order to gain heaven. Such religion is worth nothing. . . . A profession of Christ without this deep love, is mere talk, dry formality, and heavy drudgery."—*Steps to Christ* (Pocket ed.), pp. 44, 45.

May all our works be motivated by a desire to serve through love.

Life and Love   *June 5*

LOVE IS KIND AND HUMBLE

Charity suffereth long, and is kind; charity envieth not; charity vaunteth not itself, is not puffed up. 1 Cor. 13:4.

"Love is forbearing and kind. Love knows no jealousy. Love does not brag; is not conceited" (Weymouth's translation). "This love of which I speak is slow to lose patience. It looks for a way of being constructive. It is not possessive. It is neither anxious to impress nor does it cherish inflated ideas of its own importance" (Phillips' translation).

Here we have brought to light some of the identifying marks of true love. There is a great difference between true love and infatuation. There are young people who have asked: "How can we tell if our love for each other is true love?" Our text today gives us a good test. True love is patient and kind. The patient and kind way is the constructive way, the redemptive way, to deal with life situations. This is the way of love. When this world reached its darkest hour, the unfallen worlds expected Jehovah to arise and sweep away the inhabitants of the earth. But instead of destroying the world, God sent His love to save it. That is love's way. True love is unselfish, whereas immature love is based on selfishness—is conceited and jealous.

Let us remember that there is no love apart from a person. What we read here about love must be true of the person who loves. Love is patient and kind only as the person who loves is patient and kind, and these qualities in an individual have their roots in love. When these qualities are absent, love is lacking. Selfishness has taken the place of love. Actually, we consider the opposite of love as hate, but hatred is only one manifestation of selfishness. A selfish person is impatient, unkind, jealous, possessive, conceited, and cannot love. Only when by the grace of God the heart has been changed and filled with the love of Christ, can true patience, kindness, and unselfishness be manifest in all relationships.

Life and Love   *June 6*

LOVE BASIC TO TRUE REFINEMENT

Doth not behave itself unseemly, seeketh not her own, is not easily provoked, thinketh no evil. 1 Cor. 13:5.

True refinement and culture have their roots in love, and they are the marks of true love. One who truly loves treats all with refinement and delicacy as the sons and daughters of God. Christianity will make a man a gentleman. On one occasion a well-meaning man came to church in dirty clothes. Being conspicuous in the midst of others who were clean and nicely dressed, he said to a bystander after the service, "That's one thing about Christian love, it brings us all down to the same level." "No, friend," replied the bystander, "Christian love brings us all *up* to the same level." An ill-mannered person, a discourteous person, is a selfish person.

It is possible to put on an outward form of extreme politeness for a selfish end. However, this is soon detected. "The most careful cultivation of the outward proprieties of life is not sufficient to shut out all fretfulness, harsh judgment, and unbecoming speech. True refinement will never be revealed so long as self is considered as the supreme object. Love must dwell in the heart. A thoroughgoing Christian draws his motives of action from his deep heart love for his Master. Up through the roots of his affection for Christ springs an unselfish interest in his brethren. Love imparts to its possessor grace, propriety, and comeliness of deportment. It illuminates the countenance and subdues the voice; it refines and elevates the whole being."—*The Ministry of Healing,* p. 490.

True love is not easily provoked. It is not touchy. People who need to be handled with kid gloves, as it were, have not learned to love. Self rules within, and a wounded self makes one difficult to live with. Sensitive people need not be selfish people. In fact, lovely women are sensitive women. When one's sensitive nature is turned inward, he becomes the touchy person; if this is turned outward, he is then very sensitive to others' needs and becomes a most delightful individual.

Life and Love   *June 7*

LOVE REJOICES IN TRUTH

Rejoiceth not in iniquity, but rejoiceth in the truth. 1 Cor. 13:6.

Why do people enjoy hearing about the evil things in others? Why do we seem to get satisfaction out of another's fall? Why do we seem to enjoy juicy bits of gossip that are passed from one to another, even though we know that often a life is broken and discouraged? Could it be that our own ego is inflated because by comparison we seem better than they? Could it be that love is lacking?

Am I more ready and happy to pass along the good things I know and hear about a person than those not so good? Am I quick to take up reports of evil deeds, and slow to recognize the kind and loving actions manifested? How about it? Do I find myself taking for granted all the nice things, all the helpful things, another does for me, and do I find fault with every little mistake and weakness I see in that person's life and action? So often those with whom we are most closely associated in our homes are those who suffer at our hands more than any others. True love rejoiceth not in iniquity, but rejoiceth in the truth.

"If we noticed little pleasures, as we notice little pains;
If we quite forgot our losses and remembered all our gains;
If we looked for people's virtues, and their faults refused to see,
What a pleasant, cheerful, happy place this world would be!"

When true love fills the hearts of two lovers, they love each other because they inspire each other to higher and nobler living. They love each other, not because they see perfection in each other, but because they can overlook the little faults and appreciate the finer virtues that are manifest. They love each other because they have confidence in each other. They see not that petty narrowness that is the result of selfishness, but that lovely wholesomeness that comes from a manifestation of the fruit of the Spirit in the life.

Love Endureth

Beareth all things, believeth all things, hopeth all things, endureth all things. 1 Cor. 13:7.

In the eastern part of the United States there lived a man, his wife, and two lovely children. They were well fixed financially, and seemed to live together in perfect harmony. One day a piece of literature was left at their door. Mother read it, and began to study her Bible. Father wasn't interested, but didn't object until, because of her convictions, Mother would not go to certain places of amusement with him. When she decided to keep the Sabbath, her husband finally left.

Every day Mother and the children prayed for Daddy. One day, when he heard that his wife was moving to California, he thought about his children, and the prospects of not seeing them troubled him. He arranged for his attorney to call on his wife to see whether some legal grounds could be found to keep his children. The attorney questioned her about her husband, saying, "Do you suppose, since your husband has left you, he is finding other associations?" Other questions were asked, to which the wife replied that she deeply loved her husband and believed sincerely in his integrity. In no sense did she feel that he was anything but a gentleman in all his conduct, and just because he did not see fit to stay with her and the children, on account of their religious convictions, she did not love him any less; moreover, if the attorney were half as much a gentleman as her husband, he would not imply misconduct on her husband's part without evidence.

In reporting the conference the attorney said, "Man, what are you trying to do—involve me in a libel suit? That woman would not let me say one thing that would reflect on your character!" Then he told about the interview. The husband sat there speechless. He could not understand how his wife had loved him through all the abuse and desertion. Her love broke his heart. He went home to her that night, and the whole family went to California, where they are united in a bond of Christian love, the kind of love that stands when all else has failed.

Life and Love

LOVE NEVER FAILETH

Charity never faileth: but whether there be prophecies, they shall fail; whether there be tongues, they shall cease; whether there be knowledge, it shall vanish away. 1 Cor. 13:8.

The thirteenth chapter of First Corinthians is right in the heart of Paul's discussion of spiritual gifts. He discusses God's plan of endowing men and women with various gifts to be exercised and developed for the realization of divine purposes. Each has its place. We are admonished to covet earnestly the best gifts. Then Paul continues, "And yet shew I unto you a more excellent way." Following this statement, we have this wonderful thirteenth chapter on love.

Paul is saying, then, simply this: All other gifts are temporary. They are given to fulfill a specific purpose, that of preparing us for the kingdom of heaven. When their work is done, they are no longer necessary. Not that prophecies will fail in the sense that we cannot depend on them, nor does he say that the time will come when no one will be able to speak a word in the sense that tongues shall cease to speak. What he does say is made plain in Phillips' translation of our text: "For if there are prophecies, they will be fulfilled and done with, if there are tongues the need for them will disappear, if there is knowledge it will be swallowed up in truth."

More important than all these is love—for it never fails.

"O love of God, how strong and true!
Eternal, and yet ever new;
Uncomprehended and unbought,
Beyond all knowledge and all thought.

"O love of God, our shield and stay
Through all the perils of our way!
Eternal love, in thee we rest,
Forever safe, forever blest."

—HORATIUS BONAR

Life and Love · June 10

MATURE LOVE

When I was a child, I spake as a child, I understood as a child, I thought as a child: but when I became a man, I put away childish things. 1 Cor. 13:11.

Too many people never grow up emotionally. As we grow in stature, increase in knowledge, and become older in years, our love should become more mature. Someone might ask, "Should we not have a childlike faith and love, as Christians?" Yes, but there is a world of difference between a childlike love and a childish love. Childish reactions on the part of adults are manifested in resentment and bitterness, refusing to admit one's faults, selfishness, jealousy, pouting, sulking, and nagging. Unhappy homes result from emotional immaturity.

Childish people look for heaven on earth but are never able to find it, because it isn't heaven to them unless their own selfish desires are always satisfied; and since their wants are constantly changing, there can be no lasting happiness for them. If two childish people fall in love and marry, the chances of their establishing a happy home are very poor. Each expects the other to be perfect and to satisfy his own childish needs. A marriage is threatened when one or both are unwilling to endure the childishness of the other.

The young person asks, "How can I be sure of a mate whose love is mature?" Make sure that you are mature yourself, and you will not need an immature love to bolster your own. Here is a good test. Is your love characterized more by anxiety than by deep-seated joy? Does every move revolve around your own wishes and desires? Do you live more by emotional reactions than by intelligence? Do you find yourself becoming more and more attached to one who has no love for God, and who sees no attraction in the religious life? Does your love lessen your efficiency for usefulness, or decrease your love for things spiritual? If you must admit that the answer to these questions is Yes, yours is not a mature love. Face the truth about yourself, and begin at once to put away childish things.

Life and Love

June 11

Then Shall I Know

For now we see through a glass, darkly; but then face to face: now I know in part; but then shall I know even as also I am known. 1 Cor. 13:12.

No matter how much we love one another, we still cannot see all that is down deep in one another's hearts. And it is a good thing we cannot. That our vision is limited is a blessing, for two reasons. In the first place, there are within each of us so many possibilities for and tendencies to evil, so many evidences of narrow selfishness that need yet to be purified and ennobled, that it is well they are concealed. Then, too, we are not big enough, not mature enough yet, to overlook all the faults we might see in another, should his life be an open book to us. Even Jesus kept some things from His disciples, because, as He said, "Ye cannot bear them now." But there is coming a time when we shall no longer know in part, but we shall know even as also we are known. Then there will be no dark veil between. Because we know only in part, we can love only partially. But then, we shall know one another as we are known. At that time, cleansed from sin, we shall love more fully, for we shall be like Him. Until then, let us recognize our limitations, and so love as to feel safe with one another.

"O, the comfort, the inexpressible comfort, of feeling safe with a person—having neither to weigh the thoughts nor measure the words, but pouring them all right out, just as they are, chaff and grain together, certain that a faithful hand will take and sift them; keep what is worth keeping, and then, with the breath of kindness, blow the rest away."—T. L. Haines and L. W. Yaggy, *The Royal Path of Life,* p. 406.

"At present all we see is the baffling reflection of reality. We are like men looking at a landscape in a small mirror. The time will come when we shall see reality whole and face to face. At present all I know is a little fraction of the truth. But the time will come when I shall know it as fully as God now knows me" (Phillips' translation).

Life and Love   *June 12*

LOVE THE LORD

And thou shalt love the Lord thy God with all thy heart, and with all thy soul, and with all thy mind, and with all thy strength: this is the first commandment. **Mark 12:30.**

Wouldn't it be a wonderful thing to have Jesus say to you, "You are not far from the kingdom of God." He said that one day to a man. A lawyer came to Him, and asked Him, "Which is the first commandment of all?" And Jesus answered him, "The first of all the commandments is, Hear, O Israel; the Lord our God is one Lord: and thou shalt love the Lord thy God with all thy heart, and with all thy soul, and with all thy mind, and with all thy strength: this is the first commandment. And the second is like, namely this, Thou shalt love thy neighbour as thyself. There is none other commandment greater than these."

And the scribe said unto Him, "Well, Master, thou hast said the truth: for there is one God; and there is none other but he: and to love him with all the heart, and with all the understanding, and with all the soul, and with all the strength, and to love his neighbour as himself, is more than all whole burnt offerings and sacrifices." It was then that Jesus said to him, "Thou art not far from the kingdom" (Mark 12:28-34).

When we learn that far more important than all our outward acts of worship, ritual, or ceremonies is a heart that loves, we too may hear Jesus say to us, "You are not far from the kingdom."

Why did Jesus say, "Not far"? Why didn't He say, "You are in"? The scribe needed one thing more. He needed to recognize the divine character of Christ and through faith in Him to receive pardon and the ability to love. It is only thus that we can truly love God and our neighbor. Jesus has made provision then for us not only to be close to the kingdom but also to have the kingdom of God within.

May that be your experience and mine today.

Life and Love *June 13*

LOVE THY NEIGHBOR

And the second is like, namely this, Thou shalt love thy neighbour as thyself. There is none other commandment greater than these. Mark 12:31.

This text reminds us of two statements of Jesus. The first, the golden rule. "Whatsoever ye would that men should do to you, do ye even so to them" (Matt. 7:12). We can learn to love our neighbor as ourselves when we learn to treat him as we would want him to treat us. This is basic.

We are also reminded of the parable of the good Samaritan. Jesus told this story in answer to the question "Who is my neighbor?" Obviously, the answer is that anyone who needs our help is our neighbour.

I like the words of Florence Jansen, published in *Think,* entitled "These Are My Neighbors":

> "These are my neighbors, these who fall and rise,
> Who dream and wake, who dread, and hope, and yearn,
> Who, bound by earthly care, envision skies;
> Whose patience fails, and who are slow to learn.
> I see the print of striving on their brow
> And sense that they and I are one in quest;
> Their soaring hopes and blind despair, somehow,
> Find quick response upwelling in my breast.
> These are my neighbors, these in whom I see
> A spirit proud, rebellious, selfish, vain,
> Or nearly noble, all a part of me;
> In upward striving runs our common strain.
> Against discordant tricks of circumstance
> Our human oneness triumphs over chance."

When I recognize in a neighbor the same human heartbeat with all its hopes and fears and needs, and then realize that my Lord loves him as He loves me, I can begin to love him as myself.

Life and Love June 14

PERFECTING THE ART OF LOVING

No man hath seen God at any time. If we love one another, God dwelleth in us, and his love is perfected in us. 1 John 4:12.

There are a number of reasons why human love is imperfect and why we so desperately need the love of God within to perfect our love. Too often love is confused with sex appeal or with the purely sentimental and romantic feeling one experiences when "falling" in love. True love, however, should be based not on impulse but on principle.

In his book *The Art of Loving* Dr. Eric Fromm points out that most people see the problem of love primarily as that of being loved, rather than that of loving—one's capacity to love. In seeking love they follow different paths. Men try to be successful, powerful, and rich. Women try to make themselves attractive. Both sexes try to develop pleasant manners, cultivate interesting conversation, and make themselves lovable.

Many people think that to love is simple, but that to find the right object to love is difficult. Instead of concentrating on their own ability to love, they search constantly for someone who is to be the object of their love. They are not as concerned as they should be about their own faculty of loving.

People think, too, that the experience of "falling in love" is to be sought after, and they fail to recognize that the permanent state of being in love or "standing" in love is what is desirable. Many people who fall in love are attracted by an intense infatuation, and the intensity of the infatuation—this being crazy about each other—is often in proportion to the degree of their preceding loneliness.

While Dr. Fromm does not believe in a personal loving heavenly Father, he does see man's need of a more mature love. We believe that mature love is attained only as the love of God transforms our selfish hearts. Then we can begin to love as He loved, and God's love will be perfected in us.

Life and Love
June 15

A New Commandment

A new commandment I give unto you, That ye love one another; as I have loved you, that ye also love one another. John 13:34.

In what sense was the commandment of Jesus a new commandment? Moses had given a commandment to love one another. In Leviticus 19:18 we find recorded these words, "Thou shalt not avenge, not bear any grudge against the children of thy people, but thou shalt love thy neighbour as thyself."

One can see in what sense Jesus' commandment was a new commandment when he compares the two. At the time of Moses, self-love was a love people could at least partially understand. Hence, they were told to love their neighbors as themselves. Jesus now says, "Love one another as I have loved you." The life of Jesus brings to light a new type of love. "In the light from Calvary it will be seen that the law of self-renouncing love is the law of life for earth and heaven; that the love which 'seeketh not her own' has its source in the heart of God."—*The Desire of Ages* (1940), p. 20.

Love takes on new meaning in the light of a life of love. Only when experienced can it be fully understood. Violet Woods in her book *Great Is the Company* tells how Missionary Hensey sought to translate the Scriptures into the Mongo-Nundo language. As he studied the language he found no words for love, hope, or peace. After years of patient study he still found no word for love. There was an expression he heard the Bantu mothers use in speaking tenderly to their littlest children—*ok'eefe'*. He asked, "What does *ok'eefe'* mean?" "*Ok'eefe'* means that I care for this little girl of mine so much that when I think of what is going to befall her when she grows up, it hurts me."

In the life of our Lord Jesus Christ we have a true concept of love revealed, a new concept. We are to love one another not only as we love ourselves but as Christ loved us, who even gave Himself for us. Self-sacrificing love takes on new meaning in the light of His self-sacrificing life.

Life and Love   *June 16*

LOVE THE TEST OF DISCIPLESHIP

By this shall all men know that ye are my disciples, if ye have love one to another. **John 13:35.**

"How these Christians love each other!" This was the observation made by the pagans concerning the early Christians. Can this be said of us in our day, in our communities? In our text today Jesus makes loving one another the test of discipleship. But the question may come to our minds, "Are Christians the only people who can love? Isn't a pagan mother able to love her child? Do not Mohammedans love one another, some of them at least?" Yes, even a pagan loves those who love him. But Jesus said, "For if ye love them which love you, what reward have ye? do not even the publicans the same?" (Matt. 5:46).

That which is the test of Christianity is the ability to love those who are not so lovely and who do not love in return. This comes only through a transformation of heart. Will you notice that Jesus does not say to love one another is a prerequisite to discipleship. If it were, none of us would be disciples, inasmuch as the natural heart is selfish. True love for our fellow men, including our enemies, is the result of discipleship and is the outflowing of Christ's love from within.

Once we catch a glimpse of God's love, once we learn to love Him, something happens inside us. In the first place, we get a glimpse of the sinfulness of our own heart. "A view of our sinfulness drives us to Him who can pardon; and when the soul, realizing its helplessness, reaches out after Christ, He will reveal Himself in power."—*Steps to Christ* (Pocket ed.), p. 65. When Jesus reveals Himself to us He changes the heart and then He abides within. This makes it possible for us to look upon all men as He looks upon them. We are enabled to appreciate and enjoy all that is true and good and beautiful in men and to see them as they may be, transformed by the grace of God. Because Jesus loves them, we too will love them; and we will be interested in their salvation, even though they may be very unlovely in their present state.

Life and Love   *June 17*

LOVE YOUR ENEMIES

But I say unto you, Love your enemies, bless them that curse you, do good to them that hate you, and pray for them which despitefully use you, and persecute you. Matt. 5:44.

To be cursed, hated, despitefully used, and persecuted is difficult to bear. But to love those who so treat us is still more difficult from a human point of view.

How can this be done? H. Stanley Jones tells how one Armenian girl had been enabled to forgive a Turk. She and her brother had been attacked by Turks; and although she had escaped, her brother had been brutally killed before her eyes. Later, while nursing in a hospital, she recognized one of her patients as the very Turkish soldier who had murdered her brother. Her first feeling was revenge. He was very ill, just hovering between life and death. The slightest neglect would result in his death, and no one would know. His life was absolutely in her hands. But instead of revenge, she decided for Christ's sake to forgive him. She fought for his life, and won, nursing him back to health.

When he was convalescing she told him who she was. The Turkish soldier looked at her in astonishment, and said, "Then why didn't you let me die?" "I couldn't," answered the girl. "I just couldn't, for I am a Christian, and my own Master forgave His enemies who crucified Him. I must do the same for His sake." "Well," said the Turk in astonishment, "if that is what it means to be a Christian, I want to be one."

Had someone said to the Armenian girl, "Listen, you must love that Turk; love him now, or you will never be saved," under no circumstances would a command to love have created love within her heart for him. It is only as the light of the gospel of Jesus Christ shines into the heart, and the individual follows that light, that love awakens, especially for one's enemies. It was when she heard those words from Calvary, "Father, forgive them, for they know not what they do," that she was led to be like Him.

The Fruit of the Spirit

But the fruit of the Spirit is love, joy, peace, longsuffering, gentleness, goodness, faith, meekness, temperance: against such there is no law. Gal. 5:22, 23.

All Christian graces or qualities have their roots in love. The apostle Paul could have said, "But the fruit of the Spirit is love, which manifests itself in joy, peace, long-suffering, gentleness, goodness, faith, meekness, and temperance." Where there is love there is deep-seated joy. There is no peace of mind that can compare with the peace that is the result of having the love of God in the heart. Observe how patient a mother is with her crippled child, whom she loves. Gentleness and kindness are the language of love. We trust and have confidence in those we love. Humility and self-control are expressions of true love, with all the powers of one's being disciplined and devoted in all their keenness and strength and maturity to the one loved.

These virtues mentioned are positive virtues, not negative. Against such there is no law. We need laws to protect society against the fruits of the flesh, such fruits as are listed in verses 19-21: adultery, fornication, uncleanness, envyings, murders, drunkenness; but not against the fruits of the Spirit.

Fruit is the product of the tree. The character of the tree determines the fruit. Notice that it is the Holy Spirit that brings the harvest. These Christian graces are not prerequisite to the outpouring of the Holy Spirit, they are the products. Nor are they necessary in order to gain His love. They are the outgrowths of that love that develop in our lives as the result of our fellowship with Him. It is as a result of fellowship that we learn to trust and believe and have confidence in and love those near and dear to us. Love comes through fellowship with Christ, through the operation of His Spirit in our heart.

Life and Love   *June 19*

LOVE FOR GOD'S LAW

O how love I thy law! it is my meditation all the day. Ps. 119:97.

At first it may seem strange to associate love and law. But David found that the two go hand in hand. One reason why it is so difficult to learn to love is that we seem to have an inherent dislike for restrictions, rules, and regulations. The selfish human heart rebels against law. This, of course, is what sin has done to the human heart.

One of Satan's great objectives is to destroy the law of God. Where he has been successful in doing so there is little or no love, only fear and hate. We have seen that in some parts of the world there is not even a word for love in the language. The reason for this rebellion against law is the feeling that it interferes with selfish desires. Basically this is not true. Laws are necessary to make possible the fulfillment of our desires.

Downtown in the heart of busy traffic we find red lights and white lines and other restrictions that seem to interfere with our progress. But just imagine what would result without these. There would definitely be no progress whatsoever. If you have ever been caught in a traffic jam, you know what this means, and you thank God for traffic laws and regulations. God's laws are ordained to ensure us life. They become agents of death only as we refuse to live in harmony with them. Actually, policemen are our friends and protectors in a world of sin. It is too bad when children are taught to fear and despise them.

Love is much more than a mere feeling or impulse, love is a principle—a principle laid down by the great Creator, whose laws make love possible and meaningful. Like David, once we learn to know God and understand His laws, we see that they are great principles that make for love. And like David, if we would meditate on God's law all the day, we would find our lives greatly enriched in love for God and for our fellow men.

LOVE THE FULFILLING OF THE LAW

Love worketh no ill to his neighbour: therefore love is the fulfilling of the law. Rom. 13:10.

In an atmosphere of love the law of God, instead of being negative, becomes positive. The Ten Commandments are statements of constructive results, and a life in harmony with the great truths listed therein is a life of happiness and joy. Just put the words "If you love God" in front of each of the first four commandments and "If you love your fellow men" in front of the last six, and it will be clearly seen how love is the fulfilling of the law.

If you love God, you will have no other gods before Him. Why? Because when you know Him, you know there are no other gods. If you love Him, you will not make any graven images. Why? Because when you know and love Him, no image is adequate. Perhaps the best representation of the Christian Deity is a crucifix. But this is not adequate, because it portrays a *dead* Christ. We serve a *living* Christ. If you love God, you will not take His name in vain. Why? Because you respect that name too much to dishonor it. If you love Him, you will gladly lay aside your daily work at the time appointed for prayer and worship, for the Sabbath day becomes a joy and a pleasure because it is an opportunity for fellowship with the One you love.

When we love our fellow men the same positive results follow. If we love our parents, we will honor and respect them. If we love, we will not hate, and therefore we will not kill, for hatred precedes murder. If we love, we will not steal. If we truly love, we cannot commit adultery, for that would betray our love. If we love our neighbor, we will not bear false witness against him. If we love others, we will not covet, for we will be glad and rejoice with them in their blessings, successes, and joys. Truly, love is the fulfilling of the law.

Life and Love June 21

SINCERE LOVE

Seeing ye have purified your souls in obeying the truth through the Spirit unto unfeigned love of the brethren, see that ye love one another with a pure heart fervently. 1 Peter 1:22.

"Now that, through your obedience to the truth, you have prepared your souls by purification for sincere brotherly love, you must love one another heartily and fervently" (Weymouth's translation).

Of all the fair graces and virtues that are important, I think *sincerity* is the queen of them all. It is the virtue the human heart instinctively craves and hopes for. And yet how common is insincerity. What a miserable old humbug of a world we are living in—full of trickery, dishonesty, and deceit of every kind. We say what we do not mean; we express emotions we do not feel; we praise when we secretly condemn; we smile when we have a frown in our heart; we strive so often to make people think we are other than we are.

Thank God, however, there are hearts here and there upon whom we can depend. Life would not be worth living if there were no one on earth sincere. There are some things we cannot be and many things we cannot do, but being sincere is within reach of us all.

Jesus' sincerity was very appealing when He was among men. Nothing was so abhorrent to Him as falsehood, and no other class so stirred His wrath as men who were hypocrites. It was because of Jesus' incorruptible sincerity that we have from His lips such a remarkable outpouring of plain words. He spoke exactly what He meant. What He taught, He was. Not very often does an ordinary man put his whole self into his speech. His words reveal him, but they also conceal him. There is often a discrepancy between what the soul is and what the mouth declares. But not so with Jesus—what He thought, He said; what He felt, He declared. This was because He was sincere. That is why He could say, "I am the truth." What He says, we can believe; what He tells us, we can depend on. That should be said concerning you and me. May your love and mine be sincere, brotherly love.

Life and Love   *June 22*

LOVE AND KINDNESS

Be kindly affectioned one to another with brotherly love; in honour preferring one another. **Rom. 12:10.**

What is kindness? Nick Kenny's answer is quite inclusive. Think it through.

> "Kindness isn't sacrifice, or giving alms, my lad—
> It's simply sharing happiness with someone who is sad.
> Kindness is a soothing light that seeks out darkened hearts,
> And makes them flame with new-found hope, new joy—
>   and then departs.

> "Kindness is a merry song turned loose upon the air—
> A musical guardian of our joy—a foeman of despair.
> Kindness is unselfish thought, unselfish, friendly deed,
> Inspired by the wish to help some brother who's in need.

> "Kindness is forgetfulness of our own worldly aims,
> Forgetfulness of all but this: our needy neighbor's claims.
> Kindness is a loving guide that shows us how to live,
> A treasure which the more we spend, the more we have to
>   give."

When "in honour preferring one another" we rejoice in another's successes, we can let the other fellow get the credit for something that perhaps we shared in accomplishing. We will not be hurt personally, because the joy we see in the other fellow's heart will surprisingly enough well up in our own. The secret fullness of happiness that comes from making another happy is a greater joy by far than the superficial pleasure that comes from the credit, fame, and applause of men that might be ours at someone's expense.

Kindness to others brings a reward that only those who are kind can know, and kindness always begets kindness.

Life and Love *June 23*

LOVE AND DISCERNMENT

And this I pray, that your love may abound yet more and more in knowledge and in all judgment. **Phil. 1:9.**

Knowledge and judgment, or discernment, are needed in every sphere of life. In meeting temptations we need to discern right from wrong. In efficient service of any kind we need knowledge and insight. However, in the field of love relationships these qualities are needed more than anywhere else. Knowledge and discernment are perfectly compatible with love. It has been said that love is blind. This is not true. Only as one faces reality can he truly love. True love sees both the faults and the good qualities of the one loved, and evaluates with both in mind.

Most criticisms are due to misunderstanding and lack of discernment. Note how lack of insight brings heartache into the home. There is the speech made by a little girl to her mother some time ago:

"Say, Mother," she said, "may I go over to Mrs. Brown's house?" "Why, JoAnn, there are no children to play with there." "Oh, I know, Mother, but you see, Mrs. Brown is alone; and she wants me. She makes her work a game that we both play. Or she tells me stories while she works. When the work is finished, she wears nice dresses and reads to me. She looks so nice, I just love to be with her. Of course, I love you, Mother, but you see you are always so busy, you don't seem to have any time to pretend work is a game, or to tell stories, or to read to me—not even time to put on one of your nice dresses. And I'm sure I only bother you while I'm here."

These childish words hurt more than the little girl will ever know, because they were true. And why? All because of a lack of insight on the part of the mother—insight into the heart of the little girl, insight into her own heart, insight into what are the important things in life, and insight into the best methods of inspiring little girls.

May your love and mine abound more and more in knowledge and in all judgment.

Life and Love June 24

PERFECT LOVE CASTS OUT FEAR

There is no fear in love; but perfect love casteth out fear: because fear hath torment. He that feareth is not made perfect in love. 1 John 4:18.

A surgeon's little daughter was being teased one day by a visitor. He said to her, "Do you know what your daddy does? He takes people and stretches them out on a long table. Then he puts them to sleep. When they are sound asleep, he takes a sharp knife, cuts open their tummies and takes things out of them. Then he sews them up again. Isn't he a terrible man?"

"Ah," said the little girl, "you can't scare me. I know my daddy, and I love him."

Perfect love trusts, and casts out all fear. There is so much fear in this world because there is so little love. If men loved one another, they would not be afraid of one another. It is because people have not learned to love that they are tormented with fears, envies, jealousies, hatreds, and discontent.

Many people are afraid of God and of the coming judgment. Notice Weymouth's translation of our text for today and the two verses preceding it: "God is love, and he who abides in love abides in God, and God abides in him. In this will love in its perfection be displayed in us, in our being fearless on the day of judgment. . . . Love has in it no fear; but perfect love drives away fear, because fear involves punishment, and if a man fears, there is something imperfect in his love."

I fear the day of judgment only if my conscience bothers me. Isaiah tells us that only the wicked will be afraid when the day of the Lord cometh (Isa. 13:8). Selfishness and hatred, with all their fruits, bring fear. If I love God and my fellow men, I have no need to fear. In perfect confidence I can rest assured that all will be well. Not only need I not fear the judgment, but I need not fear as others do along life's road, because Jesus walks with me by the way.

Life and Love   *June 25*

LOVE COVERETH ALL SINS

Hatred stirreth up strifes: but love covereth all sins. Prov. 10:12.

There is a text that says, "He that covereth his sins shall not prosper" (Prov. 28:13). In the light of this text, how can our text for today be true, which says, "Love covereth all sins"? It makes a big difference who covers the sins and how they are covered. If we seek to cover them ourselves and to hide them, they will fester like a severe infection and cause endless trouble. But when the love of God covers our sins with the blood of Christ, or when our love helps cover another's mistakes, then we find joy, and peace, and happiness.

One of the most astounding texts in the Bible is Numbers 23:21: "He hath not beheld iniquity in Jacob, neither hath he seen perverseness in Israel: the Lord his God is with him, and the shout of a king is among them." Balaam made this statement under inspiration from the top of Pisgah just before Israel entered the land of Canaan. He was called by Balak to curse Israel, and all he could do was bless them. When you think back over the forty years preceding this event and recall all the murmuring and complaining, all the rebellion and disobedience, you wonder how a prophet could say, "He hath not beheld iniquity in Jacob, neither hath he seen perverseness in Israel." This can only be true because God loves His people. Isaiah tells us in chapter 63, verse 9, "In all their affliction he was afflicted, and the angel of his presence saved them: in his love and in his pity he redeemed them; and he bare them, and carried them all the days of old." God looks upon those whose sins are forgiven as though they had not sinned. This is true because of the wonderful righteousness of Christ, which covers them.

When God's love fills our hearts, "as he is, so are we in this world" (1 John 4:17). We too can overlook another's sin in the spirit of Jesus, who said, "Neither do I condemn thee: go, and sin no more." Thus we can, in love, help inspire others to nobler living.

Life and Love   *June 26*

HUSBANDS, LOVE YOUR WIVES

Husbands, love your wives, even as Christ also loved the church, and gave himself for it. Eph. 5:25.

The couple had been married four years before. Now with the two children at home with their daddy, the wife sat in a pastor's office weeping. "My husband doesn't love me any more," she said, "and I can't stand it any longer." What had happened? As she talked about their home it became evident that the following statement applied particularly to her husband: "There are many who regard the expression of love as a weakness, and they maintain a reserve that repels others. This spirit checks the current of sympathy. As the social and generous impulses are repressed, they wither, and the heart becomes desolate and cold. We should beware of this error. Love cannot long exist without expression. Let not the heart of one connected with you starve for the want of kindness and sympathy."—*The Ministry of Healing*, p. 360.

The little woman in the pastor's office was starved for want of affection. Her life had been one routine of child care and housework. Many failures in marriage result not so much from lack of love as from lack of expressing that love. This may be due to the fact that not having been loved, some don't know how to love. Taking love for granted and not taking time to express that love result in the situation described above. Each must assume full responsibility for making the marriage a success, and as Christ expresses His love for His church, so must the husband take time to express his love for his wife and family, and daily give the home the priority it deserves.

"Let each give love rather than exact it. Cultivate that which is noblest in yourselves, and be quick to recognize the good qualities in each other. The consciousness of being appreciated is a wonderful stimulus and satisfaction. Sympathy and respect encourage the striving after excellence, and love itself increases as it stimulates to nobler aims."—*Ibid.*, p. 361.

Successful marriage takes consideration, and self-sacrifice.

Life and Love

June 27

TEACH THE YOUNG TO LOVE

That they may teach the young women to be sober, to love their husbands, to love their children. Titus 2:4.

There was a documentary film made some years ago in South America that tells the pitiful story of a group of ninety-seven babies ranging in age from three months to three years who sickened and died for lack of love. These infants were neither neglected nor abused in the ordinary sense. They were adequately clothed, fed, and given proper medical attention. Competent nurses ministered to their daily physical needs. Only one element was lacking. The institution was badly understaffed, and each nurse had to care for ten or more of the helpless orphans. The nurses could do little more than feed, clothe, and bathe the children. They had no time to play with their charges, and they could give them no comfort or emotional exchange of any kind.

Within three months grave symptoms of abnormality became painfully apparent. At the end of five months deterioration had set in with accelerated swiftness. Some were even driven insane by loneliness and fear. Twenty-seven of those children died in their first year of life. Seven more died in their second year. Another twenty-one who remained in the institution managed to survive, but they were so seriously hurt by the experience that they had to be classified as hopeless neurotics or worse. Lack of normal love had laid waste the lives of more than half of the original group of infants.

The world is dying for a little bit of love, the kind of love that is not a passing ecstasy that develops without cultivation, but a basic principle of loyalty established early in life in an atmosphere of love. When a woman says, "I don't know why, but I just don't love my husband any more," she may think of love as feeling only. "Pure and holy affection is not a feeling, but a principle."—*The Ministry of Healing*, p. 358. This should be taught in childhood. Paul says, "Teach the young . . . to love."

Life and Love   *June 28*

LOVE NOT DEPENDENT UPON WEALTH

Better is a dinner of herbs where love is, than a stalled ox and hatred therewith. **Prov. 15:17.**

Love is not dependent upon wealth. In fact, love thrives better in an atmosphere of simplicity and humility than in an atmosphere complicated by the problems of wealth.

A banker's son made friends with a poor man's son while in school. He would often accompany the poor man's son home to spend the evening. Gradually he spent more time with his friend than at home. When his father was embarrassed at his spending time in this so-called poor section of town, he said, "Daddy, they have something we don't have at our house." A dinner of herbs with love is far more desirable than a great feast in a home where love is lacking.

If a young woman is faced with the problem of choosing between two lovers, one a man of wealth but lacking in his ability to express his love in kind and courteous ways, and the other a man not so well-to-do but one whose presence creates an atmosphere of Christian love, she had better choose the latter though he be poor so far as this world's goods are concerned. Marriage counselors find that no sound marriage was ever destroyed by financial worries. Statistics show that divorce declines steadily in depression years and increases as prosperity returns. The unhappiness commonly attributed to lack of money is more likely to be due to a lack of emotional stability. Success in marriage is determined not by the bank balance but by the attitudes of the partners to marriage and the depth of their true love for each other. Someone has said, "Intimidated by the brilliance of modern inventive genius, we have permitted one scientific miracle after another to be substituted for the infinitely greater wonders of the heart." There is nothing more wonderful than true love in a human heart. Yet at times this is eclipsed by things material or choked out by the cares and perplexities imposed upon us by this scientific age. Let this not be true of us today.

Life and Love   June 29

THE LOVE OF CHRIST PASSES KNOWLEDGE

And to know the love of Christ, which passeth knowledge, that ye might be filled with all the fulness of God. **Eph. 3:19.**

Lawrence Nye describes his visit to beautiful Forest Lawn Memorial Park in Glendale, California, on his honeymoon. He writes:

"There we stood in this new park, looking upon acres of green sod. . . . From somewhere near a great organ was playing the familiar strains of Victor Herbert's masterpiece, 'Ah! Sweet Mystery of Life.' . . .

"There, close to us, was a brilliant white group of statuary by Ernesto Gasseri called 'The Mystery of Life.'

"It consisted of eighteen life-sized figures, ranging in ages from that of a tiny baby in its mother's arms to an aged patriarch leaning intently forward as though attempting to keep up with the procession. The characters seemed to come to life. The children were watching the slow movements of a turtle, and two white doves. A man in his full years gazed wonderingly out into vistas of the unknown. Sweethearts embraced. An aged man sat patiently, having long ago ceased his attempts to pierce life's mysteries.

"We walked slowly away, and spoke not a word until we stood before a great temple. Inside was that renowned reproduction in stained glass of da Vinci's *The Last Supper,* executed by Mosetti. . . .

"It was silent in that room—reverently silent. Suddenly the two characters on either end of the great window seemed to disappear. Then, one by one, as the sun sank lower and lower, the disciples in turn seemed to fade from view. The picture narrowed more and more until the full power of a fading sunset was pouring through the central figure, the face of Christ. . . .

"And as the halo of light upon the head of that figure became more intense, an orderly opened a door. It was only for a moment, but long enough for the answer to come in. We heard again the strains: ' 'Tis the answer, 'tis the end and all of living! For it is love alone that rules for aye!' "

Life and Love   *June 30*

INCREASE AND ABOUND IN LOVE

And the Lord make you to increase and abound in love one toward another, and toward all men, even as we do toward you. 1 Thess. 3:12.

How can we increase and abound in love? Only as we learn to love the Lord. Listen, as Jesus talks to modern Peter:

"My son, love me." "Now wait a minute, Lord. I've been a Christian eleven years. What do you mean, 'Love me'? I do love you. What is the next step?" *"There is no other step; just love me."* "You know I love you, Lord; what do you mean?"

"Your love for me is revealed in your love to your fellow men. Do you love your biology professor?" "Well, I don't hate him, I just leave him alone. Lord, look at my love for other folks. Of course, I love You."

"Do you love your biology professor?" "Now, look. We don't get along, our personalities clash—so I avoid him." *"I died for him and live for him too."* "I know, Lord, and I would like to see him saved, but you understand that I just don't click with him."

"Do you love your biology professor?" "Oh, I respect him, and I think he respects me. I guess I do think of him as being overconfident and conceited. You know his kind, Lord. Why always talk about him, Lord? Look at all these other people I love."

"Do you love your biology professor?" "He is the one person, Lord, that I just can't stand. But I do love ———, I guess everyone else, and certainly you know I love You." *"You only love me to the extent that you love the person you like the least."*

"I really don't care about You, then. I always thought I loved You. Now I see. Lord, thank You for revealing this to me. I will truly love You now." *"You cannot, my child; how can you love me? There is no love in you. God is love."* "Then I cannot love anyone?" *"You are only the channel through which I can love anyone."* "Then, love this world through me, Lord, this world of broken men. Thou didst love through death, O Lord—love through me again!" *"Yes, I will, my man."*

This is the response of God. This is the response of a child of God.

JULY

Life With Myself   *July 1*

What Is Man?

What is man, that thou art mindful of him? and the son of man, that thou visitest him? For thou hast made him a little lower than the angels, and hast crowned him with glory and honour. Ps. 8:4, 5.

Who am I? What am I? What is man? There have been various answers to these questions. Someone has said: "Dust may be raised for a while into a little cloud and may seem considerable while held up by the wind that raises it; but when the force of that is spent, it falls again and returns to the earth out of which it was raised. Such a thing is man. Man is but a mass of dust and must return to his earth."

Man has been called various kinds of animal—a laughing animal, a cooking animal, an animal with thumbs, a lazy animal. Dr. Franklin calls him a tool-making animal. A cultivating animal is suggested by Walker. Hazlitt terms him a poetic animal. Southey calls man a dupable animal; and Adam Smith says, "No other animal is like man. Man is an animal that makes bargains. No dog exchanges bones with another."

David asks this question: "When I consider thy heavens, the work of thy fingers, the moon and the stars, which thou hast ordained; what is man, that thou art mindful of him?" (Ps. 8:3). When you look at the expanding universe above us and then look at man, in comparison he is but a speck of dust. However, he was created a high order of being and crowned with glory and honor. In man today, you see strange contradictions. As Blaise Pascal put it, "What a chimera is man! what a confused chaos! . . . a professed judge of all things, and yet a feeble worm of the earth! the great depository and guardian of truth, and yet a mere huddle of uncertainty! the glory and the scandal of the universe!"

Which will you be, the glory of the universe through Jesus Christ, or its scandal without Him?

Life With Myself   July 2

MADE IN THE IMAGE OF GOD

And God said, Let us make man in our image, after our likeness: and let them have dominion over the fish of the sea, and over the fowl of the air, and over the cattle, and over all the earth, and over every creeping thing that creepeth upon the earth. Gen. 1:26.

Of man it is said, "He is the image and glory of God" (1 Cor. 11:7), "made after the similitude of God" (James 3:9). According to Scripture, this is the high origin of man. The wise man says, "Lo, this only have I found, that God hath made man upright; but they have sought out many inventions" (Eccl. 7:29). Someone has said, "Like an old roofless temple, man is a grand and solemn ruin on the front of which we can still trace the mutilated inscription of his original dedication to God." Man in seeking out many inventions has ruined the image of God. The Lord Jesus Christ wants to re-create man and to make him "the new man, which is renewed in knowledge after the image of him that created him" (Col. 3:10). There is nothing God desires more than to recover every lost soul and "to retrace upon it His own image in righteousness and holiness."—*Christ's Object Lessons,* p. 194. This is the good news of the gospel.

A researcher of art in Italy was on the lookout for original paintings. He read that there was somewhere a portrait of Dante painted by Giotto, but no one knew where it was. He was led to suspect that it might be in an old former apartment house used as a storehouse for wood and hay and the like. He obtained permission to examine it. Clearing out the rubbish and experimenting upon the whitewashed wall, he soon detected signs of the long-hidden portrait. Little by little with loving skill he uncovered the sad, thoughtful, stern face of the old Tuscan poet. Sin has done for man what the whitewash and rubbish did to the painting. It has covered over and defaced the likeness of God upon the soul. It is only by the Spirit of God Himself that the long-hidden likeness can be manifested again.

May God grant that His image may be restored in us today.

SONS AND DAUGHTERS OF GOD

For as many as are led by the Spirit of God, they are the sons of God. Rom. 8:14.

Dr. M. Boudon, an eminent surgeon, was one day asked by Cardinal Dubois, prime minister of France, to perform a very serious operation upon him. Seeing him enter the room, the cardinal said to him, "You must not expect to treat me in the same rough manner as you treat the poor miserable wretches at your hospital, the Hotel Dieu." "My lord," replied Dr. Boudon with great dignity, "every one of those miserable wretches, as your eminence is pleased to call them, is a prime minister in my eyes."

Christianity brings to light the truth that every human being is actually a potential prime minister. Yes, and even more—a son or daughter of the Most High. Princes and princesses we are by the grace of God. "Behold, what manner of love the Father hath bestowed upon us," says John, "that we should be called the sons of God" (1 John 3:1). There is only one begotten son of God, and that is Jesus. However, you and I become sons and daughters by adoption into the royal family; and legally, an adopted child is as much a son or daughter as one born into the family. When we are "born again," we are adopted. Our baptismal certificate constitutes, as it were, our adoption papers. They were signed by the blood of Christ.

It was for the purpose of making possible our adoption as sons and daughters of God that Jesus came to this world. "When the fulness of the time was come, God sent forth his Son, made of a woman, made under the law, to redeem them that were under the law, that we might receive the adoption of sons. And because ye are sons, God hath sent forth the Spirit of his Son into your hearts, crying, Abba, Father" (Gal. 4:4-6).

Here is a privilege that calls forth the best that is in each one of us. Let us pray that we may be worthy of this high calling of God in Christ Jesus—to be children of the Most High.

Life With Myself   *July 4*

CHILDREN OF GOD

For ye are all the children of God by faith in Christ Jesus. Gal. 3:26.

"Am I really yours? Is this really our home—my home?" These are the questions asked by a little orphan boy as he walked through one room and then another in the home to which he was brought by his new foster parents. They had just been to the orphanage and had taken him home with them; and with wonder in his eyes, he walked around amazed. He had been pushed from pillar to post as a little fellow. He had no parents. Never before had he been able to say, "This is my home," but now he could. He could hardly believe it.

You and I are children of God by faith in Jesus Christ. We really belong to Him. We can believe it, because He has said so.

The story is told of a young man whose character and deeds of valor and heroism made a great impression upon his king. After a wonderful victory in battle, the king called in this young man and expressed his appreciation; and as a token of his regard, he offered him either possessions and riches, even to the half of his kingdom, or the hand of his only daughter in marriage. The young man thought it over. He had met the king's daughter, and he loved her. He was also tempted by the offer of the riches. Finally he decided, however, to marry the king's daughter, and in so doing he became heir with her of all the king possessed, not just half.

To be son and heir is far more valuable than the inheritance. Sonship is more important than wealth. What a privilege is ours! "The whole creation is on tiptoe to see the wonderful sight of the sons of God coming into their own" (Rom. 8:19, Phillips' translation). What an honor! All the intelligent beings in the universe are looking forward to the day when you and I will come into our own as members of the royal family—when we shall experience that triumphal entry into the New Jerusalem as sons and daughters of the King. Will you be there when the saints come marching in? Will I?

Life With Myself   *July 5*

TAKE HEED UNTO THYSELF

Take heed unto thyself, and unto the doctrine; continue in them: for in doing this thou shalt both save thyself, and them that hear thee. 1 Tim. 4:16.

Is it wrong to love myself? Is it selfish to want to save myself as well as others? No, Jesus said, "Thou shalt love thy neighbour as thyself." In fact, true self-love is essential to a true love for others. One of life's basic needs is the need for self-realization.

"Every human being, created in the image of God, is endowed with a power akin to that of the Creator—individuality, power to think and to do. The men in whom this power is developed are the men who bear responsibilities, who are leaders in enterprise, and who influence character. It is the work of true education to develop this power. . . . Instead of educated weaklings, institutions of learning may send forth men strong to think and to act, men who are masters and not slaves of circumstances, men who possess breadth of mind, clearness of thought, and the courage of their convictions. . . . Higher than the highest human thought can reach is God's ideal for His children. Godliness—godlikeness—is the goal to be reached."—*Education,* pp. 17, 18.

In the light of these quotations, it is clear that Christianity enables you to develop your true self without being selfish. In fact, God's ideal for you surpasses anything you can even imagine personally. You may say, "That is not for me—someone else perhaps, but not me." God is just as much interested in you as He is in any other individual. Christ would have died for you if you had been the only person who had sinned. (See *Christ's Object Lessons,* p. 187.) It is only Satan who says, "Cast thyself down." To those who listen to Satan, God says, "O Israel, thou hast destroyed thyself" (Hosea 13:9). To Ahab, Elijah said, "Thou hast sold thyself" (1 Kings 21:20). "Acquaint now thyself with him" (Job 22:21). "Keep thyself pure" (1 Tim. 5:22). "My son, give me thine heart" (Prov. 23:26).

Whose invitation will you accept today?

Life With Myself   *July 6*

Self-denial

And he said to them all, If any man will come after me, let him deny himself, and take up his cross daily, and follow me. **Luke 9:23.**

Self-denial is not self-depreciation. "While the Christian's life will be characterized by humility, it should not be marked with sadness and self-depreciation. . . . There is no evidence of true humility in going with the head bowed down and the heart filled with the thoughts of self."—*The Great Controversy*, p. 477.

"Our first duty toward God and our fellow beings is that of self-development. Every faculty with which the Creator has endowed us, should be cultivated to the highest degree of perfection, that we may be able to do the greatest amount of good of which we are capable."—*Counsels on Health*, p. 107.

What then does self-denial mean? Here is the answer: "Self-denial means to rule the spirit when passion is seeking for the mastery; to resist the temptation to censure and to speak faultfinding words; to have patience with the child that is dull and whose conduct is grievous and trying; to stand at the post of duty when others may fail; to lift responsibilities wherever and whenever you can, not for the purpose of applause, not for policy, but for the sake of the Master, who has given you a work to be done with unwavering fidelity; when you might praise yourself, to keep silent and let other lips praise you. Self-denial is to do good to others where inclination would lead you to serve and please yourself. Although your fellow men may never appreciate your efforts or give you credit for them, yet you are to work on."—*Testimonies*, vol. 4, p. 521. There is within us a perverted sinful self that always clamors for attention. This is the self that must be denied.

Simply to deny self without following the rest of our Master's instruction would produce a negative, unfruitful life. He further says, "Follow me." Following Him we find and develop our true selves transformed by His grace.

Life With Myself   *July 7*

TRUE SELF-DEVELOPMENT

For whosoever will save his life shall lose it: but whosoever will lose his life for my sake, the same shall save it. Luke 9:24.

Have you ever thought of the difference between selfishness and true self-love? When I seek to satisfy my own desires at the expense of others, my life is like an ever-narrowing circle, the diameter of which becomes smaller and smaller until eventually self is completely destroyed. But when I seek to serve others, to make them happy, I discover that *others* become *we*. Myself is included, and my life is then like an ever-expanding circle, the diameter of which becomes greater and greater; and there is no limit to the possibilities of my development. This is true only when the Holy Spirit takes possession within. "There is no limit to the usefulness of one who, by putting self aside, makes room for the working of the Holy Spirit upon his heart, and lives a life wholly consecrated to God."—*The Desire of Ages* (1940), pp. 250, 251.

There are four steps in the development of the true self from that state of selfishness in which we are born. First, I love myself for my sake. Second, I love others, but for my sake. This is an advanced step, but still selfish. I love others because of what they *mean* to me. Third, I learn to love others for their sake. I see value in them. I appreciate them for what they are, and I am not so much concerned about myself in the relationship. This is a more mature type of love. Then, fourth, I love myself for others' sake. I am concerned not so much for the happiness of the self as for the worth of the self. I want to develop the best that is in me for their sake. I want to be a good father for the sake of my children, a good husband for the sake of my wife, a good minister for the sake of my congregation, a good teacher for the sake of the students in my classes, et cetera. The difference, then, between selfishness and true self-love is the difference between one and four. When Jesus Christ takes possession of my heart, love for others takes the place of selfishness, and I find my true self complete in Him.

Life With Myself   *July 8*

I Am Crucified With Christ

I am crucified with Christ: nevertheless I live; yet not I, but Christ liveth in me: and the life which I now live in the flesh I live by the faith of the Son of God, who loved me, and gave himself for me. Gal. 2:20.

What is your cross and mine? What did Jesus mean when He said, "If any man will come after me, let him . . . take up his cross daily, and follow me" (Luke 9:23)? This matter of cross bearing has been greatly misunderstood. In fact, many people are carrying self-made crosses. "We are not to make crosses for ourselves, by wearing sackcloth, by pinching our bodies, or by denying ourselves wholesome, nourishing food. We are not to shut ourselves in monasteries, away from the world, and do no good to our fellow beings, thinking this is the cross of Christ; neither are we required to expose health and life unnecessarily, nor to go mourning up the hill of Christian life, feeling it a sin to be cheerful, contented, happy, and joyful. These are all self-made crosses, but not the cross of Christ."—*Testimonies,* vol. 4, pp. 626, 627.

There are some people who carry a chip around on their shoulder and think it is a cross. Others think some particular sickness or handicap is a cross. Suppose I consider tuberculosis to be my cross, and suppose I call in the elders of the church to pray for me, and suddenly, in a miraculous way, I am healed. What then? Jesus said we should take up our cross daily. Does this mean I should look around for some other sickness or trouble to carry? No. The only cross Jesus asks us to carry is the cross on which we crucify self—our old selfish selves. That is what Paul meant when he said, "I am crucified with Christ." That is what he meant when he said, "I die daily." This selfish nature of ours needs to be crucified. By the grace of God it can be. Then it can be buried in baptism, and we can rise to walk in newness of life, born again a new creature in Christ Jesus. With our selfish self crucified, and our true self re-created, we can be what God wants us to be.

Life With Myself   *July 9*

WHEN HE CAME TO HIMSELF

And when he came to himself, he said, How many hired servants of my father's have bread enough and to spare, and I perish with hunger! I will arise and go to my father. Luke 15:17, 18.

Children often wish to be someone else. But as they grow older the longing within becomes, "If only I could be myself!"

Many are blinded by Satan into thinking that following the path of forbidden pleasure enables one to be himself; but it always ends in losing oneself. The prodigal had been so blinded by Satan. He had wasted his substance on riotous living, and soon found himself hungry and lonely in a strange land. But it was when he really came to himself that he said in his heart, "I will arise and go to my father." It is when prodigals come to themselves that they return to God.

What happens when one, seemingly a wonderful Christian, loses out in his Christian experience and turns to the world? Jesus tells us it is because he has not root in himself. Do you remember the parable of the sower? Some seed fell into stony places. It sprouted; but when the sun was up, the plants, "because they had no root," withered away. Jesus explained: "But he that received the seed into stony places, the same is he that heareth the word, and anon with joy receiveth it; yet hath he not root in himself, but dureth for a while: for when tribulation or persecution ariseth because of the word, by and by he is offended" (Matt. 13:20, 21).

Occasionally a talented young physician, the seemingly satisfactory product of church school, academy, college, and medical school, who gives his friends every reason to expect a real contribution to the cause of God, loses his way spiritually soon after graduation. Why? He had no root in himself. His Christianity was not his own.

How important it is for us to have deeply rooted within our own heart the great principles of truth so that we may not lose our way! If we have lost our way, let us come to ourselves and arise and go to our Father, who will enable us to develop our true selves.

Life With Myself   *July 10*

I Must Discipline Myself

He that hath no rule over his own spirit is like a city that is broken down, and without walls. Prov. 25:28.

"I want to be free; I don't want to be tied down." A song, popular a few years ago, is actually in spirit the theme song of many in this generation. It was entitled "Don't Fence Me In." Often the forbidden path is labeled freedom, but when one walks therein he soon discovers a slavery from which it is practically impossible to be freed.

What young people want—actually want—is not freedom, but a channeling of their energies into lines of constructive activity. Suppose we liken our energies to a stream. We can do a number of things with it. We can put a dam across it; and as the water backs up behind the dam, the pressure increases. As it rises higher and higher, soon it will either overflow or we must build the dam higher. If we do, the pressure increases still more; and then, one of two things happens. Either the dam breaks and we have ruin and destruction on our hands, or the water finds peculiar outlets in strange ways. Or we can go to the other extreme and dispense with controls altogether and let the water go where it will. Where this condition exists, we soon have a swamp. But if we channel and harness the stream, we have light and power and beauty and all that water so directed can furnish.

So it is in the life of a young person. What he actually needs is discipline. He may not recognize his need as such, but it is nevertheless true. Not to dam up his energies, but to channel them into right lines is the purpose of restrictions and good discipline.

"Character is not the result of accident; it is not due to special favors or endowments of Providence. A noble character is the result of self-discipline, of the subjection of the lower to the higher nature, the surrender of self for the service of love to God and man."—*Education,* p. 57. One reason why so many people lack self-discipline is that they were not disciplined when they were young. If this is true in your case, you must take yourself in hand to make up for it.

My Will and God's

For it is God which worketh in you both to will and to do of his good pleasure. Phil. 2:13.

"I won't," said a little fellow to his mother when she asked him to put on his coat. In her embarrassment she explained, "My little boy has such a strong will power. I don't know what to do." Really, was it will power or won't power? So many of us are lacking in will power! We desire to do what is right, but seem unable to carry out our desires.

What is will power? "The tempted one needs to understand the true force of the will. This is the governing power in the nature of man—the power of decision, of choice. Everything depends on the right action of the will. Desires for goodness and purity are right, so far as they go; but if we stop here, they avail nothing. Many will go down to ruin while hoping and desiring to overcome their evil propensities. They do not yield the will to God. They do not *choose* to serve Him. God has given us the power of choice; it is ours to exercise."—*The Ministry of Healing,* p. 176.

Why is it that so many are weak in will power? It is because the will has not been kept awake or rightly directed; it has not been exercised. "The power of the will is not valued as it should be. Let the will be kept awake and rightly directed, and it will impart energy to the whole being."—*Ibid.,* p. 246. Often young people have not been allowed experience in making their own decisions; some have had all their decisions made for them, and as a result, they find themselves unable to make important decisions on their own.

Sin has weakened man's will power, and Satan has taken man's will captive so that man is no longer free to exercise his will. God wants to set us free. That is the good news of the gospel. If we surrender our wills to Him, He will set us free. Then we can make right decisions; because when we are consecrated to God, He will work in us to will and to do of His good pleasure.

Life With Myself *July 12*

My Conscience

And herein do I exercise myself, to have always a conscience void of offence toward God, and toward men. **Acts 24:16.**

An important part of myself is my conscience. This is the moral judiciary of my soul. This is that God-given factor in human experience that makes me a moral man. My conscience I should keep keen and alert.

> "I have to live with myself, and so
> I want to be fit for myself to know;
> I want to be able as days go by
> Always to look myself straight in the eye;
> I don't want to stand with the setting sun
> And hate myself for the things I've done.

> * * * * *

> "I want to go out with my head erect;
> I want to deserve all men's respect;
> But here in the struggle for fame and pelf,
> I want to be able to like myself.
> I don't want to think as I come and go
> That I'm bluster and bluff and empty show.

> * * * * *

> "I know what others may never know,
> I never can fool myself—and so,
> Whatever happens, I want to be
> Self-respecting and conscience free."

—"Myself" is from the book *Collected Verse* by Edgar A. Guest, copyright 1934, The Reilly & Lee Co., Chicago.

To keep my conscience "void of offence toward God, and toward men," I need to educate it with the Word of God and to cherish it in order to make it a healthy, safe guide.

Life With Myself   *July 13*

BOAST NOT THYSELF

Boast not thyself of to morrow; for thou knowest not what a day may bring forth. **Prov.** 27:1.

Bud had experienced a remarkable conversion from alcoholism. What a happy day it was when he gave his heart to the Lord! To strengthen his faith, the Lord even took away his desire for alcohol for a time. He moved away to another city and began a new life. It was a new day for his family too.

One day his business took him back to the city of his former activities and past the place of his former downfall. He met some of his old friends. They offered him a drink, but he refused, telling them of his new life and urging them to follow his example. When he returned home, he told a friend about his experience and concluded by saying, "I did pretty well, don't you think? Aren't you proud of me?"

Poor Bud! One month later his friend found him in the rear of a pool hall dead drunk. Several texts went through this friend's mind as he carried him out to the car and took him home. One was our text for today. Others were: "Let him that thinketh he standeth take heed lest he fall" (1 Cor. 10:12); "For men to search their own glory is not glory" (Prov. 25:27); and "Without me ye can do nothing" (John 15:5).

We have no reason to boast, because within us is no good thing. It is only by the grace of God that we can expect to be overcomers. Paul tells us, "For if a man think himself to be something, when he is nothing, he deceiveth himself" (Gal. 6:3). We are ciphers, as it were, zeros in value; but when we put One before us, even Christ, then as ciphers we become valuable. Our lives increase in value in proportion to our association and fellowship with Christ.

May God help us not to boast, but to realize our own weaknesses, to humble ourselves before the Lord, and to keep our hearts and lives in tune with Him, so that His purpose for us can be realized, and we can rejoice in being of value to Him.

Life With Myself   *July 14*

KEEP THY HEART WITH ALL DILIGENCE

Keep thy heart with all diligence; for out of it are the issues of life. Prov. 4:23.

William Stidger tells how Elsie Robinson was walking along the streets of San Francisco when she came to a corner where her favorite, happy Tony, was selling the flowers he loved. While she was trying to decide which flowers she wanted, she noticed that Tony was dampening his gardenias with misty spray. She asked him why he was dampening the petals and leaves when the stems and roots were already deep in cool, refreshing water. Tony grinned, his eyes widening in amazement that she seemed to know so little about the needs of flowers; and he said to her, "Why, Miss Robinson, don't you know, it's not enough to feed just the roots and stems; the heart too must be fed?"

It is so important to feed the heart properly, for out of it are the issues of life. To satisfy the longings within, the desires of the heart, men do what they do. Thoughts precede action, good or bad. If one's deeds are to be great, his thinking must be. If one's actions are to be noble and glorious, his thinking must be. If one's words are to be pure and true, his thinking must be. Think how many of the issues of life are determined by words—words in the home, in business, in social intercourse, and in romance. Words spring from the heart. "Out of the abundance of the heart the mouth speaketh" (Matt. 12:34).

We read, "For from within, out of the heart of men, proceed evil thoughts" (Mark 7:21). A person who likes to tell smutty stories and loves to hear them, shows he has a smutty heart. How important it is, then, for one to keep his heart pure and clean. For what he is at heart, that his life will be. "As he thinketh in his heart, so is he" (Prov. 23:7). The Lord looks on the heart, not on the outward appearance (1 Sam. 16:7). Let us choose carefully what we feed these hearts of ours so that we may never have to wonder about the caliber of the issues of life that proceed from within. For if the heart is right, all will be right.

Life With Myself   *July 15*

My Heart Is Fixed

My heart is fixed, O God, my heart is fixed: I will sing and give praise. Ps. 57:7.

Roland Hayes, the well-known Negro tenor, while still a poor boy working in a box factory in the South, sang in a church choir each Sunday. He was heard by an influential white man, who took him home to dinner one Sunday. After dinner he heard records of some of the great singers—Sembrich, Melba, and Caruso. Up to that eventful day Roland Hayes had never heard a great singer and had never seen a phonograph. The colored boy listened spellbound. Not long ago he told of that boyhood experience and summed it all up in a sentence, saying, "That night when I heard Caruso sing, it was as though a bell rang in my heart."

A friend says: "Roland Hayes has a feeling that his voice belongs to God and that it is merely his to use. That feeling has made him able to look upon himself as an instrument through which his art speaks. His art? Rather his Creator's, for he is intensely religious." Hayes sings from his heart. When our hearts are right, when our hearts are fixed, it is then that God can fulfill His purpose in our lives.

A city pastor was spending his vacation at a summer resort. He was weary with the year's arduous work; and when invited to occupy the pulpit of the little church, he felt it his duty to decline. Toward the close of his vacation he yielded to an urgent appeal and preached a sermon of great eloquence and power. A country lad sat in one of the pews that day and listened. He had never heard anything like it before, and it thrilled him. It awakened impulses within him whose meaning he could not understand. That day the preacher was to him God's special messenger, who seemed to open up before him a vista down which his life was to pass. That day his heart was "fixed." He decided to prepare for the ministry, and today he is the pastor of one of our large churches.

May our heart today be fixed on things above.

Life With Myself *July 16*

OUR DECEITFUL HEARTS

The heart is deceitful above all things, and desperately wicked: who can know it? **Jer. 17:9.**

In the unique way, God revealed to Moses the natural sinfulness of the human heart. At the burning bush God talked to Moses, and Moses talked to God. God was ready for Moses to deliver His people from the Egyptians. Moses was almost ready, but he had some lessons to learn. "The Lord said . . . , Put now thine hand into thy bosom. And he put his hand into his bosom: and when he took it out, behold, his hand was leprous as snow" (Ex. 4:6). What a symbol of the natural selfishness of the human heart! This is a hard lesson to learn.

Moses had had to spend forty years herding sheep for his father-in-law in order to learn this lesson. He was convinced that he was called to deliver Israel. He supposed it would be by force of arms. He expected to lead the Hebrew host against the armies of Egypt; and he had great plans. It was then, you recall, that he murdered the Egyptian. He was proud and self-sufficient, and he needed to learn in the school of self-denial and hardship the lessons of patience and self-control. Moses was well aware of his weakness; and out in the desert in the presence of God, overshadowed by His power, Moses' pride and self-sufficiency were swept away.

After Moses recognized the leprous condition of his hand, the Lord said, "Put thine hand into thy bosom again. And he put his hand into his bosom again; and plucked it out of his bosom, and, behold, it was turned again as his other flesh" (Ex. 4:7). This time his hand was clean, symbolic of the cleansing power of God.

Oh, how these hearts of ours do deceive us! The wise man wrote, "There is a way that seemeth right unto a man, but the end thereof are the ways of death" (Prov. 16:25). This is true, because the heart is so deceitful. What we need, then, is to have our hearts renewed by the grace of God. We need a burning-bush experience to reveal to us the true nature of our hearts and the cleansing power of the Holy Spirit.

Life With Myself   *July 17*

By Beholding We Become Changed

But we all, with open face beholding as in a glass the glory of the Lord, are changed into the same image from glory to glory, even as by the Spirit of the Lord. 2 Cor. 3:18.

A man was walking down the street one day, scanning the heavens as he walked along, trying to find a jet plane that he heard overhead. Suddenly he bumped into a little newsboy. The little fellow jumped up and said, "Say, Mister, go where you're lookin'." We smile, for probably the boy meant, "Look where you're going," but perhaps there's more truth than we realize in what he actually said.

Men do have a tendency to go where they're looking, and they tend to become like that which they behold. It is by beholding that we become changed. With every new vision there comes a change in our thinking and in our living. It is by beholding the universe through the telescope and the microscope that theories and ideas have changed; and consequently, everyday living is different from what it used to be. Beholding new scientific facts has changed the world. When a traveler beholds a sign and sees he has been going the wrong way, he changes his course. When we get our eyes open, our attitudes also change.

Job said, "I have heard of thee with the hearing of the ear: but now mine eye seeth thee. Wherefore I abhor myself, and repent in dust and ashes." It was when Isaiah saw the Lord high and lifted up that he too had a change of heart and outlook. It was when the prodigal son came to himself that he saw his true condition and began his journey homeward. The change we so desperately need comes from a new vision of God through Jesus Christ and a new understanding of our own needs. We need to open our eyes to the exceeding sinfulness of sin, to the true nature of our selfish hearts, to the truth about God and His plan of salvation, to eternal values, to a realization of what God would have us do, and to the issues in the great controversy, particularly during the closing scenes.

Once we behold these things, our lives will be changed.

Life With Myself   July 18

Transformed by the Renewing of Your Mind

And be not conformed to this world: but be ye transformed by the renewing of your mind, that ye may prove what is that good, and acceptable, and perfect, will of God. Rom. 12:2.

The transformation of my life can be brought about only by the grace of God in the renewing of my mind. If my life is to be changed, my thinking must be. Paul tells us in Ephesians 4:17-24 that the basic difference between a Christian and a non-Christian is one of understanding and thinking. Of the Gentiles he says they walk "in the vanity of their mind, having the understanding darkened, being alienated from the life of God through the ignorance that is in them, because of the blindness of their heart." The Christian, he points out, has been taught the truth as it is in Jesus and has been renewed in the spirit of his mind.

Those who would go forth as Jehovah's messengers to bring to men the light of God must "give a new direction to their thoughts."—*The Desire of Ages,* p. 100. "He [Christ] saw that new ideas and impulses must control them; that new principles must be practiced by them; through His life and death they were to receive a new conception of love."—*Ibid.,* p. 677. Jesus spent much time teaching the people, because He knew they needed a new way of thinking and they were thus transformed by the renewing of their minds.

Someone may say, "Is it not the power of the Holy Spirit that transforms men's lives?" Yes, but remember the Holy Spirit is called the Spirit of truth. He teaches men as He transforms them. Someone may say, "Is it not heart religion that we need, rather than head religion?" Yes, but "there is hard work to be done in dislodging error and false doctrine from the head, that Bible truth and Bible religion may find a place in the heart."—*Gospel Workers,* p. 81.

Since the mind is the measure of the man, we need to have our minds and hearts cleansed and renewed by the Holy Spirit. We need to fill our minds with those things that build them up in the holy faith.

Life With Myself   July 19

CONTROLLING MY THOUGHTS

Casting down imaginations, and every high thing that exalteth itself against the knowledge of God, and bringing into captivity every thought to the obedience of Christ. 2 Cor. 10:5.

The theologian Anselm says: "Our heart is like a mill, ever grinding, which a certain lord gave in charge of his servant, enjoining that he should only grind in it his master's grain, whether wheat, barley, or oats; and telling him that he must subsist on the produce. But that servant has an enemy who is always playing tricks on the mill. If any moment he finds it unwatched, he throws in gravel to keep the stones from acting, or pitch to clog them, or dirt and chaff to mix with the meal. If the servant is careful in tending his mill, there flows forth a beautiful flour, which is at once a service to his master and a subsistence to himself. But if he plays truant and allows his enemy to tamper with his machinery, the bad outcome tells the tale. His lord is angry, and he, himself, is starved."

The mill ever grinding is the heart and mind. On the produce of this mill you and I must live. We must be careful what we put into this mill. "The mind, the soul, is built up by that on which it feeds; and it is up to us what it shall be fed." The watchful enemy who is always playing tricks on the mill is obviously Satan. He is ever seeking to tamper with the machinery and to throw in bad thoughts.

"Those who would not fall a prey to Satan's devices, must guard well the avenues of the soul; they must avoid reading, seeing, or hearing that which will suggest impure thoughts. The mind must not be left to dwell at random upon every subject that the enemy of souls may suggest. The heart must be faithfully sentineled, or evils without will awaken evils within, and the soul will wander in darkness."—*The Acts of the Apostles,* p. 518.

May God help us today to guard well the avenues to our souls, so that we can bring into captivity every thought to the obedience of our Lord and Master.

Life With Myself *July 20*

FEAR THOU NOT

Fear thou not; for I am with thee: be not dismayed; for I am thy God: I will strengthen thee; yea, I will help thee; yea, I will uphold thee with the right hand of my righteousness. Isa. 41:10.

An Arab folk tale relates that Pestilence, on his way to Baghdad, once met a caravan. "Why," asked the Arab chief, "must you hasten to Baghdad?" "To take five thousand lives," Pestilence replied. On the way back from the city of the caliphs, Pestilence and the caravan met again. "You deceived me," the sheik cried angrily. "Instead of five thousand lives, you took fifty thousand." "Nay," said Pestilence, "five thousand, and not one more. It was Fear who took the rest."

Every day fear takes its toll in human misery. Young and old fear many things—real and imaginary. Some are afraid of the dark, of disease, of war, of death; others fear losing their money, their job, or their loved ones. Fear of punishment or fear of failure, fear of people or fear of God—all kinds of fears cripple and destroy. There is, of course, a normal fear, a healthy response to a danger situation. The kind of fear of which we speak today, however, we might better call anxiety, a kind of fear that paralyzes rather than safeguards.

One of the most miserable of fears is the fear of being left alone, of being rejected or of not being wanted. This fear underlies many others. For such, God says, "Thou art not alone, I am with thee." A sense of inadequacy causes many other fears; and for those, God says, "I am thy God: I will strengthen thee; yea, I will help thee." For those fears that grow out of lack of confidence and fear of failure, God says, "I will uphold thee with the right hand of my righteousness."

Many fears have their roots in guilt feelings associated with the inability to measure up to what one knows to be right. For such a one, God says, "I will uphold thee with the right hand of my righteousness." It is not a matter of having to develop righteousness on our own and finding ourselves unable; it is a matter of faith in God and being clothed with His righteousness.

Life With Myself   *July 21*

WHOM THEN SHALL I FEAR?

The Lord is my light and my salvation; whom shall I fear? the Lord is the strength of my life; of whom shall I be afraid? Ps. 27:1.

One of the most common fears is the fear of people. No matter where you go in this world you will find that fear existing in the hearts of men, particularly among the natives in heathen lands. But once they learn to know the Lord, they no longer fear men.

There is a thrilling story that comes out of New Guinea. Ordinarily the peoples of this land fear to go beyond their limited boundaries because of certain ambush and death; but one of our workers, Tamange by name, went scouting far afield for God. He was the first missionary to go among the wild natives who lived around the foot of jagged Mount Piori. The people in several villages welcomed him. They longed to stop fighting among themselves, but they knew no other way of life. Passing through one village, he was treated with suspicion; and shortly the cry went up, "Kill him, kill him!" The women fled for shelter, while the men dashed to their huts for bows and arrows, but Tamange with his interpreter continued to walk calmly on. The natives, with drawn bows, appeared on the steep slopes of a gully, dancing a war dance. Suddenly, one in their midst rushed down to Tamange shouting angrily, but telling him and his companion to follow the path to the right rather than the main one. From the bank above, the natives shouted to this man to step aside so they could shoot, but he did not heed their demands. And so Tamange and the interpreter passed on unharmed. With eyes shining with conviction Tamange tells the story and says, "Me no fright. Angel belong God showum me road. Now me no die."

When the Lord becomes our light, whom shall we fear? David said, "I sought the Lord, and he heard me, and delivered me from all my fears" (Ps. 34:4).

Therefore Will Not We Fear

God is our refuge and strength, a very present help in trouble. Therefore will not we fear, though the earth be removed, and though the mountains be carried into the midst of the sea. Ps. 46:1, 2.

In these days of great earth-shaking events, with a power in the hands of man that can literally blow mountains into the depths of the sea, "men's hearts are failing them for fear, and for looking after those things that are coming upon the earth."

Scientific discoveries supposed to alleviate man's suffering and reduce his fears in the name of progress, have actually intensified them. To illustrate: Leslie Weatherhead, who preached in London during the bombings of World War II, in his book entitled *This Is the Victory,* asks us to picture a man wrapped in skins, snatching up his club and making for his cave because his enemy is in sight; and to put this picture side by side with that of a friend of Mr. Weatherhead's, who is snatching his gas mask and making for a cave dug in his garden, because enemy planes are in sight. "My friend," he says, "may have been educated at Oxford, may have in his cave a radio set, modern sanitation, electric light, and heat; but while one admits development, I wonder if the word 'progress' is the right word to use. Last night in London life was more terrifying, harassing, and sleepless, physical safety and peace of mind were harder to find, danger was more widespread, the kind of death that threatened more horrible, the scale of disaster more appalling, than was the case before the Romans invaded Britain."

For the Christian, however, there is a message of hope that casts out fear, that does something to human hearts and enables them to say, "Therefore will not we fear, though the earth be removed, and though the mountains be carried into the midst of the sea." We need not fear the present, because God is our refuge and strength and a very present help in trouble, and we need not fear the future, for that is in God's hands. Someday soon Jesus is coming again to put an end to war and all its horror and to establish His kingdom of peace.

Life With Myself   July 23

THE FEAR OF THE WICKED

The fear of the wicked, it shall come upon him: but the desire of the righteous shall be granted. **Prov. 10:24.**

Our fears and our desires move us to action. If in avoiding our fears and achieving our desires we do wrong, our fears will come upon us; whereas, if we are righteous, our desires will be granted. Let's see how this works in life. Through fear of failure and a desire for success a young man cheats in an examination. If he follows this course consistently, he will discover that the very thing he feared—failure—will be his lot, since deception never makes for success. However, if he refuses to cheat, he may fail one test; but he stands a much better chance of realizing his ambition—success. If for fear of losing the admiration of a new-found friend, a young woman is untruthful in her statements concerning herself, she will discover in time that she will lose his admiration. But if she is frank in admitting her limitations, her humility will command his respect and increase his admiration.

When Israel was divided after Solomon's death, and Jeroboam became king of the ten tribes in the north, he was afraid that the people of his kingdom, if they went to Jerusalem to sacrifice, would desert him for Rehoboam, king of Judah. To avoid this, he made two calves of gold and said, "It is too much for you to go up to Jerusalem: behold thy gods, O Israel, which brought thee up out of the land of Egypt. And he set the one in Beth-el, and the other put he in Dan" (1 Kings 12:28, 29). In 2 Chronicles 11:14-17 we read, "The Levites left their suburbs and their possession, and came to Judah and Jerusalem. . . . And after them out of all the tribes of Israel such as set their hearts to seek the Lord God of Israel came to Jerusalem, to sacrifice unto the Lord God of their fathers. So they strengthened the kingdom of Judah, and made Rehoboam the son of Solomon strong, three years: for three years they walked in the way of David and Solomon." The very thing Jeroboam feared came upon him, and he lost the best of his kingdom to Rehoboam.

Life With Myself *July 24*

Do Not Fear the Future

Take therefore no thought for the morrow: for the morrow shall take thought for the things of itself. Sufficient unto the day is the evil thereof. Matt. 6:34.

Most of our worries and fears have to do with tomorrow; and because we cannot see into the future, we are prone to worry even though God has promised to take care of our needs.

Henry Ward Beecher gives us the following illustration in substance: I promise a young man and maiden that on their wedding day they shall have fruits and flowers from my garden, and in December they go into my garden to see what the chances are. Where are my fruits and flowers? They are all under the ground fast asleep. The two come to me and say, "You promised us flowers together with various kinds of fruits from your garden, and we see no prospect of your being able to fulfill your promise." I say to them, "My friends, January will come after December, February will come after January, March will come after February, April will come after March, and May will come after April, and every one of these months is going to have a hand in fulfilling my promise. January will talk to the flowers, February will coax them out, March will help them up, and at last they will arrive at a state of perfection. The trees also will respond to the fine influence of these months. First the leaves will come out as much as ever, the blossoms will be in about as great a hurry as the leaves, and then the fruit will be developed out of the blossom."

God promises you for the future, "I will take care of you." It seems to you like December as you look forward, but there will be spring months; and in His own good time God will see to it that when you come to the place where your need arises, it will be supplied; and though you fear your trials will be greater than you can bear, circumstances will have developed to prevent those trials, or to strengthen you for them. God says to you, "As thy days, so shall thy strength be." "Take, therefore, no anxious thought for tomorrow."

Life With Myself   July 25

THE TRUTH SHALL MAKE YOU FREE

And ye shall know the truth, and the truth shall make you free. John 8:32.

"If only I could be free—free from fears, from worries, from heavy burdens, free from guilt, free from the habits that make me a slave!" Jesus came into the world for the purpose of setting you free. As He began His ministry, He said, "The Spirit of the Lord God is upon me; because the Lord hath anointed me . . . to proclaim liberty to the captives, and the opening of the prison to them that are bound" (Isa. 61:1). Jesus desires "to loose the bands of wickedness, to undo the heavy burdens, and to let the oppressed go free, and that ye break every yoke" (Isa. 58:6).

One cause of fear of the unknown is an exaggeration of danger. A stranger approaches you in the dark, points a gun at you, and says, "Stick 'em up." You tremble with fear. If you could know that the stranger is your friend Jim, who has disguised his voice, and that the "pistol" is only a toy or a pencil, you could smile calmly and say, "Hi, Jim!" Many fears are like that. Once you see their true nature, they become powerless. When you learn the truth about them, the truth makes you free. A child is afraid of the dark. He has been told that something dreadful will grab him in the darkness. When he learns the truth about these things, he is no longer afraid.

Jesus came to teach us the truth that we need to fear only one thing, and that is sin. Nothing else can harm us eternally. The truth about forgiveness sets us free from guilt. The truth about faith and trust in God sets us free from fear of the future. The truth about the character of our loving heavenly Father sets us free from fear of the judgment. And the truth about His abiding presence releases us from fear of loneliness and rejection. Not only does Jesus tell us the truth, but He also says, "I am the truth; I will set you free, and "if the Son therefore shall make you free, ye shall be free indeed" (John 8:36).

Life With Myself   *July 26*

Perfect Peace

Thou wilt keep him in perfect peace, whose mind is stayed on thee: because he trusteth in thee. Isa. 26:3.

A king had just built a magnificent palace. As he sat in the throne room one day, he noticed in front of him a blank wall, and he thought, "Wouldn't it be wonderful to have a picture on that wall that would bring peace of mind in the midst of all the problems that arise in connection with the affairs of state?" He decided to call in the artists of the realm and have them create a picture that would convey the thought of peace. This was done, and the artists began their work.

One artist portrayed a beautiful pastoral scene—meadows with sheep and cattle grazing quietly; lying in the shade of a tree was a carefree boy rejoicing in the peace and quiet of a summer afternoon. Another depicted a quiet mountain lake in which were mirrored snow-capped peaks and tall, green pines—a very beautiful and majestic scene reminding one of the eternal hills.

There were other portrayals, but the picture that won the prize was the painting of a stormy scene on a seacoast. The high waves were beating upon the rocks, and the trees were bending in the wind. The sky was dark, and lightning was flashing. It was obviously a picture of a great storm. However, in a cleft of a rock sat a dove peacefully resting in her nest. Peace in the midst of the storm!

This is the peace that Jesus offers us. "Peace I leave with you," said Jesus, "my peace I give unto you: not as the world giveth, give I unto you. Let not your heart be troubled, neither let it be afraid" (John 14:27). Again, "These things I have spoken unto you, that in me ye might have peace. In the world ye shall have tribulation: but be of good cheer; I have overcome the world" (John 16:33). We may trust in God and know the perfect peace that passeth all understanding—peace that comes from a clear conscience, a task well done, a thankful heart, a trust in God, a forgiving spirit, and confidence in our fellow men—all through Jesus Christ our Lord.

Life With Myself   *July 27*

STRENGTH THROUGH TRUST

Trust ye in the Lord for ever: for in the Lord Jehovah is everlasting strength. Isa. 26:4.

William H. Ridgeway tells the story of a little girl who had to undergo a serious operation. When this little girl was brought into the operating room, she saw the doctors and nurses in their white masks and robes, and she was afraid. She said to the nurse, "I want my mamma, I want my mamma. I'm afraid." The surgeon, hearing her cry, said to her, "My dear child, we are going to put you to sleep gently, just as you go to sleep every night." "And what are you going to do when I get to sleep?" asked the little girl, her mind acute to the unusual situation as children's minds usually are. "Well, you know how you have been suffering so long from that mean old pain that makes you cry so often? We are going to take it all away from you so you can run about and play like other children, and your side will not hurt you ever again; and we are going to do that while you are asleep so you will never know what happened to you."

The doctor spoke kindly, gently, for he had a little girl of his own at home, and therefore knew how to deal with children. When the child suddenly sensed what was to happen, that she was really to go to sleep, she looked up at the doctor and said, "Why, Doctor, I never think of going to sleep without first saying my prayers on my knees beside my bed." So nothing would do, but the little child had to be lifted down from the stretcher, and there she knelt, put her little hands in front of her face, and prayed, "Now I lay me down to sleep, I pray the Lord my soul to keep; if I should die before I wake, I pray the Lord my soul to take. Amen." They lifted her up onto the operating table, and she quietly went to sleep under the anesthetic. Her simple childlike faith and trust in God and in the surgeon gave her peace of mind and took away all fear.

It's just that kind of simple faith, simple trust in God, the faith of a little child, that will cast out fear and give peace of mind and heart.

Life With Myself   *July 28*

Drawn Away

But every man is tempted, when he is drawn away of his own lust, and enticed. James 1:14.

Why do temptations have so strong an appeal for us? Why is sin so enticing even though it always results in heartache, frustration, and ultimate death? "The way of transgressors is hard," we are told. Yet strange as it may be, it seems easier to do wrong than to do right. What are the desires within us that move us to action? All our desires are based on God-given needs. So is every temptation.

Hunger is based on the need for food. The desire to be successful is based on the need for self-realization. The desire for love is based upon the need for affection, implanted within the human heart by the Creator. There are other desires, but notice that temptation is focused upon them also and we seek to satisfy them illegitimately.

The desires for food, beautiful things, and wisdom are all God-given desires. Satan capitalized upon these and sought to persuade Eve to satisfy them illegitimately, and as a result, destructively. God had made, and does make, provision for the satisfaction of all man's needs. "My God shall supply all your need according to his riches in glory by Christ Jesus" (Phil. 4:19).

Since all our desires arise from these needs, Satan's only hope of getting us to follow him is to make us think that in so doing these needs are met. Our sinful, selfish nature leads us to satisfy these needs quickly and for our own pleasure only. Satan is ever at hand to entice us; and when our selfish hearts respond to the enticement, we sin.

Remember that temptation is not sin. Jesus was tempted in all points like as we are, yet without sin. It is when we yield to temptation that we sin. We may not be able to keep the birds from lighting upon our heads, but we can keep them from building a nest in our hair. We will often be unable to keep temptations from entering our minds, but we can keep from harboring them, cherishing them, and yielding to them.

Life With Myself

"I KEEP UNDER MY BODY"

But I keep under my body, and bring it into subjection: lest that by any means, when I have preached to others, I myself should be a castaway. 1 Cor. 9:27.

Among the strongest of temptations are those appealing to our physical desires, those arising from physical needs. Perverted appetites and passions give us no end of trouble, and they always will as long as we live in these bodies of ours.

We are told: "The declension in virtue and the degeneracy of the race are chiefly attributable to the indulgence of perverted appetite."—*Testimonies,* vol. 3, p. 486. And again: "The controlling power of appetite will prove the ruin of thousands, when, if they had conquered on this point, they would have had moral power to gain the victory over every other temptation of Satan."—*Ibid.,* pp. 491, 492. This being true, how important it is that we should discipline ourselves, keep our appetites and passions under control.

Many a young person, and older one as well, has been puzzled by the statement of Jesus in the Sermon on the Mount, when He said, "I say unto you, That whosoever looketh on a woman to lust after her hath committed adultery with her already in his heart" (Matt. 5:28). Normal, healthy young men and women have natural desires that are God-given. We were made sexual beings before sin entered; therefore, sex is not sin. It is only the perversion of sex—satisfying this desire illegitimately—that is sinful. Often when a young person struggles with temptation along this line, he prays, "O God, take away the desire!" God does not want us to become abnormal individuals, without healthy desires. He wants us to recognize that these impulses have their place, but that they need to be kept under control. We should pray not "O God, take these away," but, "Lord, give me strength to keep them under control and in proper perspective." God does not ask us to ignore the physical but to recognize that there are higher needs to be met and that lower needs must be kept subordinate.

Life With Myself   *July 30*

A Way to Escape

There hath no temptation taken you but such as is common to man: but God is faithful, who will not suffer you to be tempted above that ye are able; but will with the temptation also make a way to escape, that ye may be able to bear it. 1 Cor. 10:13.

Some years ago a young minister was thrown out of a night club in one of our large cities because of his conduct with the waitresses. This was a terrible blow to many. Some young people lost faith. They reasoned, "If Elder So-and-so cannot go straight, how can he expect us to?" Naturally he lost his credentials, and the weeks that followed were weeks of heartache and disappointment for him and his family.

Months later a friend of his found him and said, "Tell me, George, what happened? Why did you do it?" "Well," he replied, "I was alone in the city, tired, and discouraged. When I passed by that night club, a power stronger than I took me in. I just couldn't help it." "But George," said his friend, "God doesn't allow men to be tempted above that which they are able to bear; what do you mean, you couldn't help it?" George had confidence in his friend; so he told him his experience.

For years he had indulged mentally. Whenever he was waiting in a barbershop or elsewhere, he would look through magazines that suggested thoughts that only made temptation harder to resist. He could preach powerful sermons against the evils of the night club and worldly pleasures, but he failed to turn from his own mental indulgence. A power stronger than his own did take him in that night. And why? Because "even one wrong trait of character, one sinful desire, persistently cherished, will eventually neutralize all the power of the gospel."—*Steps to Christ* (Pocket ed.), p. 34.

Notice carefully, it is the wrong thought *cherished* that neutralizes God's power in the life, not the thought that comes into the mind as a temptation. It is when we cherish that thought and yield to it mentally that it becomes sin. God's promise is true. We must, however, cooperate and not place ourselves in the way of temptation.

Life With Myself   *July 31*

How Shall I Cleanse My Way?

Wherewithal shall a young man cleanse his way? by taking heed thereto according to thy word. . . . Thy word have I hid in mine heart, that I might not sin against thee. Ps. 119:9-11.

Jesus memorized our text for today. In fact, He memorized whole sections of the Bible, and great texts came to His mind when He needed them. In temptation Jesus had but one answer—"It is written."

Have you ever been accused of cowardice for refusing to unite with your friends in some forbidden act? Perhaps you have heard words like these, "Oh, come on. You're afraid, you're scared, you're chicken!" Jesus faced this. It is quite possible that He replied, "It is written, the fear of the Lord, that is wisdom; and to depart from evil is understanding" (Job 28:28). Jesus' answer was, in substance, "No, I'm not a coward. I'm just being sensible. To depart from evil is the wise thing to do. Cowardice? No, just good sense, wisdom, and understanding."

It was when they pronounced Him narrow and strait-laced that Jesus answered by quoting our gem for today. People said in effect to Jesus, as some do to us today, "Oh, don't be so narrow-minded." Jesus said in effect, "No, it's not narrow-mindedness; it's the only way to keep from being trapped by sin and enslaved. The only way to keep from sinning is to hide God's Word in one's heart and take heed thereto." Often He was asked, "Why are you bent on being so singular, so different from us all?" Again He probably replied with a text, "Blessed are the undefiled in the way, who walk in the law of the Lord" (Ps. 119:1). "It isn't that I just want to be different. It's simply this: The Lord's way is the only way, it's the happy way. That's why I do the things I do," He explained, adding, "It is written: I have rejoiced in the way of thy testimonies, as much as in all riches" (Ps. 119:14).

There is genuine pleasure only in following the instruction in God's Word. Your success and mine in meeting temptation today will depend upon our filling our minds and hearts with the truths found therein. It's the only way you and I can be successful.

AUGUST

Life in the World Around Us   *August 1*

Not Out of the World

I pray not that thou shouldest take them out of the world, but that thou shouldest keep them from the evil. John 17:15.

Some people have the idea that in order to be a Christian one must withdraw from the world into a sort of concentration camp, mingling only with the saints. Some have withdrawn from the world into monasteries because they thought they might be defiled by contact with sinners. Some, of course, were simply escapists; but many were deceived by Satan. This was a subtle way of his to cancel the effectiveness of the influence of the sincere life.

For a number of reasons Jesus does not take us out of the world. That is where His lost sheep are, and He identifies Himself with lost humanity. He says, "Inasmuch as ye have done it unto one of the least of these my brethren, ye have done it unto me" (Matt. 25:40).

"The example of Christ in linking Himself with the interests of humanity should be followed by all who preach His word, and by all who have received the gospel of His grace. We are not to renounce social communion. . . . In order to reach all classes we must reach them where they are. . . .

"As disciples of Christ we shall not mingle with the world from a mere love of pleasure, to unite with them in folly. Such association can result only in harm. . . . But those who try to preserve their religion by hiding it within stone walls lose precious opportunities of doing good. . . .

"Social power, sanctified by the grace of Christ, must be improved in winning souls to the Saviour. Let the world see that we are not selfishly absorbed in our own interests, but that we desire others to share our blessings and privileges."—*The Desire of Ages,* p. 152.

Perhaps we should be like a ship in the sea. The ship belongs in the sea, but trouble arises when the sea gets into the ship.

Life in the World Around Us　　　　　　　　　　　　　　*August 2*

THE LIGHT OF THE WORLD

Ye are the light of the world. A city that is set on an hill cannot be hid. Matt. 5:14.

William Stidger tells that while in Switzerland he was sitting one evening on the porch of a hotel that commanded a beautiful view of the Alps. Suddenly he became conscious of the distant ringing of a church bell. A tall, stately steeple high up on the cliffs some distance away was pointed out to him. Twilight was fast settling into darkness, but still there was no light in the church. He inquired of the proprietor, "If they are expecting to have a service, why are there no lights in the church?"

"Ah," said the man, "that is a very interesting story. In a few minutes you will see people winding their way toward the church, each one carrying a light. You see, the man who gave that church to this community, gave it with the understanding that there was never to be any artificial light installed in it. So the custom is for everybody to bring with him when he comes to divine service, a lighted candle of his own."

Soon Stidger saw the little lights flickering along the pathway high up on the Alps. People from all directions were winding their way toward the house of worship. First, there was only a faint light in the church; and then it became brighter and brighter until soon it was streaming out through gorgeous stained-glass windows; and the whole building was ablaze with light.

What a fitting picture this is of Christian men and women all over this dark world! Surely darkness covers the earth and gross darkness many people, but Christians are to be lights in the darkness. And as one by one we go forth throughout the world, we soon should fill the whole earth with the light of the truth of the gospel of Christ.

Revelation 18:1 reads: "And after these things I saw another angel come down from heaven, having great power; and the earth was lightened with his glory."

May nothing dim that light in our heart today.

LIGHTS IN THE WORLD

That ye may be blameless and harmless, the sons of God, without rebuke, in the midst of a crooked and perverse nation, among whom ye shine as lights in the world. Phil. 2:15.

There are certain qualities of light that make it a fit symbol of the Christian in the world. First of all, light is illuminating. It dispels darkness and makes objects discernible and understandable. There are more answers to the world's great need in the lives of God's saints than in all the artificial light of great philosophers and teachers. All true light is but a reflection of Him who said, "I am the light of the world." And it becomes manifest more in the lives of Christian men and women than in abstract statements and theories. All of us know from experience how many a dark experience has been lightened by the cheerful smile of a Christian friend. The darkness of fear gives way to the light of faith and trust in the countenance of God's children.

Light is colorful too. The rainbow in the cloud and the band of colors on the wall as the sunshine streams through a prism bring to our attention beauties we would not see otherwise. Life would be very colorless were it not for men and women through whose lives true beauty is manifest as through a prism. Light is warming. How we do like the warm sunshine after a dark, cold night! The Christian should be like that. There is something heart warming about every true follower of Jesus. The warmth of true love melts icy hearts.

Light has therapeutic value. There are light treatments of various kinds that bring release from pain and new strength and hope to the sick. Most disease germs do not thrive in the sunlight. In the same manner association with a genuine Christian has therapeutic value. Many a heartache, many a heavy burden, has been eased by the friendly touch of one who knows the Lord. Often the germs of hatred, envy, and revenge have been destroyed in the atmosphere of love created by a humble follower of Jesus.

Does your life and mine have these qualities?

Life in the World Around Us   *August 4*

LET YOUR LIGHT SO SHINE

Let your light so shine before men, that they may see your good works, and glorify your Father which is in heaven. Matt. 5:16.

While the author of the book *Protestant Saints* was writing the manuscript, his little nephew came to him one day and said, "Uncle, what are you doing?" He replied, "I'm writing a book." "Well, what's the name of your book?" "My book is called *Protestant Saints*. Do you know what a saint is?" The boy thought a moment and thinking of the beautiful windows in his church said, "Oh! I know, Uncle, saints are the men the light shines through at the church."

"The God of High Endeavor gave me a torch to bear.
I lifted it high above me in the dark and murky air;
And straightway with loud hosannas the crowd proclaimed its light
And followed me as I carried my torch through the starless night.
Till drunk with the people's praises and mad with vanity
I forgot 'twas the torch that they followed and fancied they followed me.

"Then slowly my arm grew weary upholding the shining load
And my tired feet went stumbling over the dusty road.
And I fell with the torch beneath me. In a moment the light was out.
When lo! from the throng a stripling sprang forth with a mighty shout,
Caught up the torch as it smoldered and lifted it high again,
Till fanned by the winds of heaven it fired the souls of men.

"And as I lay in the darkness the feet of the trampling crowd
Passed over and far beyond me, its paeons proclaimed aloud,
And I learned in the deepening twilight the glorious verity,
'Tis the torch that the people follow whoever the bearer may be."

—*Author Unknown*

Life in the World Around Us *August 5*

THE SALT OF THE EARTH

Ye are the salt of the earth: but if the salt have lost his savour, wherewith shall it be salted? it is thenceforth good for nothing, but to be cast out, and to be trodden under foot of men. Matt. 5:13.

Jesus always spoke in terms that all could understand. He used concrete illustrations of abstract truths and spoke of objects familiar to people everywhere.

When Jesus said, "Ye are the salt of the earth," what did He mean? How is a Christian like salt? Food without salt is tasteless and insipid. As salt adds flavor to that with which it comes in contact, so Christianity keeps life from becoming meaningless. A life without Christ is like food without salt.

Salt loses itself for the good of the food in which it is placed. It brings out the flavor. A true Christian loses himself for the good of others. He becomes so absorbed in helping others and bringing out their good qualities that he quite forgets himself in the process. What a fitting illustration of what Christians ought to be!

Salt is also a preserving agent. It is used in preserving hides and foods. The Christian is really the preserving agent of the world. It is the Christian who keeps society from destroying itself. The cities of Sodom and Gomorrah would have been preserved had there been found in them ten righteous men. There is no way of estimating the value of a Christian man in a community.

Salt works quietly and imperceptibly. Its influence is felt rather than seen. Some Christians are like light—a flash of glory, brilliant, illuminating, and seen by all. We need Christians like that, but others are more like salt. They don't say much, one doesn't see much of them, but calmly and quietly their influence is made known.

Salt is stable. It does not lose its distinctiveness. If a Christian loses his stability, loses contact with the Divine, he becomes as useless as salt that has no savor.

May God help us to be the salt of the earth today.

Life in the World Around Us August 6

As Dew From the Lord

And the remnant of Jacob shall be in the midst of many people as a dew from the Lord, as the showers upon the grass, that tarrieth not for man, nor waiteth for the sons of men. Micah 5:7.

Have you ever had the idea that a Christian has to be a so-called wet blanket whenever people are enjoying themselves? Is it necessary always to be against something? Is your religion only a negative affair? Do you live for Christ by simply refusing to do wrong or is there a positive element in your Christianity?

There are circumstances and times when refusals are necessary; in fact, we need to say No to some things in order to say Yes to better things later. But the Christian life is not primarily negative.

Our text today makes it plain that the remnant, we who live in the last days, are to be as refreshing as the dew and as welcome as the rain to thirsty flowers. In spite of the fact that Jesus' young companions "were impatient at His scruples, and pronounced Him narrow and strait-laced," "they enjoyed His presence and welcomed His ready suggestions."—*The Desire of Ages*, p. 89.

It is true that a Christian's life by its contrast is a rebuke to that of the sinner, but there will be a warm and loving spirit manifested.

Only the narrow individual whose selfish, personal interests are threatened is irritated by the coming of needed rain to a thirsty land. So only he whose sinful life is exposed when placed in contrast to a pure life will be irritated at the presence of the Christian. However, in order for our lives to be as refreshing as the dew upon the grass, we need that heavenly refreshing ourselves.

So today we might pray the words of John Greenleaf Whittier:

> "Drop thy still dews of quietness,
>   Till all our strivings cease,
> Take from our souls the strain and stress,
> And let our ordered lives confess
>   The beauty of thy peace." Amen.

Life in the World Around Us   *August 7*

ROCKS IN A WEARY LAND

And a man shall be as an hiding place from the wind, and a covert from the tempest; as rivers of water in a dry place, as the shadow of a great rock in a weary land. Isa. 32:2.

A great rock in a weary land reminds us of Jesus, the Rock of Ages. Since, however, "as he is, so are we in this world" (1 John 4:17) you and I may be the shadow of a great rock in a weary land. Dr. Adam Smith makes this figure take on new meaning. "As we observe a peculiar phenomenon in the Near East where the desert touches a river valley or an oasis, the sand is in a continual state of drift from the wind. Often because of the infiltration of the river or spring, plants spring up through the sand in the region nearby and give promise of flourishing, particularly if there happens to be a shower or two of rain; but it never lasts. Down comes the periodic drift, and life is stunted or choked out. Here and there, however, there is a great boulder on the leeward side of which a garden can grow. This is possible because the rock arrests the drifts."

By arresting the drifts men can be like rocks in a weary land. Deadly forces, blinding and fatal as the desert wind, sweep down human history. Great men serve the whole human race by arresting these. In Abraham, for example, all nations were blessed because he arrested the drift of heathenism and idolatry. We might mention other great men through the years. Certain personalities today are a real source of inspiration to many.

Either we arrest the drifts or we are blinded and destroyed by them—the drift of materialism, the drift of indifference, the drift toward worldliness, the drift toward a lack of concern for others. Men and women are needed who can recognize these drifts and who can stand for the right even though the majority are being overcome. To do this we need to be anchored to the Rock of Ages. Then in the shelter of our fellowship others will find great help—shelter from the tempest, from the wind, from the burning sun.

Life in the World Around Us   *August 8*

Peculiar People, Zealous of Good Works

Who gave himself for us, that he might redeem us from all iniquity, and purify unto himself a peculiar people, zealous of good works. Titus 2:14.

A group of young people were returning to their college after giving a program at a distant academy. It was late at night. Everyone went to sleep but the driver, and soon he too became sleepy. Suddenly his car headed up a steep incline off the road, turned over and over, and finally came to rest upside down on the road some distance farther on. The young people were obviously shaken and bruised. Fortunately, no bones were broken. One by one they crawled out through one of the windows.

Two men were driving behind them just in time to see the accident. They stopped to render aid, of course; and one of the men offered the young people a bottle of whisky—to warm them up and quiet them down, he said. They refused, saying, "No thank you, sir, we don't drink." The other man offered them cigarettes—to calm their nerves, he said. Again they refused, saying, "We don't smoke." Finally they all climbed into the strangers' car to be taken to the next town's hospital for a checkup. As they rode along one of the men said, "Where have you kids been? To a dance?"

"No, sir, we don't dance. We just gave a musical program at ——— Academy, and we are on our way back to our home college."

"Well, what kind of people are you anyway? You don't drink, you don't smoke, you don't dance, and we haven't heard any of you swear. Why, I never saw the like. Funny people! Funny people!" he repeated as he drove along.

Although God's people seem peculiar to the world, the word in our text does not mean "odd" or "funny." Actually it means "particularly His own." Weymouth translates it nicely in these words, "to . . . purify for Himself a people who should be His own, zealous for good works." Let us not disappoint our Lord today.

222

Life in the World Around Us   *August 9*

As He Is, So Are We in This World

Herein is our love made perfect, that we may have boldness in the day of judgment: because as he is, so are we in this world. 1 John 4:17.

"As he is, so are we in this world." "But," you say, "Jesus was a special character, and His life on earth was a definite fulfillment of specific prophecies. Even the very time of His appearance was foretold." Did you ever stop to think that our time was also foretold in prophecy? This age in which you and I live is the focal point of all the telescopes of prophecy through the ages. Perhaps you say, "Yes, but Jesus had a special work to do. His definite mission was the subject of specific prophecies." Yes, so is our mission a subject of prophecy!

Consider the prophecy of the coming of Elijah, before the "great and dreadful day of the Lord" (Mal. 4:5, 6), which states that in these last days there will arise young men and women who will go forth in the spirit and power of Elijah to proclaim the word of the Lord and prepare the way for His coming. Yes, young friend, your mission is the subject of prophecy too. "As my Father hath sent me," said Jesus, "so send I you." Jesus came to reveal to the world the true character of God. This you and I are also to do.

Since "as he is, so are we in this world," He has left us an example that we should follow His steps. This is your high privilege and mine. How can we fulfill it? From such a responsibility we might recoil, but we need not. The promise of help is also given in our text for today. Notice Phillips' translation, "So our love for Him grows more and more, filling us with complete confidence for the Day when He shall judge all men—for we realise that our life in this world is actually His life lived in us." If we try in our own strength to be what He was, we shall miserably fail; but as we properly relate ourselves to Him, our lives will actually be His life lived in us. This gives us confidence; we need not fear for the future. Our love for Him will grow until we shall stand together in the judgment and hear His words, "Well done, thou good and faithful servant: . . . enter thou into the joy of thy lord."

YE ARE MY WITNESSES

Ye are my witnesses, saith the Lord, and my servant whom I have chosen: that ye may know and believe me, and understand that I am he: before me there was no God formed, neither shall there be after me. Isa. 43:10.

The great sculptor, Lorado Taft, had a summer home in New England. One evening the artist called a few friends to his mountain cabin porch to see the sunset in all its glory. He pointed out the infinite variety of the colors changing and shifting on the horizon; and his trained senses enabled him to see more than the average man could see.

The maid interrupted shortly and said, "Mr. Taft, may I run down the road? I want to go home a minute."

"Well, bless your heart," Mr. Taft replied, "why do you want to go?"

"Oh! I want to show my mother the sunset," was the explanation.

"Why, my dear girl," said the great man, "your mother has lived here a good many years. She has seen many sunsets."

"Oh, no," was the earnest reply, "we never saw the sunsets here until you came."

How true it is in life! Many never see things beautiful, things spiritual. Thousands never catch a glimpse of the beauty of the Sun of Righteousness until someone points Him out to them. To many the Bible is a dark, deep mystery, though it may occupy a prominent place in their libraries. Here is where you and I can be of real service to the Lord—His witnesses, if you please. We can give to benighted men and women a new understanding of God's Word, bringing them new hope and happiness. We can help open the eyes of the blind who never seem to see the light of the glorious truth of the gospel, and what a thrill will come to you and to me when sometime somebody will say, "You know, I never knew the Lord Jesus until you came."

We are the only Bible many people ever will read. We are living epistles known and read of all men, living witnesses. "Ye are my witnesses," says the Lord. Let us be faithful witnesses today.

Life in the World Around Us   *August 11*

NOT ASHAMED OF THE GOSPEL

For I am not ashamed of the gospel of Christ: for it is the power of God unto salvation to every one that believeth; to the Jew first, and also to the Greek. Rom. 1:16.

The writer of these words was not one whose vision was narrow, whose experience was limited, or whose mind was inferior. Paul was a highly educated man and had traveled a great deal. His contacts with men of all walks of life brought him in touch with the best everywhere. He could discuss philosophy, history, or literature with the most learned men of his day. This background gives weight to his words. If in the face of all this he could still say, "I am not ashamed of the gospel of Christ," they are not idle words. See him, for instance, at Athens—the most sacred shrine of art and center of philosophy—talking religion and philosophy to the descendants of Plato, Socrates, and Aristotle.

As he spoke, all the past glory of Athens meant nothing in comparison with the glory of the gospel. All the outstanding names in Greek philosophy sank into insignificance before the name of Christ.

Sometimes folks seem to be ashamed of their Christianity. Some young people, for example, after accepting Christ while away at boarding school, look forward with dread to going home and meeting old friends and relatives who are not Christians. They fear the finger of scorn or ridicule. Paul considered it a privilege to be a Christian. You and I, too, should consider it so. If we have been disgraced, it is hard to face people; but if we have been promoted, it is easy. Think of Christianity as the power of God unto salvation, and we can face all unashamed.

Should a fine automobile be ashamed of its power and its lines? Should a diamond be ashamed of its brilliance? Should a rose be ashamed of its fragrance, or an orchid its beauty? Should the sun be ashamed of its light, or the sunset its color? No more should you and I be ashamed of the Lord Jesus Christ. For he who is ashamed of Jesus, is ashamed of His life.

Life in the World Around Us August 12

CALL NO MAN COMMON

And he said unto them, Ye know how that it is an unlawful thing for a man that is a Jew to keep company, or come unto one of another nation; but God hath shewed me that I should not call any man common or unclean. Acts 10:28.

God hath made of one blood all nations. Jesus saw infinite possibilities in every human being, and sought to bring out the best that was in each and to redeem them by His grace. All souls are precious in His sight, and He wants us to regard them as such. Sinful men have built up walls of prejudice and hatred between themselves, but Jesus breaks down these walls. "He is our peace, who hath made both one, and hath broken down the middle wall of partition between us" (Eph. 2:14). Caste systems, iron curtains, bamboo curtains, railroad tracks, social classes, salary brackets, religious backgrounds, and even denominational barriers have separated men from each other, causing uncalculated heartache and sorrow. The Christian will recognize all men as sons of God, and therefore brothers. Christ loves them all; why shouldn't we?

An outstanding scholar was driven from France into Lombardy during the seventeenth century. Before he was able to establish himself, he took sick. Ragged and unkempt, he sought help from physicians who, believing him to be a worthless vagabond, held a consultation in Latin, the language of scholars, and said, "Let us experiment with this worthless fellow."

The scholar was startled, and asked in perfect Latin that astonished the physicians, "Dare you call a man worthless for whom Christ did not disdain to die?"

The power of God is able to take a man we might call most filthy and hopeless, transform him, and place him by the throne of God. God has no favorites. You and I as Christians in this world should be like Jesus. He identified Himself with the least of men and said, "Inasmuch as ye have done it unto one of the least of these my brethren, ye have done it unto me" (Matt. 25:40).

Life in the World Around Us   *August 13*

GOOD CITIZENS

Honour all men. Love the brotherhood. Fear God. Honour the king. 1 Peter 2:17.

The Christian will be a good citizen. He will recognize that "the powers that be are ordained of God," and he will accept the counsel that "every soul be subject unto the higher powers. For there is no power but of God" (Rom. 13:1). The best citizen is the conscientious citizen. The Christian is a good citizen of his country no matter what that country may be. Even if he does not agree with the administration and with the rulers of his country, he will still be loyal in rendering tribute to whom tribute is due. Jesus said, "Render to Caesar the things that are Caesar's."

What if the "king" is engaged in evil practices? A Christian will still be a good citizen. Jesus, Peter, and Paul lived under the Caesars. They were not in harmony with all the activities of the Roman Empire, yet they were good citizens. A Christian will also recognize his heavenly citizenship. When the requirements of the kingdom of heaven conflict with the requirements of the earthly kingdom, he will "obey God rather than men" (Acts 5:29).

God honored the stand of those who were good citizens, yet who were loyal to Him when conflicts arose. Shadrach, Meshach, and Abednego, in days of old, were ordered to appear for the dedication of the golden image. As good citizens they appeared that day; but when Nebuchadnezzar commanded them to worship the golden image, that was something different. God honored their stand and delivered them from the burning fiery furnace.

The Christian who honors all men, loves the brotherhood, is loyal to the church, fears God, is true to his conscience, and honors the king, is obviously a good citizen. The secret of good citizenship is "Fear God." The man who fears God, respects His law, loves the Lord Jesus, and has the Holy Spirit in his heart can be none other than a good citizen, not only of this world but also of the earth made new.

Life in the World Around Us August 14

WE WRESTLE AGAINST WICKED SPIRITS

For we wrestle not against flesh and blood, but against principalities, against powers, against the rulers of the darkness of this world, against spiritual wickedness in high places. Eph. 6:12.

Although the idea of a literal devil and literal evil angels is ridiculed by many, they are in reality foremost among the foes of a Christian.

Two boys were talking, and one said to the other, "Do you believe in the devil?" "Oh, no," said the other, "he's like Santa Claus; he's your daddy." We smile as we think of it; but people who do not believe that he exists are more likely to be deceived by him; for the Bible makes it very plain that Satan goes about like a roaring lion, seeking whom he may devour. The forces of evil are very real.

"There are multitudes today as truly under the power of evil spirits as was the demoniac of Capernaum. All who willfully depart from God's commandments are placing themselves under the control of Satan. Many a man tampers with evil, thinking that he can break away at pleasure; but he is lured on and on, until he finds himself controlled by a will stronger than his own."—*The Ministry of Healing,* pp. 92, 93.

"Satanic agencies took possession of men. The bodies of human beings, made for the dwelling place of God, became the habitation of demons. The senses, the nerves, the organs of men were worked by supernatural agencies in the indulgence of the vilest lust."—*Ibid.,* p. 142.

Satan is not a being with hoofs, horns, and a tail. He was once the highest angel in the courts of heaven; and he still appears at times as such, deceiving men. As we approach the last days, spiritualism will become more active in subtle ways. Under the guise of hypnotism, Christian Science, mental telepathy, and magic many will be led astray. We need not, however, fear Satan's power, for he is a conquered foe. We are told that even "the prey of the terrible shall be delivered," and that even the devils are subject unto us through the name of Jesus.

Life in the World Around Us

August 15

Put on the Whole Armor of God

Put on the whole armour of God, that ye may be able to stand against the wiles of the devil. **Eph. 6:11.**

To enable us to be successful in our struggle with the forces of evil in this world, the Lord has provided certain protective measures or pieces of equipment with which we may be prepared to come out victorious. Here they are: "Stand therefore, having your loins girt about with truth, and having on the breastplate of righteousness; and your feet shod with the preparation of the gospel of peace; above all, taking the shield of faith, wherewith ye shall be able to quench all the fiery darts of the wicked. And take the helmet of salvation, and the sword of the Spirit, which is the word of God" (Eph. 6:14-17).

Note the various pieces of equipment. First, if our loins are "girt about with truth," we will not be deceived. Second, if we are wearing the "breastplate of righteousness," we will not be swept away by the temptations of the world. Third, having our "feet shod with the preparation of the gospel of peace" we will be prepared to share our faith wherever we go. Our attitude will not be negative, but positive. Fourth, against "the shield of faith" all the darts of the enemy have no effect, because we trust in God. Fifth, the helmet of salvation provides a protection against all the brainwashing attempts of the enemy. When we keep uppermost in mind the principles of salvation, which alone can resist the subtle reasoning of the enemy, we need not fear all the delusions and finespun theories that are abroad everywhere. Finally, with the "sword of the Spirit, which is the word of God," we will be prepared to live triumphantly.

If we combine these six items of the armor of God with prayer and watching as Paul admonishes, "Praying always with all prayer and supplication in the Spirit, and watching thereunto with all perseverance and supplication for all saints" (Eph. 6:18), we will then have the secret of successful Christian living in a world filled with the forces of evil.

Life in the World Around Us August 16

LOVE NOT THE WORLD

Love not the world, neither the things that are in the world. If any man love the world, the love of the Father is not in him. **1 John 2:15.**

This text is, at first sight, very puzzling to the person who sees so much that is beautiful and good in the world. We sing:

"This is my Father's world, and to my listening ears,
All nature sings, and round me rings the music of the spheres.
This is my Father's world; I rest me in the thought
Of rocks and trees, of skies and seas; His hand the wonders wrought."

Every true Christian cultivates the ability to look for the better things—the beautiful, the true, the worth-while things around him. Is this the text of a pessimist? By no means. The verses that follow tell us clearly on what in this world we should not set our affections: "For all that is in the world, the lust of the flesh, and the lust of the eyes, and the pride of life, is not of the Father, but is of the world." Only those things in this world that appeal to our perverted, sinful nature are to be shunned.

"A man cannot love the Father and love the world at the same time. For the whole world-system, based as it is on men's primitive desires, their greedy ambitions and the glamour of all that they think splendid, is not derived from the Father at all, but from the world itself. The world and all its passionate desires will one day disappear. But the man who is following God's will is part of the Permanent and cannot die" (Phillips' translation).

We still can sing:

"This is my Father's world, O let me ne'er forget
That though the wrong seems oft so strong, God is the Ruler yet.
This is my Father's world; why should my heart be sad?
The Lord is King; let the heavens ring! God reigns; let the earth be glad."

Life in the World Around Us   *August 17*

WHY DO THE WICKED PROSPER?

For I was envious at the foolish, when I saw the prosperity of the wicked. . . . Until I went into the sanctuary of God; then understood I their end. Ps. 73:3, 17.

Why do the wicked prosper? This question has puzzled the hearts of men down through the ages. Job asked it long before David's day. "Wherefore do the wicked live, become old, yea, are mighty in power? Their seed is established. . . . Their houses are safe" (Job 21:7-9), their cattle multiply, their children are happy. "What is the Almighty, that we should serve him? and what profit should we have, if we pray unto him?" (verse 15).

Jeremiah put it this way: "Righteous art thou, O Lord, when I plead with thee: yet let me talk with thee of thy judgments: Wherefore doth the way of the wicked prosper? wherefore are all they happy that deal very treacherously?" (Jer. 12:1). In Malachi's day the people were saying: "It is vain to serve God: and what profit is it that we have kept his ordinance, and that we have walked mournfully before the Lord of hosts? And now we call the proud happy; yea, they that work wickedness are set up; yea, they that tempt God are even delivered" (Mal. 3:14, 15).

What is the answer? As David thought about it his feet "were almost gone," his steps "had well nigh slipped" (Ps. 73:2), and he said, "When I thought to know this, it was too painful for me; until I went into the sanctuary of God; then understood I their end" (verses 16, 17). It was in the sanctuary that he saw that the wages of sin is death.

Does it pay to serve God? Listen to the word of the Lord: "They shall be mine, saith the Lord of hosts, in that day when I make up my jewels; and I will spare them, as a man spareth his own son that serveth him. Then shall ye return, and discern between the righteous and the wicked, between him that serveth God and him that serveth him not" (Mal. 3:17, 18).

Life in the World Around Us *August 18*

THE WAY OF TRANSGRESSORS IS HARD

Good understanding giveth favour: but the way of transgressors is hard. Prov. 13:15.

Although it may seem that the wicked are the ones who prosper in the world, their prosperity and happiness is only temporary and superficial. The Bible talks about the pleasures of sin. Sin can give pleasure, but not lasting joy and peace. Often you hear folks say, "Why is it so hard to do right and so easy to do wrong?" Actually, the way of transgressors is hard. Jesus said, "Take my yoke upon you, and learn of me. . . . For my yoke is easy, and my burden is light." There is no burden heavier than the load of guilt carried by the transgressors, and no joy that compares with leaving that heavy load at the foot of the cross and walking away with a light heart, free in Christ Jesus.

The way of the transgressor is hard because it enslaves. It leaves scars that cannot be erased. It hurts so many. It neutralizes the power of God in the soul and keeps men and women from being true to themselves and true to their Creator. It keeps them out of heaven and makes them responsible for hindering others as well. It is the deceptive way. You think you see a cup of cool, refreshing water on a hot day; and when you drink it, you discover it is a cup of poison. You think you see a rare and beautiful gem with varying hues of light and color; but as you try to grasp it you discover it is only a bubble.

Someone has said, "Sin is a sweet poison; it tickleth while it stabbeth. The first thing that sin doth is to bewitch, then to put out the eyes and take away the sense and feeling, then make a man drunk and then . . . he doeth he knoweth not what."

Another has said, "Sin is like Delilah that sings the Nazarite asleep and delivers up the strength of God into the hands of the uncircumcised." One of the saddest pictures in all the Bible is that of Samson, a man of tremendous potentialities, blind and shackled, grinding away at the mill. The way of the transgressor is hard.

Life in the World Around Us August 19

RESIST NOT EVIL

But I say unto you, That ye resist not evil: but whosoever shall smite thee on thy right cheek, turn to him the other also. Matt. 5:39.

In imagination we can just see the perplexed expressions on the faces of His listeners as Jesus spoke these strange words in the Sermon on the Mount. They still challenge us. What does He mean, "Resist not evil"? Shall we simply tolerate the evil around us? Are we not partakers with the evildoers if we do nothing to stop them? What does "turn the other cheek" mean?

Jesus makes it clear that we are not to resist evil with evil—we are not to return in kind, insult for insult. The law, "An eye for an eye, and a tooth for a tooth," never was applicable to individual relationships. "It is true that the rule, 'Eye for eye, tooth for tooth,' was a provision in the laws given through Moses; but it was a civil statute. None were justified in avenging themselves; for they had the words of the Lord: 'Say not thou, I will recompense evil.'"—*Thoughts From the Mount of Blessing* (1956), p. 70. Nor are these words against legitimate self-defense. There are times when we would be doing a man a favor by preventing him from doing damage, and we are not to stand by and allow damage to be done if we can stop it and be of service. The Christian attitude toward evil in the world is a redemptive attitude. To fight evil with evil is simply to make two evils instead of one, and both are increased in the process.

Paul says, "Recompense to no man evil for evil." "Be not overcome of evil, but overcome evil with good" (Rom. 12:17, 21). "If thine enemy hunger, feed him; if he thirst, give him drink: for in so doing thou shalt heap coals of fire on his head" (verse 20). See Proverbs 25: 21, 22. The best way to destroy an enemy is to make a friend of him, and this can be done only by love. As we turn the other cheek, we take the enemy by surprise. As Christians let us overcome evil with an atmosphere of redemptive good will and a positive spirit of love.

"VENGEANCE IS MINE," SAITH THE LORD

Dearly beloved, avenge not yourselves, but rather give place unto wrath: for it is written, Vengeance is mine; I will repay, saith the Lord. Rom. 12:19.

"I'll get even with you." "You'll pay for this." "Just wait until——" "You'll be sorry." These are the expressions of hearts filled with revenge. The disposition to avenge wrong is a perversion of a keen sense of justice and an energetic spirit. The resentful person should "be taught that God is the eternal guardian of right. He has a tender care for the beings whom He has so loved as to give His dearest Beloved to save. He will deal with every wrongdoer.

"'For he that toucheth you toucheth the apple of His eye.' Zechariah 2:8.

"'Commit thy way unto the Lord; trust also in Him; and He shall bring it to pass. . . . He shall bring forth thy righteousness as the light, and thy judgment as the noonday.' Psalm 37:5, 6. . . .

"Let the impulsive, the self-sufficient, the revengeful, behold the meek and lowly One, led as a lamb to the slaughter, unretaliating as a sheep dumb before her shearers. Let them look upon Him whom our sins have pierced and our sorrows burdened, and they will learn to endure, to forbear, and to forgive."—*Education*, p. 257.

When some of the courtiers of Philip the Good tried to persuade him to punish a man who had used him ill, he declined saying, "It is a fine thing to have revenge in one's power, but it is a finer thing not to use it." This is the spirit of Jesus. By indulging the spirit of retaliation, we only injure ourselves and grieve our Lord. The Lord says, "Vengeance is mine; I will repay." He is the only one who can do it in love. If, therefore, we feel like "getting even with someone," let us forgive him; turn him over to the Lord; do something nice for him; pray for him; and help him to know that because God is kind, longsuffering, and merciful to us, so we should be to others.

Life in the World Around Us   *August 21*

THE CARES OF THIS LIFE

And take heed to yourselves, lest at any time your hearts be overcharged with surfeiting, and drunkenness, and cares of this life, and so that day come upon you unawares. Luke 21:34.

Cares have multiplied with the increase of knowledge in this generation manyfold. Man's wants today number ever so many more than our fathers could even imagine. In this fast-moving age streamlined methods and high-pressure activities have greatly increased heart failures.

Someone has written:

> "Hurry the baby as fast as you can.
> Hurry him, worry him, make him a man.
> Off with his baby clothes, get him in pants,
> Feed him on brain foods and make him advance.
> Hustle him, soon as he's able to walk,
> Into a grammar school: cram him with talk.
> Fill his poor head full of figures and facts:
> Keep on a-jamming them in till it cracks.
> Once boys grew up at a rational rate,
> Now we develop a man while you wait.
> Rush him through college, compel him to grab
> Of every known subject a dip and a dab.
> Get him into business and after the cash
> All by the time he can raise a mustache.
> Let him forget he was ever a boy,
> Make gold his god, and its jingle his joy.
> Keep him a-hustling and clear out of breath,
> Until he wins—nervous prostration and death."
>
> —*Author Unknown*

One of the finest ways to take heed to ourselves is to spend a little moment every day with our Lord.

In the World, Tribulation

These things I have spoken unto you, that in me ye might have peace. In the world ye shall have tribulation: but be of good cheer; I have overcome the world. John 16:33.

With tragedy and suffering on every hand, we are continually aware of the truth of Jesus' statement, "In the world ye shall have tribulation." Why is this true? Why does a God of love allow it? Could He not have made a world incapable of suffering? We must remember that the world operates according to certain fundamental laws. To violate these laws knowingly or ignorantly is to put ourselves out of harmony with them and to suffer the consequences. We would not want it otherwise. The laws of nature are dependable. It would be disastrous if that were not so.

Men and women were created by God as free moral agents with the power of choice. We are not mere robots on a stage operated by forces entirely beyond our control. Although created in the image of God with powers akin to those of the Creator, having the power of choice, we can make wrong decisions that lead to suffering.

Because of sin men have become the victims of selfishness. Satanic hatred often causes men to deliberately inflict hardship upon their fellow men; and the suffering resulting from strained human relationships is ofttimes hardest to bear.

There are other causes of suffering that might be mentioned. Let us remember that because of the nature of our world, because of sin, and because we have made wrong decisions, we are required to endure tribulation until we learn our lessons and until we can live in a new heaven and a new earth wherein dwelleth righteousness, and where suffering shall be no more. In the meantime we are told to be of good cheer, for Jesus has overcome the world. Even in the midst of tribulation the Christian can know a peace of mind that passeth understanding.

By the grace of Christ we can triumph over suffering.

Life in the World Around Us *August 23*

ALL THINGS WORK TOGETHER FOR GOOD

And we know that all things work together for good to them that love God, to them who are the called according to his purpose. Rom. 8:28.

Many years ago, an eminent French engineer was detained in the Mediterranean by a tedious quarantine. It was hard for one of his active temperament to endure such confinement. However, as he waited on the deck of the vessel, he read; and a book to which he gave special attention inspired the conception of the Suez Canal, the execution of which has made him famous and has been of great service to the world.

Did De Lesseps afterward regret those dragging days of quarantine? No. Little did he realize at the time how that experience could ever work out for good; but it did.

Our text does not say all things are good. It does say, however, "all things work together for good to them that love God," and that is the promise the child of God can claim. Not everything that happens is God's will, but nothing can happen to defeat His will. Our sufferings at the hands of Satan, or at the hands of selfish men and women, are not from God; neither are they good. But God permits them and uses them in developing our characters and in polishing and refining us in the process of Christian growth.

What a wonderful promise is our text! And what is more wonderful, not one of God's promises has every failed. Even though we cannot now see how all our circumstances can work out for good, we can trust Him and know that someday we shall understand.

Two Christians were once speaking of their experiences and one said, "It is terribly hard to trust God and realize His hand in the dark passages of life."

"Well, brother," said the other, "if you cannot trust a man out of your sight, he is not worth much. And if you cannot trust God in the dark, it shows that you do not trust Him at all."

Life in the World Around Us *August 24*

LEARN OBEDIENCE THROUGH SUFFERING

Though he were a Son, yet learned he obedience by the things which he suffered. Heb. 5:8.

Because men suffer they seek for the cause of that suffering and thereby discover the laws of life that govern these bodies of ours. Many people are awakened by pain to the fact that they have been violating one of the basic laws of health. Many of us would already have destroyed ourselves were it not for the warning given by pain. When men learn to appreciate pain and to profit from it by seeking for a better understanding of the laws of health, that they may live in harmony with them, they learn obedience through suffering. Even Jesus as a boy had to learn obedience by the things that He suffered, though, of course, He was without sin.

You and I are born in sin. The essence of sin is selfishness, and selfishness in the heart is like a cancer. Often one is not aware of its presence until it is too late. All of us need to be awakened to the terrible malignity of sin, and God uses suffering for that purpose.

"Trials and obstacles are the Lord's chosen methods of discipline and His appointed conditions of success. He who reads the hearts of men knows their characters better than they themselves know them. He sees that some have powers and susceptibilities which, rightly directed, might be used in the advancement of His work. In His providence He brings these persons into different positions and varied circumstances that they may discover in their character the defects which have been concealed from their own knowledge. He gives them opportunity to correct these defects and to fit themselves for His service. Often He permits the fires of affliction to assail them that they may be purified."—*The Ministry of Healing,* p. 471.

Let us not rebel against the painful experiences of life, but profit by them and so relate ourselves to them that we can by God's grace overcome the selfishness within our hearts and be fitted for service. This prepares us also for sonship in the family of heaven.

Life in the World Around Us *August 25*

Made Perfect Through Suffering

But the God of all grace, who hath called us unto his eternal glory by Christ Jesus, after that ye have suffered a while, make you perfect, stablish, strengthen, settle you. 1 Peter 5:10.

In human experience many are embittered by suffering rather than made perfect by it. What does it mean to be made perfect through suffering? First, we need to define perfection. Perfection is not some static state beyond which there is no room for progress. It is not a state of completeness beyond which no more growth is possible. A continual development with constant progress—that is perfection. The expression "made perfect through suffering," then, means that a Christian grows through suffering.

How is this accomplished? How do we grow through suffering? First, it gives us a better understanding of the laws of life. Second, we are made conscious of the exceeding sinfulness of sin; and we learn to hate sin, because it causes pain. Third, we are made perfect through suffering by gaining a new scale of values. How different things material look when sickness comes!

We are enriched through suffering, for it gives us a fuller understanding of others, a deeper appreciation of fellowship. There is something about comradeship in suffering that ties hearts together in a way that no other experience can do. The boys in the armed forces who fight side by side are buddies for life. We never forget those who have suffered with us through tragic experiences. Christ suffers with us when we suffer; and if we have followed Him, we can pray with Paul, "That I may know him and the fellowship of his suffering." "Of all the gifts that Heaven can bestow upon men, fellowship with Christ in His sufferings is the most weighty trust and the highest honor."—*The Desire of Ages,* p. 225. There is no spiritual growth comparable to that which comes through fellowship with Christ in His sufferings. This the true Christian will understand more fully as the days go by.

Life in the World Around Us — August 26

PARTAKERS OF CHRIST'S SUFFERINGS

But rejoice, inasmuch as ye are partakers of Christ's sufferings; that, when his glory shall be revealed, ye may be glad also with exceeding joy. **1 Peter 4:13.**

Suffering gives us a keener appreciation of redemption. It makes us conscious of the results of sin and helps to create a longing for the day when sin shall be no more. Peace after pain is an experience that none but those who have suffered can appreciate, and the resurrection becomes more meaningful in the light of Calvary, as does the crown in the light of the cross. Fellowship with Christ in His sufferings is a privilege that not even angels have.

"No angel breathes the anguish cry,
   'My God forsakes. Oh, why! Oh, why!'
No angel knows that midnight hour
   Of blood-damp agony's crushing power.
No angel feels sin's dreadful loss
   And staggers 'neath his heavy cross,
Or falls across the door of hope
   Sees iron dungeon's gateway ope';
Sees blackest darkness wake in light,
   When God's bright morning swallows night.
No angel drops the cross of strife
   To enter into endless life.
No angel sees God's soothing balm,
   No angel needs His brooding calm.
Peace after pain to man alone
   Unfelt by angels round the throne.
Let gratitude a welling fount
   Beyond all measure and all count
Flow from the hearts of His redeemed
   That man should be thus high esteemed."

—L. A. REED

Life in the World Around Us   *August 27*

IN ALL THEIR AFFLICTION, HE WAS AFFLICTED

In all their affliction he was afflicted, and the angel of his presence saved them: in his love and in his pity he redeemed them; and he bare them, and carried them all the days of old. Isa. 63:9.

"It is true that all suffering results from the transgression of God's law, but this truth had become perverted. Satan, the author of sin and all its results, had led men to look upon disease and death as proceeding from God, as punishment arbitrarily inflicted on account of sin." —*The Desire of Ages,* p. 471.

Suffering from pain caused by disease, from heartache caused by the attitude of her husband, from an inability to discipline her children properly, and from worry and insecurity arising from her husband's threat to leave her, a woman came to consult her pastor. Moreover, she carried a heavy burden of guilt, thinking God was punishing her because of a past mistake. When it was explained to her that "sickness, suffering, and death are work of an antagonistic power; Satan is the destroyer; God is the restorer" (*The Ministry of Healing,* p. 113), she said, "Then God is not thus punishing me? My heart feels ten pounds lighter already. Thank you so much."

Satan has distorted "the wages of sin is death" to read "the wages of God is death," as if God were responsible for all the heartache in this world. If that is true, physicians are working contrary to His purpose in alleviating suffering. What right have doctors and nurses to step in and interfere with God's disciplinary measures? Disease is the work of Satan, "and the physician is warring against his work and power."—*Counsels on Health,* p. 324.

Not expecting man to go through anything that He would not go through Himself, God, in Christ, came into the world to suffer with man, to die for him, and to give him the opportunity of sharing with Him in demonstrating to the universe His great love.

Life in the World Around Us

COMFORT THOSE IN TROUBLE

Who comforteth us in all our tribulation, that we may be able to comfort them which are in any trouble, by the comfort wherewith we ourselves are comforted of God. 2 Cor. 1:4.

Everybody in the office watched the new man with interest. He came in on time and seemed to do his work well. However, when the noon whistle blew he left immediately and did not return until one o'clock sharp. He was never late, but never a minute early. When five o'clock came he left just as quickly. After a few days the office force circulated ideas concerning the new man's character and made fun of him. "Is he afraid he might work a minute extra?" Finally, one of the more understanding workers learned that the newcomer had a very difficult situation at home. He had the burden of caring for a very sick wife and several young children who had to be ready for school early. At noon he had but one hour to provide for his wife's needs, and at five the children were home and needed his supervision. This accounted for his hurrying away; and greater understanding resulted in practical assistance for the family, arranged by a man who himself had had a similar experience.

Those best capable of comforting others are those who have themselves suffered. A silent handshake from one who has likewise suffered means more than many beautiful words spoken by those who have never known sorrow. Many a minister has been greatly enriched in his ministry by personal experiences of suffering. If once you have laid to rest a loved one of your own, your heart beats in unison with those who sit in the mourner's seat as it never did before.

One reason why we are so critical is the fact that we misunderstand. Our attitudes change when our eyes are opened, and nothing opens our eyes like experience. Therefore, the man who has suffered is less critical of his fellow men, because suffering gives him an understanding heart. He then is able to comfort others in their trouble by the comfort wherewith he himself has been comforted of God.

Life in the World Around Us August 29

Our Light Affliction

For our light affliction, which is but for a moment, worketh for us a far more exceeding and eternal weight of glory. 2 Cor. 4:17.

Dr. Todd tells the story of an invalid of twenty years whose sufferings were extreme. One night, as she was contemplating her continued affliction, suddenly the room was filled with light; and an angel asked, "Daughter of sorrow, art thou impatient?" "No, but I can see no end of pain, nor why I must suffer thus. I know I am a sinner, but I had hoped Christ's sufferings, and not mine, would save me. Oh, why does God thus deal with me?" "Come with me, daughter, and I will show thee." He tenderly took her and carried her to a large workshop in a far-off city. Many workmen seemed to have small brown pebbles that they were grinding, shaping, and polishing. Her guide pointed her to one who seemed to be most earnestly at work. He had in a pair of strong iron pincers a half-polished pebble that was seen to be a diamond. He grasped it as if he would crush it and held the rough stone without mercy. The stone whirled, dust flew, and the jewel grew smaller and lighter. "Please," said the sufferer, "why do you grind the jewel so hard?" "I want to grind off every flaw in it," was his reply. "If this diamond will bear the wheel long enough, it will occupy a prominent place in our king's crown. We take more pains with such. We have to grind and polish them a great while; but when they are done, they are very beautiful." Gently the angel carried the sufferer to her own bed of pain again. "Daughter of sorrow, dost thou understand the vision?" "Oh, yes," she replied, for she could become a diamond in the crown of the Great King.

We read: "The fact that we are called upon to endure trial shows that the Lord Jesus sees in us something precious which He desires to develop. . . . He does not cast worthless stones into His furnace. It is valuable ore that He refines."—*The Ministry of Healing,* p. 471.

Our light affliction, which is actually but for a moment, worketh for us a far more exceeding and eternal weight of glory.

Life in the World Around Us *August 30*

MY GRACE IS SUFFICIENT

And he said unto me, My grace is sufficient for thee: for my strength is made perfect in weakness. Most gladly therefore will I rather glory in my infirmities, that the power of Christ may rest upon me. 2 Cor. 12:9.

It is one thing to explain suffering; it is another to suffer. The sufferer discovers there are times when one needs more than an explanation. Here, then, are a few suggestions that help:

First, remember that physical and material prosperity or adversity are not related to moral worth. Do not evaluate your standing with God on the basis of how *much* you suffer, but on *how* you suffer. Second, seek to find the cause, and do everything humanly possible to remove it. This is in no way contrary to God's will, nor is it a sign of lack of faith. (See *The Ministry of Healing,* pp. 231, 232.) Third, cultivate the consciousness of God's abiding presence. Your suffering does not separate you from Him; in fact, He knows you need Him more then than at any other time. Fourth, pray not for release, but for strength. Pray, "Thy will be done," and seek to help others who suffer along the way. And, finally, look beyond the veil. There will come a time when suffering shall be no more.

"Father, to Thee we look in all our sorrow,
   Thou art the fountain whence our healing flows;
Dark though the night, joy cometh with the morrow;
   Safely they rest, who in Thy love repose.

* * * * *

"Patient, O heart, though heavy be thy sorrows!
   Be not cast down, disquieted in vain;
Yet shalt thou praise Him when these darkened furrows,
   Where now He plougheth, wave with golden grain."

—FREDERICK HOSMER

Life in the World Around Us August 31

Songs in the Night

Yet the Lord will command his lovingkindness in the daytime, and in the night his song shall be with me, and my prayer unto the God of my life. Ps. 42:8.

"In the full light of day, and in hearing of the music of other voices, the caged bird will not sing the song that his master seeks to teach him. He learns a snatch of this, a trill of that, but never a separate and entire melody. But the master covers the cage, and places it where the bird will listen to the one song he is to sing. In the dark he tries and tries again to sing that song until it is learned, and he breaks forth in perfect melody. Then the bird is brought forth, and ever after he can sing that song in the light. Thus God deals with His children. He has a song to teach us, and when we have learned it amid the shadows of affliction, we can sing it ever afterward."—*The Ministry of Healing,* p. 472.

There are times when darkness almost overwhelms the soul; when night settles down and there is not even a star on life's horizon. Storms rage and clouds are heavy. It seems there is no relief. These are the times when sorrow deepens our appreciation of spiritual values.

Many a song of Christian experience has been learned in the night. Life is not only Gethsemane; often there follows even Calvary, but then comes the resurrection. This is the hope that shines brightly in the darkness. The most beautiful song we learn in the night is the song of hope. Sometimes, however, the night seems long, and the realization of our hope seems far away. But even in the darkness the Christian can sing a song of comfort and fellowship, for he knows that Jesus was a man of sorrows and acquainted with grief. In the night we can learn to sing with Him those songs of life's deeper meanings—songs of hope, songs of comfort and fellowship, songs of redemption.

SEPTEMBER

Life and My Work September 1

TO EVERY MAN HIS WORK

For the Son of man is as a man taking a far journey, who left his house, and gave authority to his servants, and to every man his work, and commanded the porter to watch. Mark 13:34.

"Each has his place in the eternal plan of heaven. Each is to work in co-operation with Christ for the salvation of souls. Not more surely is the place prepared for us in the heavenly mansions than is the special place designated on earth where we are to work for God."—*Messages to Young People,* p. 219.

One of the basic essentials to creative living is the channeling of our God-given energies into lines of constructive activity. Everyone needs something to do. Life would become dreary and monotonous without work—not just mere labor, but the accomplishing of something worth while, in the doing of which one has the feeling that he is making a contribution of some kind. The greatest sense of satisfaction comes to one when he has accomplished something. Take, for example, a little fellow who comes running to his daddy with a windmill he has just made, and he cries out, "Look, Daddy! See what I made, and it works!" The twinkle in his eye is symbolic of the satisfaction in his heart.

Our memory text for today points out that God has made provision for this need and has given to every man his work. I think it was Thomas Carlyle who said, "Blessed is he who has found his work." How true that is. Show me the man who sings at his work, and I'll show you a happy man.

Perhaps you say, "What is that special place for me? What is my work?" May we suggest first of all that you do to the best of your ability the work that lies nearest to you. Keep in touch with God, and He will lead you. Work faithfully, and watch for His opening providences. See that what you are now doing is done well. This is the best preparation for the work He has for you tomorrow.

Talents According to Ability

And unto one he gave five talents, to another two, and to another one; to every man according to his several ability; and straightway took his journey. **Matt. 25:15.**

"The kingdom of heaven," said Jesus, "is as a man travelling into a far country, who called his own servants, and delivered unto them his goods. . . . And . . . he gave . . . to every man according to his several ability" (Matt. 25:14, 15).

The man traveling into a far country represents Christ; the servants are His followers. The talents include "all gifts and endowments, whether original or acquired, natural or spiritual."—*Christ's Object Lessons,* p. 328. These are apportioned according to the ability to use them. He who can use five talents, receives five; he who can use but two, receives two; while he who can wisely use only one, receives one. God expects returns "according to that a man hath, and not according to that he hath not" (2 Cor. 8:12).

"The talents, however few, are to be put to use. The question that concerns us most is not, How much have I received? but, What am I doing with that which I have? The development of all our powers is the first duty we owe to God and to our fellow men."—*Ibid.,* p. 329. It is not only a duty, but also a glorious privilege to develop these talents for the Master. Somehow as we consecrate them to Him He blesses us so that they multiply manyfold. The five-talented man, you remember, brought back five more talents.

Perhaps you say, "But I am like the one-talented man who buried his talent." If you are a one-talented man, you need not bury it. Another parable tells of ten servants who received just one portion each. When called to give an account, the first came, saying, "Lord, thy pound hath gained ten pounds" (Luke 19:16). Here you see a one-talented man who brought ten talents back to his Lord. He accomplished as much by the grace of God as did the five-talented man. Let us not bury our talent or talents, but use them to His glory today.

Various Gifts

And God hath set some in the church, first apostles, secondarily prophets, thirdly teachers, after that miracles, then gifts of healings, helps, governments, diversities of tongues. 1 Cor. 12:28.

When Jesus "ascended up on high, he led captivity captive ["a multitude of captives," margin], and gave gifts unto men" (Eph. 4:8). These gifts are dispensed by the Holy Spirit to those who can safely be entrusted with them. They are given for the "perfecting of the saints, for the work of the ministry, and for the edifying of the body of Christ: till we all come in the unity of the faith, and of the knowledge of the Son of God, unto a perfect man, unto the measure of the stature of the fulness of Christ" (Eph. 4:12, 13).

The Holy Spirit gives to every man severally, as He wills. Not all receive the same number of gifts, and the gifts vary. Certain people are very gifted. Maybe you have thought that you did not belong to those classified as gifted. But if you'll notice Paul's list, you'll find one little word that includes you, I am sure—the word "helps." You can always help in some way.

A mother once sent her little girl to the store to buy some bread. She told her to hurry home because it was just about suppertime. But as time went on, the little girl did not return. Finally she came running into the home with tears in her eyes; and when her mother asked what had happened and where the bread was, she said, "Oh, I'm sorry, I forgot all about the bread. You see, little Mary down the street was hurt, and I was helping her."

"Well," said Mother, "and how did you help Mary?"

"Well, I—I—I cried with her."

Perhaps we smile at the little girl's reply, but it is surprising how weeping with those who weep actually helps. In so many ways, if our hearts are right, we can help one another. That, too, is a gift.

In Paul's first letter to Timothy he wrote, "Neglect not the gift that is in thee" (1 Tim. 4:14). This counsel is for you and me today.

Life and My Work   *September 4*

A Man's Gift Maketh Room for Him

A man's gift maketh room for him, and bringeth him before great men. Prov. 18:16.

Sometimes young people worry about placement in the future. The medical student worries about being accepted for entrance to Loma Linda; the ministerial student, an internship. As each sees the number interested in those fields, he begins to wonder whether there is a chance for him.

Today's text is encouraging. "A man's gift maketh room for him." There is still a great need in all callings for men who are faithful and honest in their work. There is room for good men in every walk of life. What was true in Ezekiel's day is just as true today.

"And I sought for a man among them, that should make up the hedge, and stand in the gap before me for the land, that I should not destroy it: but I found none" (Eze. 22:30).

> "Give us men to match our mountains;
>   Give us men to match our plains.
> Men with empires in their purpose,
>   Men with throbbing, conquering brains.
>
> "Give us men to lead our nation;
>   Give us men with holy zeal.
> Men aflame with truth and vision
>   Men who bear the heavenly seal.
>
> "Give us men who follow Jesus;
>   Give us men who love their Lord.
> Men with hearts pure and courageous
>   Men led by God's eternal word."

God is still looking for Spirit-filled men. Dedicate your gift to Him; He will enable you to fulfill His purpose for you.

Life and My Work   *September 5*

Do It With Thy Might

Whatsoever thy hand findeth to do, do it with thy might; for there is no work, nor device, nor knowledge, nor wisdom, in the grave, whither thou goest. Eccl. 9:10.

"Many are dissatisfied with their lifework. It may be that their surroundings are uncongenial; their time is occupied with commonplace work, when they think themselves capable of higher responsibilities; often their efforts seem to them to be unappreciated or fruitless; their future is uncertain.

"Let us remember that while the work we have to do may not be our choice, it is to be accepted as God's choice for us. Whether pleasing or unpleasing, we are to do the duty that lies nearest."—*The Ministry of Healing,* pp. 472, 473.

God frequently uses strange ways to prepare men for important jobs. Often He leads them through trying experiences. We think of Moses. What he thought during those forty years of herding sheep for his father-in-law would probably equal what many people think today because they are doing a kind of work different from what they had planned, so different from what they are sure God wants them to do.

The wilderness experience prepared Moses for the greatest work God ever called any man to do. "He who understands us better than we understand ourselves refuses to permit us selfishly to seek the gratification of our own ambition. He does not permit us to pass by the homely but sacred duties that lie next us. Often these duties afford the very training essential to prepare us for a higher work. Often our plans fail, that God's plans for us may succeed."—*Ibid.,* p. 473.

The first step in choosing our lifework, therefore, is to do with our might what our hands find to do.

Our text should be our motto whatever our work, and "our daily prayer should be, 'Lord, help me to do my best. Teach me how to do better work. Give me energy and cheerfulness. Help me to bring into my service the loving ministry of the Saviour.' "—*Ibid.,* p. 474.

Do All to the Glory of God

Whether therefore ye eat, or drink, or whatsoever ye do, do all to the glory of God. 1 Cor. 10:31.

The artist drew aside a curtain; and the sun streamed through a beautiful, unfinished, stained-glass window. In the lower part there were many little children looking up and smiling. All about them were flowers. Above the children was an incomplete figure of a man. As the artist placed prepared pieces of glass in the window, he talked to himself, saying, "This is to be my very best. I must tell the world how much I love the Christ. It must be beautiful, to show His beauty. If I can only make it express what I feel, how glad I shall be." And he sang as he worked.

There was a little piece of glass lying in a corner in a pile of rubbish. It was discouraged, and said, "Oh, I thought I had some important place in the window. Now it seems as if I am of no value, and am only to be thrown away. All I can do is to do my best where I am. If the sunshine comes to my corner, I shall shine."

Suddenly there was a commotion in the studio as the artist went from place to place looking for something. The glass heard the artist say, "I can't finish without it. It was such a wonderful piece, and I had spent so much time and thought on it. Where can it be? I just must have it to finish the window." The glass thought, "Can it be I?"

With a cry of delight the artist pulled the bit of glass from the rubbish pile. When it was placed in the window, it became the eye of the Christ, helping to tell the world of the artist's love.

Young friend, you too, like the little bit of glass, belong to the Artist. You belong in the beautiful window. You belong in God's beautiful church. If you will "do all to the glory of God" no matter where you find yourself, you will discover that someday the Master Artist will use you in some humble way to show the world the beauty of the Christ. He knows where you are and is preparing you for a place. Ask God to help you to glorify Him in your life.

Life and My Work *September 7*

FAITHFUL IN THAT WHICH IS LEAST

He that is faithful in that which is least is faithful also in much: and he that is unjust in the least is unjust also in much. Luke 16:10.

The spray from the sink had splashed only a few drops of water into her clean pitcher, contaminating it. It was a tense moment. The impatient surgeon called, "Hot sponges! Where are the hot sponges?" The hot sterile water from the tank had almost filled the pitcher before she realized what had happened. She snatched it up, hurried into the arena, and poured the hot water over the sponges in the basin. Just as quickly, gloved hands wrung out one and laid it on the field near the wound.

The speed of the deed and the immensity of its possibilities froze Betty to the spot. Since the pitcher was contaminated, the sponges were dirty; and that would mean a contaminated wound. She shuddered. What if the patient should die? What if it meant long weeks in the hospital with an open wound in the abdomen? She had seen patients like that—weak, pale, and listless. She would be to blame. "Oh, God," she prayed, "what shall I do?"

The surgeon laid down his forceps and picked up the sponge. "Don't, Dr. Granger! Don't use that sponge. It's contaminated. The pitcher was dirty, and I poured that water into the basin."

All eyes turned in her direction. Dr. Granger's word came like an ultimatum, "You knew it was dirty; and you poured it in the basin?"

"Yes, I was afraid to make you wait a moment. No harm has been done to the patient. You'll just have to wait until we change the setup."

When the operation had ended, Betty faced the superintendent. "I'm sorry. I don't know why I did it. It was terrible."

The superintendent smiled. "It was a mistake, Betty, but you rectified it as best you could. We'll forget the incident, and remember the lesson. This I know, you will never cease to thank God for your decision tonight." She lifted the cotton pad from the patient's eyes, and Betty looked into the face of—her mother!

Life and My Work *September 8*

FAITHFULNESS IN MONEY MATTERS

If therefore ye have not been faithful in the unrighteous mammon, who will commit to your trust the true riches? **Luke 16:11.**

How faithful are you in money matters? Do you pay your honest debts? Do you keep your promises even though it may mean a loss to you? If a man is not faithful in his financial dealings, he cannot expect to have committed into his care true riches, which have eternal value.

John was the new clerk in Mr. Elliot's store. Others worked for Mr. Elliot too. After John had worked only a month, all but he received a raise. When he asked, "Why didn't I get a raise?" he was told that he hadn't proved himself yet. The others had worked for a longer time. He was assured if he would be faithful, he would, in due time, receive his raise as well. But John wasn't satisfied; he could use that extra money. It wasn't fair that Mr. Elliot did not raise his salary. He decided to get his raise, anyway. He figured what the amount should be, and took home enough goods each month to make up the difference. Poor John! Instead of getting a raise, he was fired.

They were playing a game of finance. Jim was the banker. Whenever he saw he was losing, he took a one-hundred-dollar bill instead of a fifty-dollar bill from the bank. No one seemed to notice. Finally, of course, he won. The game was over, and all but one player thought no more about it. That one was Jim's new girl friend. When the evening was over, she thanked him. Jim left her hoping for another date soon, but she refused all his invitations. A mutual friend asked her one day why she wasn't seen with Jim any more, and she told him the story of the evening. When Jim heard her reaction he said, "Why, it was only a game. Why let that make such a difference?" Yes, it was only a game; but if one is unfaithful in a game, may it not be an indication that he will also be unfaithful in the game of life?

"If therefore ye have not been faithful in the unrighteous mammon," in the things that are of lesser consequence, who will commit to your trust the true riches—things of eternal consequence?

WILLING TO LIVE HONESTLY

Pray for us: for we trust we have a good conscience, in all things willing to live honestly. Heb. 13:18.

There are many ways of being dishonest, ranging from a small boy's telling a deliberate lie to his mother to a man's reporting a false income to the tax collector. One can be dishonest by keeping silent when a courageous word would correct a false impression. Even a lifted eyebrow can create a wrong impression, though we say no word at all. We can be dishonest by telling only a part of the truth, and thus convey a distorted idea of the facts. One man excused this kind of lying by saying that he presented different aspects of the truth to different people. This, of course, is only fair language describing a foul deed. We can also be dishonest by saying words which, taken by themselves, may be strictly true, but which will result in the wrong conclusions being drawn.

A man once employed a genealogical expert to trace his ancestry. When asked to suppress the fact that the man's grandfather had been electrocuted for murder, the expert refused, but agreed to tell it in more elegant language. He reported that the grandfather had always had a great interest in electricity, and at length came to occupy the chair of electricity in one of the large institutions of New York State. He said that the man "died in harness" and gave his life for electricity. Every word was true, but the account gave a false impression.

We hear that "honesty is the best policy," but he who acts upon this principle because of policy only is not an honest man. Such action implies an ulterior motive, and it is motive that gives character to an act. To be truly honest, one must be so at heart.

"Johnny," said a man winking slyly at a dry-goods clerk of his acquaintance, "you must give me good measure. Your master is not in."

Johnny looked solemnly into the man's face and replied, "My Master is always in." Johnny was a Christian. Christ dwelt in his heart; he was fundamentally honest.

Life and My Work — September 10

Prove Your Own Work

But let every man prove his own work, and then shall he have rejoicing in himself alone, and not in another. Gal. 6:4.

Every man's work is to be tested. Some tremble at the thought, but one need not fear inspection if he has tested and proved his own work. There is wonderful security in work well done. Those who prove their arithmetic problems know they are right and need not fear the grade. More important than all is the work of building character. We are to build the right material on the right foundation.

The apostle Paul puts it this way, "For other foundation can no man lay than that is laid, which is Jesus Christ. Now if any man build upon this foundation gold, silver, precious stones, wood, hay, stubble; every man's work shall be made manifest: for the day shall declare it, because it shall be revealed by fire; and the fire shall try every man's work of what sort it is. If any man's work abide which he hath built thereupon, he shall receive a reward" (1 Cor. 3:11-14).

It is well for us to develop the habit of daily self-examination. Every night like the philosopher Sextus, we should ask ourselves, "Wherein have I transgressed today? What good have I done?"

> "If I have wounded any soul today,
> If I have caused one foot to go astray,
> If I have walked in my own willful way,
>   Dear Lord, forgive!
>
> "If I have uttered idle words or vain,
> If I have turned aside from want or pain,
> Lest I myself should suffer through the strain,
>   Dear Lord, forgive!

—C. M. Battersby

Words and music copyright, 1911, renewal, 1939. The Rodeheaver Co., owner. All rights reserved. Used by permission.

Life and My Work — September 11

Sowing and Reaping

Be not deceived; God is not mocked: for whatsoever a man soweth, that shall he also reap. Gal. 6:7.

The story is told of a Frenchman who persuaded some Missouri Indians to exchange fur for gunpowder, representing that they could obtain a fine crop by sowing it. The Indians prepared a field and sowed the powder according to instructions and set a guard to watch it. As it did not come up, in due time they saw that they had been deceived. Some time later the partner of the deceiver visited these Indians with a large stock of goods for the purpose of trade. The Indians came, and each took such things as pleased him until all were gone, but they refused to pay for the goods. The Frenchman went to the head chief and demanded redress. The chief assured him that full justice would be done as soon as the harvest of gunpowder could be gathered. Life has interesting ways of bringing men face to face with the truth, "Whatsoever a man soweth, that shall he also reap."

> "Sow a Thought, and you reap an Act;
> Sow an Act, and you reap a Habit;
> Sow a Habit, and you reap a Character;
> Sow a Character, and you reap a Destiny."

Sometimes we don't think too much about the harvest when we are sowing, and the tragedy is that it is too late to change the crop when the harvest is ripe. Why not, then, let us sow seeds of kindness, of love, of truth, and good will that will ensure for us the kind of harvest in which we can rejoice.

Paul continues in Galatians 6:8, 9, "He that soweth to his flesh shall of the flesh reap corruption; but he that soweth to the Spirit shall of the Spirit reap life everlasting. And let us not be weary in well doing: for in due season we shall reap, if we faint not."

Our text is not only a warning, but a promise. If we sow well, we need not worry about the harvest. What will you sow today?

DILIGENT IN HIS BUSINESS

Seest thou a man diligent in his business? he shall stand before kings; he shall not stand before mean men. **Prov. 22:29.**

According to the linguists, diligence comprises both the impulse of the bowstring that dispatches the arrow and the feather that keeps it true to its aim. *Diligo,* the Latin word from which diligence is derived, means "I choose, select, or love." To be diligent, therefore, is to resemble an eager hunter who selects the fattest of the herd, and leaving the rest, pursues and captures that one.

Napoleon Bonaparte won his victories chiefly by rapid concentration of his forces on one point of the enemy's line. This is diligence. Diligence involves an objective and the desire and energy to accomplish it. It involves careful planning and good hard work in executing the plan. It involves focusing all one's forces on one point. A burning glass, for example, is powerful because it focalizes a mass of sunbeams on one point. So in all departments of our activity, if we have one thing to do and do it well, we will be successful.

Satan always selects his disciples from men who are idle. Our Saviour, however, chooses His while they are busy, diligent in their business. In days of old He chose the twelve from men who were busy. They were either mending their nets or casting them into the sea or were sitting at the tax collector's booth. Jesus Himself was busy when He received the call from the wilderness to begin His sacred work. He was a diligent carpenter.

Benjamin Franklin said, "Diligence is the mother of good luck," and "God gives all things to industry." "Plough deep while Sluggards sleep; and you shall have corn to sell and to keep." "One today is worth two tomorrows," and "Never leave that till tomorrow which you can do today."

"He shall stand before kings," is the promise, "he shall not stand before mean men." He who is diligent in business, serving the Lord, will one day stand before the King of kings. Where will you stand?

Life and My Work   *September 13*

LOVE NOT SLEEP, OPEN THINE EYES

Love not sleep, lest thou come to poverty; open thine eyes, and thou shalt be satisfied with bread. **Prov. 20:13.**

The wise man is simply telling us to wake up. He is not talking to the man who earns a good night's sleep, but to the lazy man.

A beggar once presented himself to some men with tears and lamentable gestures, expressing to them his miserable poverty, telling of a private disorder that shame prevented him from uncovering. They all pitied the man and gave him something. As he departed, one man ran after him, inquiring what his private infirmity might be, and said, "I see nothing whereof you have reason to complain."

"Alas," said the beggar, "my disease is such as you cannot see. It hath crept over my whole body. It is passed through the very veins and marrow of me. This is called by some idleness or laziness."

Alert men make great contributions to progress. "Why do you put ground glass in your windows?" asked Benjamin Tilghman once of a lighthouse attendant. "Wouldn't clear glass give a better light?"

"Yes, it would," the attendant answered, "and we do put clear glass in the windows, but the strong winds blow the sand up against the windows and soon it is all ground glass again." Tilghman thought, "Here is nature's method of grinding glass." Many others had observed the same phenomenon but did not learn anything from it. This one man was on the alert. He contrived an apparatus that would blow jets of steam, air, and sand against glass with such force as to roughen the glass almost instantly. In 1870 he sold part of his patents for $400,000.

From watching a lamp swinging in a church, Galileo discovered the law of the pendulum—a most valuable law in the construction and use of certain instruments and machines. From watching the lid of a teakettle constantly rising and falling, James Watt soon realized that steam had power to lift the lid. We all know the results of that observation.

If we would get the most out of life, we too must wake up in order to accomplish great things for God and for our fellow men.

Life and My Work   *September 14*

NEITHER SLOTHFUL NOR WASTEFUL

He also that is slothful in his work is brother to him that is a great waster. **Prov. 18:9.**

Let us learn a parable of idleness. Among the disciples of Hillel, the wise teacher of the sons of Israel, was one named Saboth who gave himself up to idleness. Hillel was grieved and resolved to cure him of his fault. He took him to a pool of snakes and vermin covered with muddy weeds. "Here," said Hillel, "let us rest."

"Oh, not here," said the youth. "Dost thou not perceive what poisonous vapors it exhales?"

"Thou art right, my son. This bog is like the soul of the slothful man." Hillel then took the youth to a waste field producing thorns and thistles. "This," he said, "has good soil to produce all that is good and pleasant, but it is forgotten and neglected. A little while ago thou didst see the soul, now behold the life of an idle man." Saboth was so impressed that he began to lead a new life.

Then Hillel took him into a fertile valley beside a clear brook that flowed between fruitful trees and flowery meadows, and said, "This is the picture of thy new, industrious life. Nature that warned thee will now reward thee. Her beauty and grace can only give joy to him who sees in her life a picture of his own."

"Gather up the fragments that remain," said Jesus after feeding the five thousand, "that nothing be lost." These words meant more than putting the bread into baskets. The lesson was twofold. First, nothing was to be wasted. We are to let slip no temporal advantage. We should neglect nothing that will benefit human beings. Let everything be gathered up that will feed earth's hungry ones. Second, when the baskets of fragments were collected, the people thought of their friends at home. They wanted them to share in the bread that Christ had blessed. The fragments were distributed among the eager throng, and were carried away into all the region round about.

Such blessings neither the slothful nor the wasteful can enjoy.

Life and My Work   *September 15*

Do Your Own Business

And that ye study to be quiet, and to do your own business, and to work with your own hands, as we commanded you. 1 Thess. 4:11.

There are three interesting statements in today's text. The first one: "that ye study to be quiet." How great is this need in this complex, busy world in which we live! "In quietness and in confidence shall be your strength" (Isa. 30:15). We need to pray with John Greenleaf Whittier: "Drop Thy still dews of quietness, Till all our strivings cease; Take from our souls the strain and stress, And let our ordered lives confess The beauty of Thy peace."

The second statement is "do your own business." Many people look too much to the business of others and not enough to their own. One day after Jesus had given some instruction to Peter concerning his work, Peter turned, and seeing John following, said to Jesus, "Lord, and what shall this man do? Jesus saith unto him . . . What is that to thee? follow thou me" (John 21:21, 22). Let us mind our own business today and not be sidetracked into that of others.

The third expression is, "work with your own hands." The men who have been successful, not only in the world but also in the cause of God, have been men who have not been afraid to work. "Men give me credit," said Alexander Hamilton, "for genius. All the genius I have lies just in this: when I have a subject in hand, I study it profoundly. Day and night it is before me. I explore it in all its bearings. My mind becomes pervaded with it; then the effort which I make, the people are pleased to call the fruit of genius. It is the fruit of labor and thought."

Edison worked about twenty hours a day for at least seven months on his phonograph in order that it might properly pronounce the single word *specia*. He held firm and finally succeeded. The pianist, Falberg, said he never ventured to perform one of his celebrated pieces in public until he had played it at least fifteen hundred times.

Take together the three expressions of our text today, and you are bound to be a success in whatever you do.

Remember the Sabbath Day

Remember the sabbath day, to keep it holy. Ex. 20:8.

Perhaps you wonder why this text should be included in a collection of texts on "Life and My Work." The very first word is the reason. The Sabbathkeeping Christian will keep uppermost in his mind all week long his appointment with his Lord at the end of the week. Just as a lover looks forward to his appointment with his beloved, all week long the Christian will plan his work so it will not interfere with the Sabbath appointment.

On one occasion the local elder of a rural Seventh-day Adventist church made arrangements with a distant neighbor to buy some hay. The neighbor said he would be glad to deliver the hay at the end of the week, and the good elder said, "Fine, I'll help you unload it when you bring it," not thinking that he might bring it on Sabbath. He thought no more of it until Sabbath afternoon when he was sitting on the veranda of his country home. He happened to look up from reading the *Review* and saw his neighbor coming with the load of hay. What should he do? He thought it over carefully, went into the house, changed his clothes, and went out and helped the man unload the hay. Then he explained to his neighbor that he was a Seventh-day Adventist, that he did not work on Saturdays, but that he had broken the commandment on Monday. He had failed to *remember* the Sabbath day; and he must now ask his Lord to forgive him. While some may not agree that he should have helped unload the hay, here was a man who was sincere in his Sabbathkeeping. He was also thoughtful of his neighbors. This made a great impression upon the neighbor.

In our choice of a lifework we must keep in mind that there are some things a Sabbathkeeping Christian cannot do. We need also to recall that the commandment says, "Remember the sabbath day, to keep it holy." We cannot keep a day holy without being holy. Holiness and faithfulness in all that we do during the week is important to proper Sabbath observance.

Life and My Work   *September 17*

SIX DAYS SHALT THOU LABOR

Six days shalt thou labour, and do all thy work. Ex. 20:9.

The Sabbath commandment is a commandment not only to rest from our labors, but also to work. God expects us to do our work faithfully and well. He says, "Six days shalt thou labour." When Adam sinned, among other things God said, "In the sweat of thy face shalt thou eat bread." "And the life of toil and care which was henceforth to be man's lot was appointed in love. It was a discipline rendered needful by his sin, to place a check upon the indulgence of appetite and passion, to develop habits of self-control. It was a part of God's great plan for man's recovery from the ruin and degradation of sin."—*Patriarchs and Prophets,* p. 60. In reality, labor is a blessing.

"The youth should be led to see the true dignity of labor."—*Education,* p. 214. When Lysander, a Lacedaemonian general, brought magnificent presents to Cyrus, he saw and much admired the royal gardens. In answer to his inquiries Cyrus replied that he himself had drawn and marked out the plan of the gardens and had planted many of the trees with his own hands.

"What," exclaimed Lysander with atonishment, viewing Cyrus from head to foot, "is it possible that with those purple robes and splendid vestments, those strings of jewels, and bracelets of gold, those buskins so richly embroidered, is it possible that you could play the gardener and employ your royal hands in planting trees?"

"Does that surprise you?" said Cyrus. "I assure you that when my health permits, I never sit down to my table without having fatigued myself either in military exercise, rural labor, or some other toilsome employment to which I apply myself with pleasure."

Lysander, still more amazed, took Cyrus by the hand and said, "You are truly happy and deserve your high fortune, since you united it with virtue."

Even Cyrus the Great appreciated the blessings and dignity of labor. All great men do. We need never be ashamed of work.

Life and My Work   *September 18*

SLEEP OF A LABORING MAN IS SWEET

The sleep of a labouring man is sweet, whether he eat little or much: but the abundance of the rich will not suffer him to sleep. Eccl. 5:12.

William Stidger tells the following story: In England each year they have hiring fairs, to which farmers go to hire their help. After a certain farmer had interviewed many boys unsuccessfully, he finally found a boy who was wholesome, big, and strong. But when he asked that boy whether he knew anything about farming, all the boy would say was, "If you please, sir, I knows how to sleep on a windy night."

"Well, that's no great qualification for a farmer's man. Most of my men have been able to do that too well, unfortunately," said the squire. He could get no other answer from that boy. Finally he hired him.

Soon after, there came one of those night storms common in the hilly districts of Yorkshire. The squire lay awake thinking of other windy nights when great damage had been done, and waited for the boy to go to see whether everything was shipshape, but the boy did not stir. The squire called him, but he only turned over and began to snore.

Then the squire remembered what he had said about being able to sleep on a windy night. He said to himself, "He does that, and no mistake!" Planning to discharge him the next day, the farmer dressed and went out himself to see the damage he was sure had been done. Everywhere he went he found things in good shape. Every rope and peg of every haystack was secure. The doors and windows of the stable were fastened down tightly. The gates were fastened, and every detail was cared for with wise forethought. It began to dawn on the squire's mind that the boy's reply to his question as to his qualifications as a farm hand was not as trivial and foolish as it had first sounded.

The result of honest labor is security and peace of mind. The sleep of a laboring man is sweet because of a healthy tiredness, a peace of mind, and proper preparedness for whatever storms may come.

May the sweet sleep of a laboring man be ours tonight.

The Laborer Worthy of His Reward

For the scripture saith, Thou shalt not muzzle the ox that treadeth out the corn. And, The labourer is worthy of his reward. 1 Tim. 5:18.

Our text today is for both employers and employees. The laborer should remember that as a Christian he should do an honest day's work. He should be worth his salary. In fact, he should do more. He should be willing to go the second mile. The man who never does more than he is paid to do will never get paid for more than he does. Some employees reason as follows: "Since I am paid only 75 cents an hour, I will do only 75 cents' worth of work." These never succeed because they cannot agree with their employer as to what constitutes 75 cents' worth of work.

The man who is more interested in the pay than in the service he performs is only a timeserver and is generally never satisfied with his pay. He is a potential troublemaker. Should someone else be paid more or receive as much for less work, he shouts immediately, "Unjust, unfair." He is like the men in Jesus' parable who complained because all were paid the same wages at the end of the day, although some went to work at a later hour. The greatest satisfactions in life come from work well done, from having made a contribution, and from having performed a needed service. The man who concentrates on the pay rather than the service misses this satisfaction. The true Christian will be worth his salary because uppermost in his mind is service. Obviously, the pay is important, but is not everything.

Employers, too, should take note. They should pay men their just wages. There would be no conflicts between capital and labor if both were Christian and both served each other in the spirit of Christ and the golden rule. If an "ox that treadeth out the corn" is not to be muzzled, what about a man? Is an ox more valuable than a man? If instead of seeing how much money we can save or how much money we can make, we would think rather of how much good we can do, what a blessing it would be for all of us.

Provide for Your Own

But if any provide not for his own, and specially for those of his own house, he hath denied the faith, and is worse than an infidel. 1 Tim. 5:8.

To say that a man has denied the faith and is worse than an infidel is no small statement. Yet, this is said of the man who does not provide for his own house. God expects us to give the home priority.

"The restoration and uplifting of humanity begins in the home. The work of parents underlies every other. Society is composed of families, and is what the heads of families make it. Out of the heart are 'the issues of life' (Proverbs 4:23); and the heart of the community, of the church, and of the nation is the household. The well-being of society, the success of the church, the prosperity of the nation, depend upon home influences."—*The Ministry of Healing,* p. 349.

To provide for one's own household means more than merely to finance it. Someone has said, "Too many fathers are only house guests. They drop in occasionally." Actually a man's family is more important than his vocation. If work and money are more important, something is wrong with one's sense of values. Is bread more important than the lives of those for whom it is provided? If the home is the heart of life, shall we destroy the heart because of the periphery?

Since home building is society's greatest achievement, then a man's duties as husband and father have priority. Children need fathers and mothers, not child psychologists. Let us make first things first in providing for our own. Even ministers need to understand this text. "The minister's duties lie around him, nigh and afar off; but his first duty is to his children. . . . Nothing can excuse the minister for neglecting the inner circle for the larger circle outside."—*Gospel Workers,* p. 204. This is also true of every other profession.

"A well-ordered, a well-disciplined family in the sight of God is more precious than fine gold, even than the golden wedge of Ophir." —*The Adventist Home,* p. 32.

Be Content Without Covetousness

Let your conversation be without covetousness; and be content with such things as ye have: for he hath said, I will never leave thee, nor forsake thee. **Heb. 13:5.**

There was once a young iceberg in the far north who became very much discontented with life. He had heard the seals talk about the loveliness of the south where the bright sea rippled and sparkled under the glorious sun. One day a seal said to him, "Oh, you poor iceberg, you can never see what I have seen. You can never know what light and joy really are." The young iceberg began to grumble.

"My child," said a wise old iceberg who overheard him, "believe me that the good God who created us has put us here for some wise purpose. It may not be His will to reveal it to us; but, if we are content with our circumstances, He will make us happy."

The little one would not listen to this advice. When the weather became less severe, he succeeded in freeing himself and sailed with joy toward the south. "Now I will be of some use in the world," he thought. But, alas, for his good intentions. His first act was to smash a boat in the dark. "Oh," he sighed, "I am clumsy; I am in the way." When knocked about by waves and winds, he said, "I did not know what a peaceful home I had until I lost it, and by my own willfulness."

The forlorn iceberg sighed and melted in tears of distress and anxiety. He tried to return; but as the treacherous sun looked down on him, the poor iceberg wept more and more until at last he disappeared into the lonely sea—an example to all who leave their appointed stations for a pathway chosen by themselves, which is certain to end in waste and ruin.

This is the discontent that has its roots in covetousness. The covetous man is content with what he has until he sees someone else with more. There is, however, a noble, wholesome discontent—a state in which one is not satisfied with present attainments. May that be the only kind of discontent we allow in our lives.

Poor, Yet Rich

There is that maketh himself rich, yet hath nothing: there is that maketh himself poor, yet hath great riches. **Prov. 13:7.**

Today we think of the poor rich man and the rich poor man. "Once upon a time, a rich man's farmland produced heavy crops. So he said to himself, 'What shall I do, for I have no room to store this harvest?' Then he said, 'I know what I'll do. I'll pull down my barns and build bigger ones where I can store all my grain and my goods and I can say to my soul, Soul, you have plenty stored up there for years to come. Relax! Eat, drink, and have a good time!' But God said to him, 'You fool, this very night you will be asked for *your soul!* Then, who is going to have all that you have prepared?' That is what happens to the man who hoards things for himself and is not rich where God is concerned" (Luke 12:16-21, Phillips' translation).

From this story told by Jesus it is clear that the poor rich man is the man who thinks only in terms of the material things of the present and does not take into consideration eternal riches. There will come a time when earthly riches will be worthless. "In that day a man shall cast his idols of silver, and his idols of gold . . . to the moles and to the bats" (Isa. 2:20). Then he that maketh himself rich will find that he has nothing.

The rich poor man, however, is the man who manifests the spirit of Jesus who, "though he was rich, yet for your sakes he became poor, that ye through his poverty might be rich" (2 Cor. 8:9). Paul describes himself "as poor, yet making many rich" (2 Cor. 6:10).

Not only is the poor man rich in terms of eternal values and in the light of future destiny, but there is also a richness in life that a poor man can enjoy here and now. The honorable, kindly, intelligent small farm owner may be happier than the richest man who is without the blessings the farmer can know. He and his happy, hard-working family know at eventide a peace of mind that comes only to those who work hard and who love the Lord.

Faithfulness in Tithe Paying

Bring ye all the tithes into the storehouse, that there may be meat in mine house, and prove me now herewith, saith the Lord of hosts, if I will not open you the windows of heaven, and pour you out a blessing, that there shall not be room enough to receive it. Mal. 3:10.

There is in man a tendency to say in his heart, "My power and the might of mine hand hath gotten me this wealth," but God wants us to remember that "it is he that giveth thee power to get wealth" (Deut. 8:17, 18). In Him we live and move and have our being. God wants to take us into partnership with Himself that together we may do the works of God in this world and rejoice in a service that has everlasting consequences. For this purpose He created us.

From the very beginning "the Lord placed our first parents in the Garden of Eden. He surrounded them with everything that could minister to their happiness, and He bade them acknowledge Him as the possessor of all things. In the garden He caused to grow every tree that was pleasant to the eye or good for food; but among them He made one reserve. Of all else, Adam and Eve might freely eat; but of this one tree God said, 'Thou shalt not eat of it.' Here was the test of their gratitude and loyalty to God.

"So the Lord has imparted to us heaven's richest treasure in giving us Jesus. . . . The productions of the earth, the bountiful harvests, the treasures of gold and silver, are His gifts. . . . He asks us to acknowledge Him as the Giver of all things; and for this reason He says, Of all your possessions I reserve a tenth for Myself, besides gifts and offerings, which are to be brought into My storehouse. This is the provision God has made for carrying forward the work of the gospel."—*Counsels on Stewardship*, p. 65. All that we have belongs to God, and He gives us 90 per cent commission for being His stewards. In addition, if we are faithful, He promises blessings beyond our capacity to receive. What a distinct privilege is ours to be in partnership with our Creator!

Life and My Work September 24

Where Your Treasure Is

For where your treasure is, there will your heart be also. Matt. 6:21.

The supreme affection, whatever may be its object, is the centralizing power of the soul. As in matter, so in mind, the greater force controls the lesser. In one's life the greater love always supersedes lesser loves. We need to be careful, therefore, what constitutes our greater love; for where our treasure is, there will our heart be also.

A woman came to a minister's home on one occasion and found two boys playing with their toys. "Well, boys," she said, "are these your treasures?"

"No, ma'am," said the elder of the two, "these are not our treasures; these are our playthings. Our treasures are in heaven."

The trouble with most of us is that we do not distinguish between playthings and treasures. Our playthings become our treasures, and as a result the objects of our affections are only vanity and toys. Too often we think of treasure in terms of money; but money does not merit our supreme affection. Money is powerful, but a power of well-defined and narrow limits. Someone has said, "It will purchase plenty, but not peace. It will furnish your table with luxuries, but not you with an appetite to enjoy them. It will surround your sickbed with physicians, but not restore health to your sickly frame. It will encompass you with a crowd of flatterers, but never procure you a true friend. It will bribe into silence the tongues of accusing men, but not an accusing conscience. It will pay some debts, but not the largest one of all—your debt to the law of God. It will relieve many fears, but not those of guilt and terror that crown the brow of death. He stands as grim and terrible by the dying bed of wealth as by the pallet of the poorest beggar whom piteous riches has thrust from her door."

Occasionally, perhaps, we have said concerning some spiritual activity, "I just couldn't put my heart into it." Could it be that if we invested more of our time and money and energy in spiritual things, we would find our hearts there? Let us try it and see.

Life and My Work *September 25*

LABOR NOT FOR THE MEAT THAT PERISHETH

Labour not for the meat which perisheth, but for that meat which endureth unto everlasting life, which the Son of man shall give unto you: for him hath God the Father sealed. John 6:27.

A brother came to the convent at Mount Sinai, and finding all the monks at work, shook his head and said to the abbot, "Labour not for the meat that perisheth, and remember Mary hath chosen the good part."

"Very well," said the abbot, and taking the visitor to a cell, he gave him a book. The monk sat all day reading and wondering much that no one called him to dinner or offered him any refreshment.

The night at length arrived, and hungry and weary, he left his solitary cell and repaired to the apartment of the abbot. "Father," said he, "don't the brethren eat today?"

"Oh, yes," replied the abbot, "they have eaten plentifully."

"Then how is it," said the monk, "that you could not call me to partake with them?"

"Because, brother," replied the abbot, "you are a spiritual man and have no need of carnal food. For our part, we are obliged to eat; and on that account we work. But you, brother, who have chosen the good part, are above the want of meat that perisheth."

"Pardon me, Father," said the monk. "I perceive my mistake."

Jesus does not condemn honest labor, but rather He warns against laboring for the material to the exclusion of the spiritual. Too many people are like the storekeeper who, whenever he was asked to attend prayer meeting replied, "Can't leave the store."

One day his little daughter came to her mother and said, "Mamma, will you go to heaven when Jesus comes?"

"Yes, I hope so, my child. And I hope you and Papa will go, too."

"Oh, no, Papa can't go. He can't leave the store!"

Too many of us become too absorbed in labor for things that perish. Let us take time today for things that endure unto everlasting life.

Go Ye Into All the World

And he said unto them, Go ye into all the world, and preach the gospel to every creature. **Mark 16:15.**

No matter what our work may be, our greatest objective is to fulfill the gospel commission. Jesus says to all, "Go ye."

Why should we be concerned with the people in other lands? We read, "Among the heathen are those who worship God ignorantly, those to whom the light is never brought by human instrumentality, yet they will not perish."—*The Desire of Ages,* p. 638. If they live up to all the light they have, they will be saved. Why send them more light?

First, Jesus said, "Go ye." We should go because He asks us to go. Then He also said, "Inasmuch as ye have done it unto one of the least of these my brethren, ye have done it unto me" (Matt. 25:40). Christ identifies Himself with all people, and He it is who calls, "Come over into Macedonia, and help us."

God is counting on you and me to do for others, including the heathen, what He Himself cannot do. God does not seem real to many people; we do. God cannot appear to each in person, so He sends human beings. Unconverted souls need the human touch.

"Our little world is the lesson book of the universe."—*Ibid.,* p. 19. Certain consequences are being dramatically demonstrated on this planet—the contrast between God's way and Satan's way. In sinful heathen lands men live in fear, filth, and superstition. That is what sin has done to men. When loving missionaries take to them the message of the Lord Jesus Christ, love replaces fear; and men begin to clean up. That is what the love of God does to human beings. God wants us to play well our little part in this drama, whether in the mission fields or at home supporting the missionaries with our means and with our prayers. Together we can help to demonstrate the love of God.

Are we responsible for others? Love assumes the responsibility. Shall I seek to save you merely to save myself? No. If I love you, the family reunion in heaven will not be complete if you are not there.

LABORERS ARE FEW

Then saith he unto his disciples, The harvest truly is plenteous, but the labourers are few; pray ye therefore the Lord of the harvest, that he will send forth labourers into his harvest. Matt. 9:37, 38.

"Maybe the Lord does need laborers in His harvest. But what can I do? I can't preach." It is not in talking to people that we can best win them. "Our influence upon others depends not so much upon what we say as upon what we are. Men may combat and defy our logic, they may resist our appeals; but a life of disinterested love is an argument they cannot gainsay. A consistent life, characterized by the meekness of Christ, is a power in the world."—*The Desire of Ages*, p. 142.

If you and I will begin just where we are by living a consistent Christlike life and watch for God's guidance in little openings, marvelous will be the results; great shall be the harvest.

"The disciples were to begin their work where they were. The hardest and most unpromising field was not to be passed by. So every one of Christ's workers is to begin where he is. In our own families may be those hungry for sympathy, starving for the bread of life. There may be children to be trained for Christ. There are heathen at our very doors. Let us do faithfully the work that is nearest. Then let our efforts be extended as far as God's hand may lead the way. The work of many may appear to be restricted by circumstances; but wherever it is, if performed with faith and diligence, it will be felt to the uttermost parts of the earth. When Christ was upon earth His work appeared to be confined to a narrow field, but multitudes from all lands heard His message. God often uses the simplest means to accomplish the greatest results. It is His plan that every part of His work shall depend on every other part, as a wheel within a wheel, all acting in harmony. The humblest worker, moved by the Holy Spirit, will touch invisible chords, whose vibrations will ring to the ends of the earth, and make melody through eternal ages."—*Ibid.*, pp. 822, 823.

Life and My Work *September 28*

THE JEWELRY BUSINESS

And they shall be mine, saith the Lord of hosts, in that day when I make up my jewels; and I will spare them, as a man spareth his own son that serveth him. Mal. 3:17.

In the hotel of a little north Wisconsin town, Bishop Anderson, of Chicago, once met an enterprising young salesman who, inclined to be talkative, introduced himself by remarking, "I'm a traveling man."

"So am I," replied the bishop.

"I'm in the jewelry business," volunteered the youth.

"So am I," answered the bishop, thinking of the scripture, "they shall be mine, saith the Lord of hosts, in that day when I make up my jewels."

"My father has taken me into partnership." The young man was becoming confidential.

"So has mine," returned the bishop.

"This is my first trip out."

"I have made many trips."

"I'm working very hard," the young man spoke earnestly, "for I am eager to make a good report when I get home."

And the bishop reverently responded, "So am I."

In all the world, the most important business, handling the most valuable commodity, and bearing the biggest dividends, is the business of dealing with human souls. No matter what our work may be, you and I should be in the jewelry business in partnership with our heavenly Father. Let us do our best to ensure a good report when we get home.

> "Like the stars of the morning,
> His bright crown adorning,
> They shall shine in their beauty,
> Bright gems for His crown."

BE OF GOOD COURAGE

Be strong and of a good courage, fear not, nor be afraid of them: for the Lord thy God, he it is that doth go with thee; he will not fail thee, nor forsake thee. Deut. 31:6.

As Martin Luther drew near the door that was about to admit him into the presence of his judges at the Diet of Worms, he met the celebrated George of Freundsburg. George was a courageous old general who had led his soldiers against the French Army, driving it into the Placeno, which largely decided the captivity of the king of France. This old general, seeing Luther pass, tapped him on the shoulder and shaking his head said kindly, "Poor monk. Thou art now going to make a nobler stand than I or any other captain have ever made in the bloodiest of our battles. But if thy cause is just and thou art sure of it, go forward in God's name and fear nothing. God will not forsake thee." This was truly a noble tribute paid by the courage of the sword to the courage of mind and heart.

We need both the courage of mind and the courage of action. Think of the courage of Philip, the bishop of Heraclea, who in the beginning of the fourth century was dragged by his feet through the streets, severely scourged, and then brought again to the governor who charged him with "obstinate rashness in continuing disobedience to the Imperial Decrees." But he boldly replied, "My present behavior is not the effect of rashness, but proceeds from my love and fear of God who made the world and who will judge the living and the dead, whose commands I dare not transgress. I have hitherto done my duty to the Emperors and am always ready to comply with their just orders according to the doctrine of our Lord Christ who bids us give both to Caesar and to God their due. But I am obliged to prefer heaven to earth and to obey God rather than man."

This is the kind of courage that we need today. While we marvel at the courage of the martyrs of old, we need to remember that it takes as much courage to live for God as it does to die for Him.

As Thy Days, So Shall Thy Strength Be

Thy shoes shall be iron and brass; and as thy days, so shall thy strength be. **Deut. 33:25.**

Here is a wonderful promise, "as thy days, so shall thy strength be." God has not promised strength for a week, or a year, but for one day at a time. Too many people anticipate the problems of tomorrow and faint under the load of them today. Thus they meet two sets of troubles at once—one set that is actually present, and the set that they bring in by worrying about the future. They, therefore, meet their troubles twice, once before they come and a second time when they arrive. They needlessly telescope their troubles into a double expenditure of energy; and when they break under the strain, they wonder why.

Said Jesus, "Do not be troubled about to-morrow; to-morrow will take care of itself. The day's own trouble is quite enough for the day" (Matt. 6:34, Moffatt).

"Our heavenly Father has a thousand ways to provide for us of which we know nothing. Those who accept the one principle of making the service of God supreme, will find perplexities vanish and a plain path before their feet."—*The Ministry of Healing,* p. 481.

As we look ahead perhaps we cannot see how we can carry on another day. However, these ways provided for our strength are for one day at a time, and are not for tomorrow. "The faithful discharge of today's duties is the best preparation for tomorrow's trials. Do not gather together all tomorrow's liabilities and cares and add them to the burden of today. 'Sufficient unto the day is the evil thereof.' . . . In the darkest days, when appearances seem most forbidding, have faith in God. He is working out His will, doing all things well in behalf of His people. The strength of those who love and serve Him will be renewed day by day. He is able and willing to bestow upon His servants all the help they need."—*Ibid.,* pp. 481, 482.

Claiming this promise, let us go forth with courage to our work.

OCTOBER

Life Through Giving October 1

GIVE AND IT SHALL BE GIVEN UNTO YOU

Give, and it shall be given unto you; good measure, pressed down, and shaken together, and running over, shall men give into your bosom. For with the same measure that ye mete withal it shall be measured to you again. Luke 6:38.

To give is to live. The life that will be preserved is the life that is freely given in service to God and man. Living for self is like grain that is eaten—it disappears, and there is no increase. The law of self-serving is the law of self-destruction. Jesus said, "Except a corn of wheat fall into the ground and die, it abideth alone: but if it die, it bringeth forth much fruit." The law of self-sacrifice is the law of self-preservation.

This law is manifest in all of nature. Electricity can flow in only as it flows out. When cells in our bodies begin to live for themselves alone and cancer develops, they soon destroy the whole body. "There is nothing, save the selfish heart of man, that lives unto itself. No bird that cleaves the air, no animal that moves upon the ground, but ministers to some other life. There is no leaf of the forest, or lowly blade of grass, but has its ministry. Every tree and shrub and leaf pours forth that element of life without which neither man nor animal could live; and man and animal, in turn, minister to the life of tree and shrub and leaf. The flowers breathe fragrance and unfold their beauty in blessing to the world. The sun sheds its light to gladden a thousand worlds. The ocean . . . receives the streams from every land, but takes to give. The mists ascending from its bosom fall in showers to water the earth, that it may bring forth and bud."—*The Desire of Ages,* pp. 20, 21.

This law of life through giving is the law of life for heaven as well as earth.

May God help us to learn to live by this law of life today.

Life Through Giving   *October 2*

Freely Ye Have Received, Freely Give

And as ye go, preach, saying, The kingdom of heaven is at hand. Heal the sick, cleanse the lepers, raise the dead, cast out devils: freely ye have received, freely give. Matt. 10:7, 8.

"Have you had a kindness shown?
    Pass it on;
'Twas not given for thee alone,
    Pass it on;
Let it travel down the years,
Let it wipe another's tears
Till in heaven the deed appears—
    Pass it on.

"Did you hear a loving word?
    Pass it on;
Like the singing of a bird?
    Pass it on;
Let its music live and grow,
Let it cheer another's woe,
You have reaped what others sow—
    Pass it on.

"Be not selfish in thy greed,
    Pass it on;
Look upon thy brother's need,
    Pass it on;
Live for self, you live in vain,
Live for Christ, you live again,
Live for Him, with Him you reign—
    Pass it on."

—Henry K. Burton

Life Through Giving October 3

GOD SO LOVED THAT HE GAVE

For God so loved the world, that he gave his only begotten Son, that whosoever believeth in him should not perish, but have everlasting life. John 3:16.

Giving is one of the manifestations of the glory of God. "I do nothing of myself," said Christ. "The living Father hath sent me, and I live by the Father." "I seek not mine own glory" (John 8:28; 6:57; 8:50).

"In these words is set forth the great principle which is the law of life for the universe. All things Christ received from God, but He took to give. So in the heavenly courts, in His ministry for all created beings: through the beloved Son, the Father's life flows out to all; through the Son it returns, in praise and joyous service, a tide of love, to the great Source of all. And thus through Christ the circuit of beneficence is complete, representing the character of the great Giver, the law of Life."—*The Desire of Ages,* p. 21.

"The glory shining in the face of Jesus is the glory of self-sacrificing love. . . . The love which 'seeketh not her own' has its source in the heart of God."—*Ibid.,* p. 20.

"Satan has accused God of requiring self-denial of the angels, when He knew nothing of what it meant Himself, and when He would not Himself make any self-sacrifice for others. . . . Christ came to the world to meet these false accusations, and to reveal the Father."—ELLEN G. WHITE in *The Review and Herald,* Feb. 18, 1890.

Contrary to Satan's accusations, God is Himself the embodiment of the spirit of giving and self-denial. The spirit of liberality is the spirit of Heaven. The spirit of selfishness is the spirit of Satan. The principle of *giving* manifest in actual benevolence and active service and concern for others stands out in contrast with the principle of *getting* manifest in emphasis upon receiving and active concern for self alone. The one leads to life both here and hereafter. The other leads to misery and death. God so loved that He gave. Let us learn to love and to give. This is the way of life.

Life Through Giving   October 4

EVERY GOOD AND PERFECT GIFT IS FROM ABOVE

Every good gift and every perfect gift is from above, and cometh down from the Father of lights, with whom is no variableness, neither shadow of turning. James 1:17.

Let us think for a moment today of all the wonderful gifts we receive from God. "The power of God is manifested in the beating of the heart, in the action of the lungs, and in the living currents that circulate through the thousand different channels of the body. We are indebted to Him for every moment of existence, and for all the comforts of life. The powers and abilities that elevate man above the lower creation, are the endowment of the Creator.

"He loads us with His benefits. We are indebted to Him for the food we eat, the water we drink, the clothes we wear, the air we breathe. . . . He is a bountiful benefactor and preserver.

"The sun which shines upon the earth, and glorifies all nature, the weird, solemn radiance of the moon, the glories of the firmament, spangled with brilliant stars, the showers that refresh the land, and cause vegetation to flourish, the precious things of nature in all their varied richness, the lofty trees, the shrubs and plants, the waving grain, the blue sky, the green earth, the changes of day and night, the renewing seasons, all speak to man of his Creator's love."—*Counsels on Stewardship,* p. 17.

Every good and perfect gift is from above. With our heavenly Benefactor there is "no variableness, neither shadow of turning." Some gifts are not good. They have shadows due to ulterior motives. God's gifts are not so. God is no respecter of persons. There are no shadows with His gifts. They are given fully and freely. Nor does He give only when He is "in the mood."

Life's greatest gift is also from above. The gift that brings all other blessings in its train is the gift of the Holy Spirit, which enables us to use rightly all other gifts. It is the gift that fills our hearts with the spirit of giving, causing all to rejoice.

Life Through Giving   October 5

Giving, Prompted by Love

And walk in love, as Christ also hath loved us, and hath given himself for us an offering and a sacrifice to God for a sweetsmelling savour. Eph. 5:2.

A poor Arab found a spring of sweet water. Accustomed as he was to brackish wells, he considered this water was fit for a monarch. Filling his leather bottle from the spring, he determined to present it to the king. He traveled far, and laid his offering at his sovereign's feet.

The king did not despise the gift brought to him with so much trouble. He drank some of it, and thanking the Arab with a smile, ordered him to be presented with a reward.

The courtiers were eager to taste the water also, but the caliph forbade them. After the Arab had departed, the king explained, "During the long journey the water had become impure and distasteful, but it was an offering of love. As such, I have received it with pleasure; but I well knew that had I suffered another to partake of it, he would not have concealed his disgust. Therefore, I forbade you to touch it, lest the heart of the poor man should have been wounded."

If a non-Christian caliph could be touched by the motive of a poor Arab, surely our loving heavenly Father appreciates every gift motivated by sacrificial love. That was His motive; it should be ours.

> "When I survey the wondrous cross
>   On which the Prince of glory died,
> My richest gain I count but loss,
>   And pour contempt on all my pride.
>
> . . . . .
>
> "Were the whole realm of nature mine,
>   That were a tribute far too small;
> Love so amazing, so divine,
>   Demands my life, my soul, my all."
>
> —Isaac Watts

Life Through Giving   *October 6*

Give Bountifully

But this I say, He which soweth sparingly shall reap also sparingly; and he which soweth bountifully shall reap also bountifully. 2 Cor. 9:6.

No church ever died because it gave too much. Listen to an old colored minister: "I'se knowed many a church to die, 'cause it didn't gib enough, but I neber knowed a church to die 'cause it gib too much. Dey don't die dat way. Bredren, hab any ob you knowed a church to die 'cause it gib too much? If you hab, just let me know; and I'll make a pilgrimage to dat church; and I'll climb up by de soft light of de moon to its moss-covered roof; and I'll stand dar and lift up my hands to heben and say, 'Blessed are de dead dat die in de Lord.'"

Too often we give the Lord only what is left over after we have taken care of all our wants and needs—like the little boy who was given two nickels, one for himself and one for the Lord. On his way to church one of the nickels rolled into the gutter and fell into a drain beyond his reach. "Oh, oh," said the boy, "there goes the Lord's nickel." Too many of us are like him. Some perhaps, may be like the richly clad woman who, at a meeting in behalf of homeless wanderers in New York, wiped her eyes upon an expensive embroidered handkerchief after hearing the story of their sufferings, but when the contribution box came around, gave twenty-five cents to aid the society to promote their welfare.

A dear old church member was once discussing Christianity with an infidel, who said, "You might as well drop the subject, for I do not believe a single word you say. And more than this, I am satisfied that you do not really believe it yourself, for to my certain knowledge you have not given, for the last twenty years, as much for the spread of Christianity, such as the building of churches and the forwarding of foreign and domestic missions, as your last Durham cow cost. Why, sir, if I believed one half of what you say you believe, I would make the church my rule for giving and my farm the exception."

Life Through Giving *October 7*

Give Cheerfully

Every man according as he purposeth in his heart, so let him give; not grudgingly, or of necessity: for God loveth a cheerful giver. 2 Cor. 9:7.

The story is told that when Columbus first applied to the Indians for a supply of provisions, they refused to give him anything. Foreseeing a coming eclipse, Columbus threatened them with sudden destruction; and as a sign, told them that the sun would be darkened within two days. When the eclipse came on, the Indians were filled with fear; and they came to Columbus bringing large supplies of provisions. They gave, but from the motive of fear.

This is not the kind of giving God is interested in. God wants only a cheerful giver. He does not appreciate gifts that are grudgingly given. In Edinburgh, after a sermon on giving, one member of the congregation by accident put a crown piece in the plate instead of a penny. As soon as he recognized what he had done, he asked to have it back. But he who held the plate said, "In once, in forever."

"Ah weel, ah weel," grunted the unwilling giver, "I'll get credit for it in heaven."

"Nah, nah," said the collector, "ye'll get credit only for the penny."

"I was shown that the recording angel makes a faithful record of every offering dedicated to God, and put into the treasury, and also of the final result of the means thus bestowed. The eye of God takes cognizance of every farthing devoted to His cause, and of the willingness or reluctance of the giver. The motive in giving is also chronicled."—*Counsels on Stewardship,* p. 196.

Seneca said, "We should give as we receive, cheerfully, quickly, and without hesitation; for there is no grace in a benefit that sticks to the fingers." Warwick wrote, "He gives not best who gives most; but he gives most who gives best." Even man loves a cheerful giver. How do you give—grudgingly or cheerfully?

Life Through Giving October 8

Provision for Giving

And God is able to make all grace abound toward you; that ye, always having all sufficiency in all things, may abound to every good work. 2 Cor. 9:8.

Today let us read our text again, noting the words: "all grace," "always," "all sufficiency," "all things," "every good work." What a statement! God has made every provision possible for our needs that we may prosper and share with others. Notice our text and several verses that follow in Phillips' translation: "After all, God can give you everything that you need, so that you may always have sufficient both yourselves and for giving away to other people. . . . He Who gives the seed to the sower and turns that seed into bread to eat, will give you the seed of generosity to sow and, for harvest, the satisfying bread of good deeds done. The more you are enriched by God the more scope will there be for generous giving, and your gifts, administered through us, will mean that many will thank God. For your giving does not end in meeting the wants of your fellow-Christians. It also results in an overflowing tide of thanksgiving to God."

A pious minister named Fresenius one day found his mother, who was a widow, concerned about a dollar that she much needed at the time but did not know where to get. Not being able himself to supply it, he said, "I likewise believe you must have the dollar. I accordingly turn this hourglass and assure you that if the dollar is really needed, it will positively lie here on the table before the hourglass is run down. If it does not lie here, God will convince us after this hour that it was not as indispensable as we imagined." The story is that the hourglass was scarcely run out when a messenger arrived, bringing a dollar that someone owed Fresenius.

This is the kind of faith we need in God—a faith to believe that He will supply what we need when we need it most. When things do not come just as we think they should, let us be assured that perhaps we do not need them as much as we thought.

Life Through Giving *October 9*

BRING AN OFFERING

Give unto the Lord the glory due unto his name: bring an offering, and come into his courts. Ps. 96:8.

Once there was a very good and powerful king and a poor woman who loved the king very much. She wished to give a present to her sovereign, but had only one little brown farthing. A rich neighbor came to her and said, "You can never put that dirty brown farthing among the bright gold pieces offered to the king. Here are some new silver shillings. They will not look so bad. You can put them in, and it will be all the same, for I was going to give them anyway."

But the poor woman said, "Oh, no. My gift to the king must be my own. I am sorry I have nothing better to give, but this is all I have."

So the poor woman went forward with the rest. When she passed the king she slipped her little coin quietly into the plate. As she turned away, she felt a tap on her shoulder; the king was looking down at her and smiling graciously. "My good woman," he said, "was it you who put in this costly gift?" As she looked into his hand, she saw something very much like her little brown farthing; but it began to grow brighter and brighter till she could scarcely look at it; for it was all shining with gold, diamonds, and other precious stones.

"Oh, no," said the woman, "I gave only one little brown farthing."

"Take it into your own hand and see," said the king, still smiling. So the woman took it and saw that it was her farthing, after all.

"Yes," she said, greatly surprised, "that's the very farthing. I tried hard to shine it, but I could only get it to look a little bright at the edge." So she gave it back to the king; and as soon as he touched it, it was shining and sparkling as before.

"This little farthing," said the king, "pleases me as much as the rich man's gold, for with me a man is accepted according to what he hath and not according to what he hath not."

However small our gifts, if they come from our hearts in love, in the hand of the Master they will reveal their true value.

Life Through Giving October 10

Give to the Poor

He that hath pity upon the poor lendeth unto the Lord; and that which he hath given will he pay him again. **Prov. 19:17.**

"In view of what Heaven is doing to save the lost, how can those who are partakers of the riches of the grace of Christ withdraw their interest and their sympathies from their fellow men? How can they indulge in pride of rank or caste, and despise the unfortunate and the poor?"—*Counsels on Stewardship,* p. 160.

Since Jesus identifies Himself with all of humanity when He says, "Inasmuch as ye have done it unto one of the least of these my brethren, ye have done it unto me" (Matt. 25:40) we can understand how it is that "He that hath pity upon the poor lendeth unto the Lord" (Prov. 19:17).

Now God does not put a premium upon poverty due to laziness. We are told, "The custom of supporting men and women in idleness by private gifts or church money encourages them in wrong habits. . . . Every man, woman, and child should be educated to practical, useful work."—*Ibid.,* p. 165. Therefore, the man who is poor because of his unwillingness to work is to be pitied not for his poverty, but for his laziness. Even so, you and I are to treat the poor as God treats them.

God imparts His blessings to us in order that we may share with others. This sharing is not to be limited to money. "It is God's purpose that the rich and the poor shall be closely bound together by the ties of sympathy and helpfulness."—*Ibid.,* p. 161. We are told, "Pure religion and undefiled before God and the Father is this, To visit the fatherless and widows in their affliction, and to keep himself unspotted from the world" (James 1:27). Again, "Bring the poor that are cast out to thy house" (Isa. 58:7). "In the story of the good Samaritan, Christ illustrates the nature of true religion. He shows that it consists not in systems, creeds, or rights, but in the performance of loving deeds, in bringing the greatest good to others, in genuine goodness."—*The Desire of Ages,* p. 497.

Life Through Giving   *October 11*

GIVE TO HIM THAT ASKETH

Give to him that asketh thee, and from him that would borrow of thee turn not thou away. Matt. 5:42.

So often when we are asked to give to certain ones in need, we are prone to ask, "Are they Christian? Are they trying to do what's right? If they are not, why should we give to them?"

An old Jewish allegory goes something like this: One day Abraham sat at his tent door as his custom was, waiting to entertain strangers, when he saw a man who was a hundred years old—stooped, leaning on his staff, weary with age and travel—coming toward him. Abraham received him kindly, washed his feet, caused him to sit down, and provided supper. The old man ate, however, without asking God's blessing and giving thanks. When asked why he did not worship the God of heaven, the man told Abraham that he worshiped fire only and acknowledged no other god; at which answer Abraham grew so zealously angry that he thrust the old man out of his tent, exposing him unguarded to the darkness, evils, and dangers of the night. God called Abraham and asked where the stranger was. He replied, "I thrust him away, because he did not worship Thee."

God answered, "I have suffered him these hundred years though he dishonored me, and couldest thou not endure him for one night when he gave thee no trouble?" Whereupon, says the story, Abraham called him back again and gave him hospitable entertainment and wise instruction.

"As we see men and women in need of sympathy and help, we shall not ask, 'Are they worthy?' but 'How can I benefit them?' Rich and poor, high and low, free and bond, are God's heritage. He who gave His life to redeem man sees in every human being a value that exceeds finite computation. . . . We are to discern His estimate of the value of the soul. When we do this, we shall feel that human beings, however degraded, have cost too much to be treated with coldness or contempt."
—*The Ministry of Healing,* pp. 162, 163.

Life Through Giving   *October 12*

GIVE, NOT TO BE SEEN OF MEN

Take heed that ye do not your alms before men, to be seen of them: otherwise ye have no reward of your Father which is in heaven. Matt. 6:1.

The aim in giving should not be to secure praise and honor of men.

Naber, an Arab, owned a beautiful horse that was coveted by a Bedouin named Daher. Daher offered Naber his camels and much of his wealth for the horse, but in vain. At length he decided on a plan. He disguised himself as a lame beggar and went to wait for Naber to pass by. When he saw Naber approaching on his beautiful steed, he pleaded, "I am a poor stranger. For three days I have been unable to move from this spot to seek food. I am dying. Help me, and Heaven will reward you." Naber kindly offered to take him home upon his horse but the rogue replied, "I cannot rise. I have no strength left."

Naber, in compassion, dismounted, and with difficulty set the impostor on his horse; but no sooner did Daher feel himself in the saddle than he set spurs to the horse and galloped off, calling out as he did so, "It is I, Daher. I have got the horse and am off with it!"

Naber called after him to stop and listen. Certain of not being pursued, Daher turned and halted a short distance from Naber, who was armed only with a spear.

"You have taken my horse," said the latter. "Since Heaven has willed it, I wish you joy of it, but I do pray you never to tell anyone how you obtained it."

"And why not?" asked Daher.

"Because," said Naber, "another man might be really ill; and men would fear to help him. You would be the cause of many refusing to perform an act of charity for fear of being duped as I have been."

Shamed by these words, Daher was silent; then, springing from the horse, he returned it and embraced Naber. Naber invited him to his tent where they spent a few days together and became fast friends for life.

Life Through Giving October 13

SCATTERING AND WITHHOLDING

There is that scattereth, and yet increaseth; and there is that withholdeth more than is meet, but it tendeth to poverty. Prov. 11:24.

The truth of our text today is demonstrated in many ways whether we are dealing with money, with ideas, or with words and deeds of kindness. "There is that scattereth, and yet increaseth; and there is that withholdeth more than is meet, but it tendeth to poverty."

There came out of England a century ago the story of three brothers. As boys, they were taught to give of their little store for the spreading of the gospel. Each possessed a box in which he dropped any money that he might feel inclined to give for this cause.

There came a time when the family moved; and in the confusion of moving, the boxes were mislaid. A certain portion of their goods were long delayed. The boxes were looked for in vain. A long time afterward the boxes were unexpectedly found. When the boys opened them, they found that they contained almost the same sum of money, about ten pounds. The eldest brother had long wished to possess a watch, and without hesitation he appropriated the whole of the contents to purchase one. The second brother was of a divided mind. He spent half of his money for his own gratification, and the other half he gave to missions. The youngest brother, remembering the original purpose of the deposit in the box, gave the whole of it to the Lord.

This action on the part of these three boys was prophetic, as it were, indicative of their future course. As years went by, this was truly demonstrated. The eldest became engaged in many undertakings that seemed to promise wealth. He expended large sums of money, but at the close of his life he was a poor man and for some time dependent upon the bounty of his youngest brother. The second brother was not poor, yet neither was he rich, nor was he satisfied with his moderate circumstances. The third and youngest, however, died leaving one hundred thousand pounds after having given away at least that much for missions and other works of love.

Life Through Giving   *October 14*

THE LIBERAL SOUL MADE FAT

The liberal soul shall be made fat: and he that watereth shall be watered also himself. **Prov. 11:25.**

Unselfish liberality is a miracle of grace produced by the sanctification of the spirit. The Bible gives a number of illustrations of such liberality and the blessings that came from it.

In the poverty-stricken home in the city of Zarephath, the famine pressed sore; and the pitifully meager fare seemed about to fail. There was left only a little handful of meal in a barrel and a little oil in a cruse, and the young widow woman was out gathering sticks to prepare what appeared to be her family's last meal. The prophet Elijah approached her and asked for a drink of water and for a morsel of bread. In response to Elijah's request, the widow revealed her state of affairs. Elijah said to her, "Fear not; go and do as thou hast said: but make me thereof a little cake first, . . . and after make for thee and for thy son" (1 Kings 17:13). No greater test of faith could have been required. The widow had hitherto treated all strangers with kindness and liberality; and now, regardless of the suffering that might result to herself and her child, and trusting in the God of Israel to supply her every need, she did according to the saying of Elijah; and wonderful was the result. "The barrel of meal wasted not, neither did the cruse of oil fail, according to the word of the Lord, which he spake by Elijah."

The widow shared her morsel with Elijah; and in return, she and her son were preserved. "And to all who, in time of trial and want, give sympathy and assistance to others more needy, God has promised great blessing. He has not changed. His power is no less now than in the days of Elijah."—*Prophets and Kings,* pp. 131, 132.

We think of Mary's beautiful, valuable, acceptable offering of the precious ointment; and we think of the widow's two mites. Liberality is not measured by the amount given, but on the basis of the amount possessed. As it was in the days of these liberal souls, so it is today. "He that watereth shall be watered also himself."

Life Through Giving October 15

Sacrifice

Gather my saints together unto me; those that have made a covenant with me by sacrifice. Ps. 50:5.

Too many Christians serve only when it is convenient. Dr. G. A. Gordon tells of a young man who wrote his fiancée this letter:

"My Dearest,

I would climb the most rugged and precipitous mountain to see the light of your eyes. I would swim any body of water far wilder and wider than the Hellespont to sit at your side. I would go through tempests and torrential rains to kneel at your feet.

Yours forever—

P.S. I will call on you again tomorrow if it doesn't rain."

The young man did not realize the incongruity of the postscript, but neither do many Christians realize the incongruity of being unwilling to sacrifice for Jesus. How inconsistent is the Christian who stays away from communion service because of bad weather. At the church is a service commemorating the sacrifice of Christ upon the cross, reminding all of His sufferings to provide for their salvation; and at home is the lazy Christian, unwilling to weather a little storm to show his appreciation. What valiant soldiers of the cross such Christians are!

"I saw that some hardly know as yet what self-denial or sacrifice is. . . . But none will enter heaven without making a sacrifice. A spirit of self-denial and sacrifice should be cherished. Some have not sacrificed themselves, their own bodies, on the altar of God. They indulge in hasty, fitful temper, gratify their appetites, and attend to their own self-interest, regardless of the cause of God. Those who are willing to make any sacrifice for eternal life, will have it; and it will be worth suffering for. . . . The far more exceeding and eternal weight of glory swallows up everything and eclipses every earthly pleasure."—*Testimonies*, vol. 1, p. 126.

Life Through Giving   *October 16*

More Blessed to Give Than to Receive

I have shewed you all things, how that so labouring ye ought to support the weak, and to remember the words of the Lord Jesus, how he said, It is more blessed to give than to receive. Acts 20:35.

"I looked upon a sea, and lo, 'twas dead,
  Although by Hermon's snows and Jordan fed.
How came a fate so dire? The tale's soon told.
All that it got, it kept, and fast did hold.
All tributary streams found there their grave,
Because the sea received and never gave.

"O sea that's dead, teach me to know and feel
That selfish grasp and greed my doom will seal.
And help me, Lord, my best—myself to give.
That I may others bless—and like Thee live."
        —*Chapman College Review*

"The best that we have is not what we've got
  But that which we give away—
A gift to make easy another's lot—
  For it all comes back some day;
The love that we showered to left and right,
  The boost that we gave some heart
That wanted the dream and the song and the light,
  As it struggled to get a start.
We count our treasures in bank and chest,
  The things we have saved—they are there,
But they do not matter, they're not the best—
  Our best are the things we share."
        —Folger Kinsey in *Warp's Messenger*

Life Through Giving — October 17

GIVE TO ALL THEIR DUES

Render therefore to all their dues: tribute to whom tribute is due; custom to whom custom; fear to whom fear, honour to whom honour. Rom. 13:7.

This matter of giving involves more than simply giving to those less fortunate than we.

In giving to all their dues, we should remember that it involves not only the giving of material things but also respect and honor. In the very heart of the Ten Commandments there is the command, "Honour thy father and thy mother." We are told that this involves more than appears merely on the surface. "The fifth commandment requires children not only to yield respect, submission, and obedience to their parents, but also to give them love and tenderness, to lighten their cares, to guard their reputation, and to succor and comfort them in old age. It also enjoins respect for ministers and rulers, and for all others to whom God has delegated authority."—*Patriarchs and Prophets*, p. 308.

It is giving respect and honor, rather than coveting and demanding it, that brings the blessing. Seeking honor brings no happiness; for if it is sought for as an end in itself, it will be found to be only a shadow.

Alexander the Great, finding Diogenes in the journal house, asked him what he was seeking. He answered, "I am seeking for your father's bones and those of my slave, but I cannot find them because there is no difference between their dust."

Those who seek honor for themselves are often challenged.

"How well I whistle!" said the wind to the keyhole.

"Well, if that isn't rich," said the keyhole to the wind. "You mean how well I whistle!"

"Get some paper," said the old woman, "and stuff up the keyhole, and stop the draft." And so neither wind nor keyhole whistled any longer.—*Leisure Hours*.

Life Through Giving   *October 18*

Give Service

And whosoever of you will be the chiefest, shall be servant of all. For even the Son of man came not to be ministered unto, but to minister, and to give his life a ransom for many. Mark 10:44, 45.

William Stidger tells a beautiful Russian legend about a golden palace said to contain everything that would please the heart of a child. Children tried every day to earn the key to the palace. One day one youngster said to the doorkeeper, "I have brushed my hair until it shines like gold, and I have woven many yards of linen."

"These do not count," said the doorkeeper. "Do something each morning for somebody else."

So the child sought someone to help. She gave an old beggar all the precious coins she had been saving for many weeks. "Now," she thought, "I have earned the golden key," and ran to tell the doorkeeper. But the old man shook his head sadly. "Try again, child," he said.

She was disappointed until she saw a poor lame woman who was climbing a hill painfully and dragging a heavy bundle upon her back. "I'll help her," thought the child. "That will surely be enough to earn the key." This she did; and when she came to the doorkeeper, he said tearfully, "You must try again, child, try again."

By now the child was discouraged; and walking home slowly, decided to give up working for the key. It was impossible to earn it. Passing through a wooded section, she heard a faint cry and found a little puppy caught in a trap. "Oh, you poor little dog," she cried, and tried to unfasten the trap. She pulled until her fingers were torn and bleeding. When the little dog was free, she tore some bandages and bound the bruised paw and trudged homeward. Suddenly there appeared before her the old doorkeeper, holding out to her the key to the palace. "Oh," she said in astonishment, "the key is not for me. I did not help the little dog for the key. I forgot all about the key."

"Dear child," he said, "the key is for those who forget themselves."

Life Through Giving October 19

GIVE ENCOURAGEMENT

They helped every one his neighbour; and every one said to his brother, Be of good courage. Isa. 41:6.

Nothing we can give is more helpful than a word of encouragement.

Barnabas' real name was Joses, but the apostles surnamed him "Barnabas, (which is, being interpreted, The son of consolation)" (Acts 4:36). He was the kind of man who was always encouraging someone. Perhaps the best example of Barnabas' encouragement of others was that of the experience of John Mark, who, when things went hard on Paul's missionary tour, quit and went home. This disgusted the apostle Paul, who refused to take Mark with him on his next journey. Barnabas, however, saw something good in Mark and determined that he should go with them. The argument between Paul and Barnabas was so great that they finally separated. Barnabas took Mark. The encouragement given Mark brought forth fruit and later Paul said, "Bring Mark along, he is profitable for the ministry."

Many a young man would bury his talents were it not for encouragement. Occasionally, some do not respond to our efforts; but we need to remember that "beneath the forbidding exterior, there are good impulses that might be reached. Without a helping hand many would never recover themselves, but by patient, persistent effort they may be uplifted. Such need tender words, kind consideration, tangible help. They need that kind of counsel which will not extinguish the faint gleam of courage in the soul."—*The Ministry of Healing,* pp. 168, 169.

Let us be of good courage and encourage others along life's way.

Life Through Giving   *October 20*

GIVE HELP TO WEARY HEARTS

The Lord God hath given me the tongue of the learned, that I should know how to speak a word in season to him that is weary: he wakeneth morning by morning, he wakeneth mine ear to hear as the learned. Isa. 50:4.

Ours is the privilege of helping weary ones along the way and speaking words in season to those who are heavyhearted.

Arthur Tavani puts it this way:

> "Scientific skills are not mine to instill,
> Nor the gift of magic cadenzas to trill.
> My hands cannot draw from ivory keys
> The series of their confined harmonies.
> Nor may I achieve with brush and paint
> A glassy sea or represent a saint.
> But I pray for the gifts of a joyful smile
> For a gesture making life more worth while.
> The boon to lift care from those whose load
> Seems to bog them down along the road
> And the knack of turning a soul from pain
> To see the lovely light again.
> I would be artful at the core,
> Giving out treasures from my store,
> Seeing in every bird and flower
> The hidden essence of a greater power.
> And best of all I'd like the gift of pens
> To keep Him living in the hearts of friends."

Jesus always knew how to speak a word in season to the weary. Let us tell weary hearts of the invitation of the Master, "Come unto me, all ye that labour and are heavy laden, and I will give you rest. Take my yoke upon you, and learn of me; for I am meek and lowly in heart: and ye shall find rest unto your souls" (Matt. 11:28, 29).

Life Through Giving   *October 21*

GIVE LIBERTY TO CAPTIVES

The Spirit of the Lord God is upon me; because the Lord hath anointed me to preach good tidings unto the meek; he hath sent me to bind up the brokenhearted, to proclaim liberty to the captives, and the opening of the prison to them that are bound. Isa. 61:1.

The words of Patrick Henry, "Give me liberty, or give me death," are the outcry of every human heart. Because of this, Satan has labeled the forbidden path Freedom; but only Jesus can truly set men free. Those who have been captives of Satan, bound by his chains, and have been set free, know true happiness and joy, for there is no slavery like being mastered by an evil habit, and there is no prison house like sin.

A traveler came one day to some cages of beautiful birds that had recently been taken captive. They ruffled their sunny plumage on the wires, struggling to be free. The traveler was a wayworn man with sad eyes. As he watched the birds, tears appeared in his eyes; and turning to the owner, he asked the price of one. When told, he paid for it and set the prisoner free. This he did until every bird was soaring to the skies and singing on the wings of liberty. Bystanders stared in amazement. He explained, "I was once a captive myself."

We, too, can bring liberty to the captives of sin by bringing men and women to a knowledge of the truth that sets them free. We can open up these prison houses of sin by opening doors of opportunity to live in fellowship with Christ. Jesus always says, "I . . . set before you an open door, which no one is able to shut." Here is a freedom that is not temporary but eternal. First, of course, we must know this freedom ourselves. And how does it come? "Put your will on the side of Christ. Will to serve Him, and in acting upon His word you will receive strength. Whatever may be the evil practise, the master passion which through long indulgence binds both soul and body, Christ is able and longs to deliver. He will impart life to the soul that is 'dead in trespasses.' He will set free the captive that is held by weakness and misfortune and the chains of sin."—*The Ministry of Healing,* p. 85.

Life Through Giving   *October 22*

GIVE BEAUTY FOR ASHES

To appoint unto them that mourn in Zion, to give unto them beauty for ashes, the oil of joy for mourning, the garment of praise for the spirit of heaviness; that they might be called trees of righteousness, the planting of the Lord, that he might be glorified. Isa. 61:3.

So much of earthly beauty turns to ashes before our eyes. What is the perfect, most beautiful gift that we can give?

William Stidger tells of a queen who loved beautiful flowers and who was dying. "There's still one thing that can save her," said the wise men. "If the loveliest rose in the world—the symbol of the purest and brightest love—is brought to her before her eyes close, she will not die."

Poets sang of the love of youth and great heroes. "But they have not named the right flower," said the wise men.

Said one mother who brought her pretty baby to the bedside of the queen, "Here in the blooming cheeks of my sweet child is the loveliest rose of love that may be found."

"Lovely is this rose," replied the wise men, "but there is a lovelier."

Another exclaimed, "I saw the loveliest rose on the cheeks of a mother who carried her sick child in her arms, and wept, and prayed."

"Holy and wonderful is this white rose of a mother's grief," replied the wise men, "but it is not the one we seek."

"The loveliest rose in the world I saw at the altar of the Lord," said the bishop, "a young maiden that went to the Lord's table, and with all the love and purity of her spirit she looked up to heaven."

"May she be blessed," said the wise men, "but not one of you has yet named the loveliest rose in the world."

Just then the queen's little son came running into the room. "Mother," cried the boy, "only hear what I have read!" The child sat by the bedside and read from the Book of the Christ of the cross. A glow spread over the cheeks of the queen, and her eyes gleamed for joy. The loveliest rose sprang from the blood of Christ shed on the cross.

Life Through Giving   *October 23*

GIVE FREEDOM FROM HEAVY BURDENS

Is not this the fast that I have chosen? to loose the bands of wickedness, to undo the heavy burdens, and to let the oppressed go free, and that ye break every yoke? Isa. 58:6.

"Whether they know it or not, all are weary and heavy laden. All are weighed down with burdens that only Christ can remove. The heaviest burden that we bear is the burden of sin. If we were left to bear this burden, it would crush us. But the sinless One has taken our place. 'The Lord hath laid on Him the iniquity of us all.'

"He has borne the burden of our guilt. He will take the load from our weary shoulders."—*The Ministry of Healing,* p. 71. While we cannot forgive sin, we can give men freedom from sin by introducing them to Jesus.

Besides this burden of sin, there are many burdens men and women have made for themselves.

"There are many whose hearts are aching under a load of care because they seek to reach the world's standard. They have chosen its service, accepted its perplexities, adopted its customs. Thus their character is marred, and their life made a weariness. The continual worry is wearing out the life forces. Our Lord desires them to lay aside this yoke of bondage. He invites them to accept His yoke; He says, 'My yoke is easy, and My burden is light.'"—*Ibid.,* p. 481.

Here again we can help by encouraging such to surrender all that they have to God, for "the surrender of all our powers to God greatly simplifies the problem of life. It weakens and cuts short a thousand struggles with the passions of the natural heart."—*Messages to Young People,* p. 30.

"That ye break every yoke." Yoked up with Satan, we carry the heavy part of the load. The yoke does not fit, and the burden becomes wearisome. Yoked up with Christ, He carries the heavy part. The yoke fits; and the burden becomes light, interesting, and challenging.

Life Through Giving October 24

GIVE BREAD TO THE HUNGRY

Is it not to deal thy bread to the hungry, and that thou bring the poor that are cast out to thy house? when thou seest the naked, that thou cover him; and that thou hide not thyself from thine own flesh? Isa. 58:7.

Zelia M. Walters wrote the story of an unemployed man named Donley, who was forced by circumstances to beg. One evening a kindly woman gave him a dollar, saying, "Buy yourself food. And don't lose courage, even if things do look hard. There's a job for you somewhere. I hope you'll find it soon."

"Thanks, lady. You've given me a fresh start and a new heart. I'll never forget your kindness." He felt like a man, not a bum.

"You'll be eating Christ's bread. Pass it on," she said.

Donley spent fifty cents at a cheap eating place and resolved to save the rest for another day. But when he thought of "Christ's bread," he could not save it just for himself; and so he shared it with an old fellow who was hungry. During the meal, Donley noticed that the old man was wrapping up part of his bread in a paper napkin. "Saving some for tomorrow, hey?" he asked.

"No—no. There's a kid down my way. He's had tough luck and was crying when I left—hungry. I aim to give him the bread."

Christ's bread! A third guest would enjoy it. The two of them took the bread to the hungry boy who began to eat greedily, then stopped and called a frightened, lost dog, "Here, Jack, you can have half of it," said the boy. The child acted like a new boy then.

Donley turned and found the lost dog nosing at his leg. He patted it and found a collar around its neck with its owner's name on it. When he returned the dog, he was given ten dollars reward. Donley looked at the bill, half dazed. "I don't like to take it. I just wanted to do the dog a good turn."

"Take it along. What you did is worth more than that to me. And do you want a job? Come to my office tomorrow."

Life Through Giving October 25

HEALTH THROUGH GIVING

Then shall thy light break forth as the morning, and thine health shall spring forth speedily: and thy righteousness shall go before thee: the glory of the Lord shall be thy rereward. Isa. 58:8.

According to our text for today, right doing and health go hand in hand; and when you read this verse following the two preceding it you find that good health comes through giving. The wise man tells us that a merry heart doeth good like a medicine. Nothing gladdens the heart like helping someone, and the joy that comes from lifting another's burden is definitely conducive to good health. It is true that it is difficult to keep sweet with a sour stomach. Yet many a sour stomach is sour because a selfish heart seeks only to get and not to give, to receive and not to share.

Someone has described the selfish wealth seeker as follows:

> "To get his wealth, he spent his health;
> And then with might and main,
> He turned around and spent his wealth
> To get his health again."

In the end such a man has neither wealth nor health. What a contrast is this to the man described in our text! He has both health and a wealth that is eternal.

"One of the surest hindrances to the recovery of the sick is the centering of attention upon themselves. Many invalids feel that every one should give them sympathy and help, when what they need is to have their attention turned away from themselves, to think of and care for others. . . . If those who are suffering from ill health would forget self in their interest for others; if they would fulfill the Lord's command to minister to those more needy than themselves, they would realize the truthfulness of the prophetic promise, 'Then shall thy light break forth as the morning, and thine health shall spring forth speedily.'"—*The Ministry of Healing,* pp. 256, 258.

Life Through Giving October 26

Such as I Have Give I

Then Peter said, Silver and gold have I none; but such as I have give I thee: In the name of Jesus Christ of Nazareth rise up and walk. Acts 3:6.

Everywhere there are souls desperately in need of help we can give. To us the Master says, "Freely ye have received, freely give." And like Peter and John we can say, "Such as I have give I." What have we to give? Some are in a position to give money. Things material are not to be ignored. There are needs that money can satisfy. Let us be glad to share with others less fortunate than we our silver and gold.

Some can give medical attention. Everywhere people need attention physically. Jesus spent more time in healing than in preaching. God wants us to combine the work of physical healing with the teaching of the word—the meeting of spiritual needs.

All can help to meet basic spiritual needs. We can give release from the bands of wickedness, from fear, worry, guilt, grief, and anxiety. This release is needed even for physical healing. These burdens break down life's forces and block the forces of healing. We can give to others a sense of spiritual realities. To many God is not real, but we are. The personal touch is necessary; this we can give, to the glory of God. We can give men and women a sense of being of value. Jesus "taught all to look upon themselves as endowed with precious talents, which if rightly employed would secure for them eternal riches."—*The Desire of Ages,* p. 91.

We can take sinners by the hand and bid them rise up and walk and face the world again, praising God for forgiveness. In the name of Jesus Christ of Nazareth, we can give faith, hope, and love. We can give the bread of life to the hungry, the water of life to the thirsty, and the knowledge of salvation to those lost in sin. We can give Christian fellowship to the lonely, courage to a fellow traveler along the way. These, by the grace of God, we have received; and these we can give.

Life Through Giving *October 27*

GIVE SOFT ANSWERS

A soft answer turneth away wrath: but grievous words stir up anger. Prov. 15:1.

When we think of soft answers turning away wrath, there comes to mind Abigail's gentle apology that disarmed David's fury (1 Sam. 25:23-31), and Gideon's mild and modest words to the angry Ephraimites (Judges 8:2, 3).

Both of these noble answers contain the element of praise. Obviously, flattery is odious; but sincere compliments fall like sweet music upon the ear, soothing many a troubled spirit. All of us like appreciation, and we know from experience how soft words of appreciation turn away wrath, and how grievous words stir up anger.

Nowhere are soft words of this kind needed more than in the home. As Fulton Oursler puts it in the *Reader's Digest,* "the wife or husband who is alert to say the heartening thing at the right moment has taken out valuable marriage insurance." He relates that one night Sir Max Beerbohm went with his aging wife to a party in London. As they entered the room, he was ambushed by a hoard of stage and film beauties all eager to impress the great critic and caricaturist. Beerbohm turned to the lady on his arm, "My dear, let's find a quiet corner. You are looking so charming tonight that I want to talk to you alone."

Children, too, are hungry for reassurance and kindly appreciation. Oursler tells of a young mother whose little daughter taught her a lesson. The child often misbehaved, but one day she had been an especially good girl. That night, after the mother had tucked her in bed and started down the stairs, the little girl began sobbing. Turning back, the mother found her head buried in the pillow. Between sobs she asked, "Haven't I been a pretty good girl today?" That question went through the mother like a knife, and she said later, "I had been quick enough to correct her when she did wrong; but when she behaved, I had put her to bed without one word of appreciation."

Let us give soft answers to all we meet today.

Give Words in Due Season

A man hath joy by the answer of his mouth: and a word spoken in due season, how good is it! **Prov. 15:23.**

A father was reprimanding his little girl for some childish misdemeanor by scolding her. She interrupted him and said, "But, Daddy, I don't like to be unpraised."

All of us enjoy words of commendation and praise. We don't like to be "unpraised." Let us think of nice things to say to people before they are gone and it is too late.

"If with pleasure you are viewing any work a man is doing,
If you like him or you love him, tell him now;
Don't withhold your approbation till the parson makes oration
And he lies with snowy lilies on his brow;
No matter how you shout it he won't really care about it;
He won't know how many teardrops you have shed;
If you think some praise is due him now's the time to slip it to him,
For he cannot read his tombstone when he's dead.

"More than fame and more than money is the comment kind and sunny
And the hearty, warm approval of a friend.
For it gives to life its savor, and it makes you stronger, braver,
And it gives you heart and spirit to the end;
If he earns your praise—bestow it; if you like him let him know it;
Let the words of true encouragement be said;
Do not wait till life is over and he's underneath the clover,
For he cannot read his tombstone when he's dead."

—Berton Braley

Life Through Giving   *October 29*

Give Pleasant Words

Pleasant words are as an honeycomb, sweet to the soul, and health to the bones. **Prov. 16:24.**

Knowing how pleasant words affect us, why do we not speak them more often? And isn't it strange how ready we are to speak careless words?

" 'Twas but a word, a careless word,
    As thistledown, it seemed as light.
It paused a moment on the air,
    And onward then it winged its flight.

"Another lip caught up the word
    And breathed it with a haughty sneer.
It gathered weight as on it sped
    That careless word in its career.

"Then rumor caught the flying word,
    And busy gossip gave it weight
Until that little word became
    A vehicle of angry hate.

"And then another page of life
    With burning, scalding tears was blurred.
A load of care was heavier made.
    Its added weight, a careless word.

"How wildly throbbed that aching heart!
    Deep agony its fountain stirred.
It calmed; but bitter ashes mark
    The pathway of that careless word."

—*Selected*

Let us today speak only pleasant words, not careless ones!

Life Through Giving October 30

GIVE FRIENDSHIP

A man that hath friends must shew himself friendly: and there is a friend that sticketh closer than a brother. Prov. 18:24.

In the Talmud there is a story of a Jewish man who had three friends. One day he was asked to go to court to defend himself against certain charges. The Jew was in terror. He went to his three friends and asked them to accompany him to the palace. The first answered, "No, I can do no good by going, either to you or to myself."

The second said, "Well, it's a very dangerous thing to stand by your side. The emperor may charge you with some offence against the law. If I am seen with you, he might think I should share your guilt. However, I will go with you as far as the palace gate."

"No, that will not help. I can keep up my courage as far as the gate."

So he went to his third friend who said, "Fear not, I will go with you right to the emperor's presence. I will tell him that I know and trust you, and I will not leave you until you are delivered, as I hope you will be." He kept his word.

The real friend is ready to help to the utmost. William Stidger, who tells this story, also recounts how a small boy, lying on an operating table ready for a serious operation, asked his father to stay with him to hold his hand as the doctor gave him ether. Just before the ether mask was slipped over his face, he looked up at his father and said with trusting confidence, "You'll go all the way with me, won't you, Dad?"

The father replied with tears of understanding, "I sure will, son."

That is what true friendship really means—going all the way.

The friend that sticketh closer than a brother, even Jesus, our best friend, is a friend who goes all the way with us. He says, "I will never leave thee, nor forsake thee" (Heb. 13:5). "I am with you alway even unto the end of the world" (Matt. 28:20).

Let us cultivate His friendship, and like Him be a true friend to all—to the friendly and the friendless.

Life Through Giving *October 31*

GIVE LOVE AT ALL TIMES

A friend loveth at all times, and a brother is born for adversity. Prov. 17:17.

Three men came to Love the Lord, asking a gift of his white fire. It was not denied. "Take it, keep it, use it," said Love the Lord.

They answered joyfully, "Yea, Lord, this will we do."

The three went forth. One came to a dark valley full of men who groped with their hands, blindly seeking the way, for they had no light. The man took his fire and made a torch to guide them into a place of day. The second man's path led over a moor where the wind blew bitterly and the rocks stood like frozen iron. Here were men shivering with cold, huddling together; for they had no fire. And the man said, "There shall be fire." He set fagots to his fire, and it blazed up brightly. The folks warmed themselves and forgot the bitter wind. But the third man hid his fire safe within his heart so no one could come to it.

When the three came to the end of the way, Love the Lord said to the first man, "What of your fire?"

He replied, "I found folks struggling in darkness and made a torch to show them the way."

He in white said, "It is well. This fire shall never die."

The second said, "I gave shivering men my fire to live."

And he in white answered again, "This fire, too, shall never die."

Then the third answered boldly, "I have brought my fire safe. Lo, see, it is here in my heart." When Love the Lord opened that man's heart, inside it was a black char lying amid white ashes.

That which we keep for ourselves, we lose. Only that which we share is preserved. Let us share today with our brothers the blessings God has given us.

NOVEMBER

The Abundant Life *November 1*

LIFE MORE ABUNDANT

The thief cometh not, but for to steal, and to kill, and to destroy: I am come that they might have life, and that they might have it more abundantly. John 10:10.

The more abundant life is not mere existence, for life is what you are alive to. As Babcock puts it, "It is not length, but breadth. To be alive only to appetite, pleasure, pride, money-making and not to goodness and kindness, purity and love, history, poetry, music, flowers, stars, God and eternal hope, is to be all but dead."

" 'Life is so tame,' said one to me,
'Nowhere to go, nothing to see.
There's nothing new, no thrills at all.
How quickly life begins to pall.'

"Yet, even as he spoke these words,
I saw the sunset, heard the birds;
And there upon the busy street,
Watched youth and age adventure greet.

"Faith, hope, and love are found out there,
And courage conquers dark despair.
Each morning facing peace and strife,
We meet adventure, meeting life.

"Oh, you, who say the days are dull,
Open your eyes; for life is full
Of romance and surprises too,
Which God keeps offering to you."

—W. J. THOMPSON

The Abundant Life   *November 2*

A New Life

Therefore if any man be in Christ, he is a new creature: old things are passed away; behold, all things are become new. 2 Cor. 5:17.

The abundant life in Christ is a new life with a new heart, a new direction to one's going, a new outlook, new objectives, new hopes, and courage. For some, it comes about dramatically like the bursting of heavy showers from angry clouds, lashing the plains and making rivers flow. God seems to address their stubborn hearts as He addressed the Israelites at Sinai amidst lightning and the thunder of His voice. Their consciences are smitten with a sense of guilt while tears of penitence flow down their cheeks like little rivers. We think of the apostle Paul on the Damascus road.

For others it comes about quietly like the forming of gentle dews in the evening air, so silent as to escape the most delicate observation. These pass from the old to the new by almost imperceptible advances, as in the growth of a blade of grass. We think of Timothy, Paul's young companion, who from a child knew the Holy Scriptures. This change from the old to the new, which we call by various terms—regeneration, the new birth, or conversion—is accomplished by the Holy Spirit; and it can no more be explained than can the movements of the wind.

"A person may not be able to tell the exact time or place, or to trace all the circumstances in the process of conversion; but this does not prove him to be unconverted. By an agency as unseen as the wind, Christ is constantly working upon the heart. Little by little, perhaps unconsciously to the receiver, impressions are made that tend to draw the soul to Christ."—*The Desire of Ages*, p. 172.

Conversion comes when we gladly surrender to Jesus and decide to follow where the Spirit leads. We experience this new creation only when we decide for Christ. He, in love, draws us to Himself.

The Abundant Life   *November 3*

THE SPIRIT-FILLED LIFE

Not by might, nor by power, but by my spirit, saith the Lord of hosts. Zech. 4:6.

We can understand how the Spirit-filled life is the abundant life when we think of the work of the Holy Spirit. He transforms character, inspires true worship, helps those who seek Jesus to find Him, imparts a sound mind, quickens all the faculties, dignifies and ennobles, brings truth to remembrance, helps disciples in conflict with Satan's forces, defends every contrite soul, reveals the deep things of God, reveals Christ in His followers, cooperates in the preaching of the Word, qualifies men for church duties, bestows upon men the gifts promised in the gospel commission, and develops in all who receive Him the marvelous graces known as the fruits of the Spirit.

The Holy Spirit is like water—cleansing, refreshing, abundant, and freely given. He is like fire—purifying, illuminating, searching. He is like the wind—independent, powerful, observable in its effects, reviving. He is like oil—healing, comforting, illuminating, consecrating. He is like rain and dew—refreshing, abundant, imperceptible, penetrating. He is like a dove—gentle, meek, innocent, forgiving. He is like a voice—speaking, guiding, warning, teaching. And like a seal—impressing, securing, authenticating.

The abundant life is the Spirit-filled life. The contrast between a life that is filled with the Spirit and one that is not may be illustrated in the difference between two needles—one of which is magnetized. Outwardly they may look alike, yet one has hidden virtues that occasion will bring to light, and the other has not. The magnetic needle, rightly balanced, will enable a man to find his way across the trackless ocean. In like manner, so may the Spirit-filled life be a guide to many travelers on the ocean of life.

The Abundant Life   November 4

THE FRUITFUL LIFE

Herein is my Father glorified, that ye bear much fruit; so shall ye be my disciples. John 15:8.

Jesus is the vine; we are the branches, and God is the gardener who expects us to bear fruit. Even children can understand this illustration.

A Sabbath school teacher was trying to show the children that Jesus is the vine and that we as the branches derive all our strength and happiness from Him. A bright little fellow of eight years said, "Teacher, if Jesus is the vine, then the grown-up people are the branches, and we children are the little buds, aren't we?"

God expects us to bear, first of all, the fruits of the Spirit: love, joy, peace, long-suffering, gentleness, goodness, faith, meekness, temperance—beautiful Christian graces (Gal. 5:22, 23). Then He expects us to multiply our talents in service to bring others to Christ that they too may be grafted into the vine and bring forth fruit.

The Gardener makes every provision for our growth and spares no pains in caring for our needs. Pruning is necessary at times to keep us from bearing nothing but leaves. Our heavenly Father deals with us somewhat after the manner of an ancient painter with his pupil. The young artist had produced a picture of much merit, which was greatly admired by all. His heart was swelled with vanity. He laid aside his palette and pencil and sat daily before his easel admiring the product of his own genius. One morning he found his beautiful creation wiped from the canvas. He wept bitterly. His master appeared and said, "I have done this for your benefit. The picture was ruining you."

"How so?" demanded the pupil.

"Because in the admiration of your own talents, you were losing your love of the art itself. Take your pencil, and try again."

The youth dried his tears, seized his pencil, and produced a masterpiece, which but for this severe trial he would in all probability never have executed.

The Abundant Life   *November 5*

THE PURPOSEFUL LIFE

But Daniel purposed in his heart that he would not defile himself with the portion of the king's meat, nor with the wine which he drank: therefore he requested of the prince of the eunuchs that he might not defile himself. Dan. 1:8.

In business, in research, in affairs of state, in military operations, purpose and decision are important. So in life. Only men of purpose and decision ever become great and really successful.

A king desired to discover which of his three sons was most worthy to succeed him. He took them, armed with their bows and arrows, to a field in which a vulture sat on a tree. Each son was asked what he saw. The first replied, "I see grass, clouds, the sky, a river, a tree, and a bird." The second said, "I see horses, the ground, a field of wheat, a tree, and a bird." The third replied, "I see the point where the wing joins the body"; and immediately he lifted his bow and arrow and killed the bird. Needless to say, he became his father's successor.

Esther Baldwin York, in *Food for Tho't,* brings us this story and then says, "When there is a job to be done, there must be a focusing on the thing to be achieved. There must also be a straightforward, unsullied, working toward it. Choose a clear goal and a clean arrow always. There is no other way to real success."

If we would live the abundant life, we must have a purpose and cultivate the ability to make decisions wisely and promptly.

"Long delays tire the angels. It is even more excusable to make a wrong decision sometimes than to be continually in a wavering position; to be hesitating, sometimes inclined in one direction, then in another. More perplexity and wretchedness result from this hesitating and doubting than from sometimes moving too hastily.... God requires promptness of action. Delays, doubtings, hesitation, and indecision frequently give the enemy every advantage.... Prompt and decisive action at the right time will gain glorious triumphs."—*Gospel Workers,* p. 134.

The Abundant Life   *November 6*

THE COMMITTED LIFE

Commit thy way unto the Lord; trust also in him; and he shall bring it to pass. Ps. 37:5.

The abundant life is the committed life. Jesus Christ is the supreme example of the committed life. Of Him we read, "Who did no sin, neither was guile found in his mouth: who, when he was reviled, reviled not again; when he suffered, he threatened not; but committed himself to him that judgeth righteously" (1 Peter 2:22, 23).

The word *commit* can also be translated *roll.* "Roll thy way upon the Lord." The same thought is expressed in Psalm 55:22: "Cast thy burden upon the Lord, and he shall sustain thee." Jesus lived in constant dependence upon God.

"To the secret place of the Most High, under the shadow of the Almighty, men now and then repair; they abide for a season, and the result is manifest in noble deeds; then their faith fails, the communion is interrupted, and the lifework marred. But the life of Jesus was a life of constant trust, sustained by continual communion; and His service for heaven and earth was without failure or faltering. As a man He supplicated the throne of God, till His humanity was charged with a heavenly current that connected humanity with divinity. Receiving life from God, He imparted life to men."—*Education,* pp. 80, 81.

The abundant life is the life completely consecrated to God and lived in communion with the Most High. "Consecrate yourself to God in the morning; make this your very first work. Let your prayer be, 'Take me, O Lord, as wholly Thine. I lay all my plans at Thy feet. Use me today in Thy service. Abide with me, and let all my work be wrought in Thee.' This is a daily matter. . . . Surrender all your plans to Him, to be carried out or given up as His providence shall indicate. Thus day by day you may be giving your life into the hands of God, and thus your life will be molded more and more after the life of Christ."
—*Steps to Christ* (Pocket ed.), p. 70.

The Abundant Life   *November 7*

THE FORWARD-LOOKING LIFE

I press toward the mark for the prize of the high calling of God in Christ Jesus. **Phil. 3:14.**

The abundant life is the forward-looking, the onward-going, the upward-pressing life. The apostle Paul describes it this way: "I do not consider myself to have 'arrived' spiritually, nor do I consider myself already perfect. But I keep going on, grasping ever more firmly that purpose for which Christ grasped me. My brothers, I do not consider myself to have fully grasped it even now. But I do concentrate on this: I leave the past behind and with hands outstretched to whatever lies ahead I go straight for the goal—my reward the honour of being called by God in Christ" (Phil. 3:13, 14, Phillips' translation).

A color sergeant of the brigade that captured Mission Ridge pressed the standard to his blouse and pushed for the top, hoping to be the first to plant his colors there. Near the top he was fatally wounded, but he could think of nothing but the accomplishment of his noble purpose. He was asked, "Sergeant, where did they hit you?"

" 'Most up the ridge," he replied.

"I mean where did the ball strike you?"

"Within twenty yards of the top. Almost up." His arm and shoulder were fearfully mangled by a shell. The shades of death were falling upon him, but his eye was still upon the prize, and at the last he murmured, "Almost up, almost up." Here was a soldier so interested in pushing on to the top that he measured all experiences, even his being wounded, in terms of the progress he was making. This should be true of every Christian soldier. He should be so eager for the prize of the high calling of God that he measures all human experience in terms of the progress he is making toward reaching this goal.

Akbar, the ancient Mogul emperor, said, "I have lived a long time, but I have yet to see a man lost on a straight road." Pressing straight ahead toward our goal, "let us run with patience the race that is set before us, looking unto Jesus" (Heb. 12:1, 2).

The Abundant Life   *November 8*

The Persevering Life

But he that shall endure unto the end, the same shall be saved. **Matt. 24:13.**

The abundant life is the persevering life—the life that endures unto the end, the life that doesn't give up.

Someone has said, "You cannot keep a determined man from success. Place stumbling blocks in his way, and he takes them for steppingstones and on them will climb to greatness. Take away his money, and he makes spurs of his poverty to urge him on. . . . Lock him up in a dungeon, and he composes the immortal *Pilgrim's Progress.* Put him in a cradle in the log cabin in the wilderness of America, and in a few years you will find him in the capital at the head of the greatest nation on the globe."

One night Robert Bruce was driven into hiding. Six times he had gone down in failure before his foes and he was despairing of success. One day he saw a spider trying to fix its web on a beam. Six times it failed. Bruce arose saying, "Now shall this spider teach me what I am to do, for I also have failed six times." The seventh time the spider succeeded. Bruce left his hiding place, rallied his followers, met and defeated an English garrison, and finally became master of well-nigh all of Scotland.

Perseverance to the end brings success, not only in the secular affairs of life, but also in the spiritual as well. Only those who endure unto the end shall be saved. That which enables us to endure, more than anything else, is looking forward to the joy at the end of the journey. Paul said, "Looking unto Jesus . . . who for the joy that was set before him endured the cross." "We need to keep ever before us this vision of things unseen. It is thus that we shall be able to set a right value on the things of eternity and the things of time."—*The Ministry of Healing,* p. 508. And this vision will enable us to endure unto the end.

The Abundant Life   *November 9*

THE LIFE WITH EVER-INCREASING INSIGHTS

But the path of the just is as the shining light, that shineth more and more unto the perfect day. Prov. 4:18.

The abundant life is a life of growth in grace and in knowledge. Someone has said, "The acorn does not become an oak in a day. The ripened scholar was not made such by a single lesson. The well-trained soldier was not a raw recruit yesterday. It is not one touch of the artist's pencil that produces a finished painting. There are always months between seedtime and harvest. Even so the path of the just is like the shining light that shineth more and more unto the perfect day."

No mediocre attainments will satisfy. A friend called on Michelangelo, who was finishing a statue. Sometime afterward he called again and the sculptor was still at his work. His friend, looking at the figure, exclaimed, "Have you been idle since I saw you last?"

"By no means," he replied, "I have retouched this part and polished that, I have softened this feature and brought out that muscle. I have given more expression to this lip and more energy to this limb."

"Well, well," said his friend, "all these are trifles."

"It may be so," replied Michelangelo, "but recollect that trifles make perfection and perfection is no trifle."

Pliny informs us that Zeuxis once painted a boy holding a dish full of grapes. It was so well done that the birds were deceived and flew to the grapes to peck at them. Zeuxis, however, was dissatisfied with the picture, for said he, "Had I painted the boy as well as he ought to have been painted, the birds would have been afraid to touch the grapes." An ordinary painter would have been satisfied with the picture of grapes that deceived even the birds. Let us not be satisfied with being ordinary Christians. Let us remember that the abundant life is the life that becomes more and more like the Master.

Let us not be satisfied "till we all come in the unity of the faith, and of the knowledge of the Son of God, unto a perfect man, unto the measure of the stature of the fulness of Christ" (Eph. 4:13).

The Abundant Life   *November 10*

THE CONFIDENT LIFE

Being confident of this very thing, that he which hath begun a good work in you will perform it until the day of Jesus Christ. Phil. 1:6.

There is a confidence, an assurance, about the abundant life in Christ that gives a security not known apart from Him. The question may be asked, "What if after I have denied myself all the pleasures of this life in order to gain the life hereafter I should lose out at the last minute and not make it? I will have had neither the joy of this life nor the privilege of enjoying the next. Why not be sure of this one, at least? It seems too risky a business to stake all you have on something that is so far in the future and so intangible, especially when the odds are against you. Can a person be sure of life eternal?" This is a reasonable question, for the insecurity that comes from uncertainty is not conducive to peace of mind.

To give us this assurance, Paul reminds us of God's promise to Abraham. Among men in those days it was "customary to swear by something greater than themselves. And if a statement is confirmed by an oath, that is the end of all quibbling. So in this matter, God, wishing to show beyond doubt that His plan was unchangeable, confirmed it with an oath. So that by two utterly immutable things, the word of God and the oath of God, Who cannot lie, we who are refugees from this dying world might have a source of strength, and might grasp the hope that He holds out to us. This hope we hold as the utterly reliable anchor for our souls, fixed in the very certainty of God Himself in Heaven, where Jesus has already entered on our behalf" (Heb. 6:13-20, Phillips' translation).

We can rest secure in His promise, "being confident of this very thing, that he which hath begun a good work in you will perform it until the day of Jesus Christ." It is no wonder Paul could say, "For I know whom I have believed, and am persuaded that he is able to keep that which I have committed unto him against that day" (2 Tim. 1:12). May this assurance be yours and mine today.

The Abundant Life   *November 11*

A LIFE OF LIBERTY

So shall I keep thy law continually for ever and ever. And I will walk at liberty: for I seek thy precepts. Ps. 119:44, 45.

The abundant life is a life of liberty within law. A strange combination to the superficial observer is this idea of liberty and law. It would seem that the two are opposites. Surely there is no liberty where there are restrictions, rules, and regulations, and laws that say "Thou shalt not." The truth is that where there is no law, there is no liberty, and laws make freedom possible. So true is this, that James calls the law of God "the law of liberty." He says, "So speak ye, and so do, as they that shall be judged by the law of liberty" (James 2:12).

Suppose you are driving in the heart of the business section of a large city during rush hour. You are late to an appointment several miles away. Traffic regulations, yellow or white lines, red and green lights bring you to halt every little while. Many others are also in a hurry to get home. Suppose you should decide that you wanted to be free of all these restrictions that interfere with your journey, and you disregard them. Let us suppose too, that others think likewise. How long do you think you would be free? Not very long. In a few minutes you would be hopelessly tied up in a traffic jam and the chances are you would not get home for hours. The very laws and restrictions you so detest as interfering with your freedom are the factors that make it possible for you to be free to go where you will.

This principle applies in all areas of life. You must say No to some desires to be able to say Yes to them later on. The expression, "thou shalt not," can be both negative and positive. It is negative when thought of as forbidding some act, such as: "Don't you dare smoke another cigarette or I'll whip you." It can be positive in that same situation when thought of as release from the evil habit which has you so in its grip that you are a slave. Being set free, you will not be a slave to habit any longer. Wondrous freedom in Christ! Let us each day seek God's precepts, for only thus can we walk at liberty.

The Abundant Life   *November 12*

FREE FROM SERVING SIN

Being then made free from sin, ye became the servants of righteousness. **Rom. 6:18.**

"You *belong* to the power which you choose to obey, whether you choose sin, whose reward is death, or God, obedience to Whom means the reward of righteousness. Thank God that you, who were at one time the servants of sin, honestly responded to the impact of Christ's teaching when you came under its influence. Then, released from the service of sin, you entered the service of righteousness" (Rom. 6:16-18, Phillips' translation). "Sin *pays* its servants: the wage is death. But God *gives* to those who serve Him: His free gift is eternal life through Jesus Christ our Lord" (verse 23).

Sin is a hard taskmaster and very deceptive.

Sin makes you think you see a cup of cool, refreshing drink on a hot day, but when you drink it you discover it is a cup of poison.

Sin makes you think you see a rare and beautiful gem, but when you grasp it you discover it is only a bubble.

Sin makes you think you are having a wonderful time with bright lights and a thrill for a night, but the next morning it all turns to ashes in your mouth. Sin pays, but its wages are death.

Jesus offers you a cool refreshing draft of the water of life, which, when you drink it, quenches your thirst with a satisfaction that surpasses anything the world has to offer.

Jesus offers you the pearl of great price, and as you grasp it you find it is genuine and more costly and valuable than you ever dreamed. And what is more, it is yours.

Jesus offers you joy and happiness unshadowed, that reach down deep into your heart, not just for a night but for eternity—joy and happiness that will increase with the passing ages.

"Choose you this day whom ye will serve." Serving Jesus, you will find yourself free from the law of sin and death; free from the tyranny of Satan and selfishness; free to be what you can be by God's grace.

The Abundant Life *November 13*

STAND FAST IN THE LIBERTY

Stand fast therefore in the liberty wherewith Christ hath made us free, and be not entangled again with the yoke of bondage. **Gal. 5:1.**

A man who once knows the abundant life of freedom in Christ and then becomes entangled again in sin, is like a dog who returns to his vomit. Not a pretty picture, this. The many who become thus entangled, Paul says, "crucify to themselves the Son of God afresh, and put him to an open shame" (Heb. 6:6).

Dr. Guthrie tells of a Roman army that lost courage and resolved to retreat. The general reasoned with his soldiers. He appealed to their love of country, to their honor, and to their oaths. By all that could revive a fainting heart he sought to animate their courage and to shake their resolution. Though they trusted, admired, and loved him, his appeals were all in vain. They were not to be moved. They were carried away as by a panic and they faced around to retreat.

It happened that they had just forced a mountain pass, had just cleared a gorge where the way between two great rocks on the one side and the foaming river on the other was but a footpath broad enough for the step of a single man. As the last resort, the general laid himself down there saying, "If you will retreat, it is over this body you go, trampling me to death beneath your feet." No foot advanced. The flight was arrested. The soldiers could face the foe, but they would not mangle beneath their feet one who loved them and had often led their ranks to victory, sharing like a common soldier all the hardships of the campaign and ever foremost in the fight. The sight was one to inspire them with decision. Hesitating no longer to advance, they wheeled around to resume their march, deeming it better to meet sufferings and to endure death itself than to trample underfoot their devoted and patriotic leader.

Let all who are tempted to turn back realize that Jesus who loves us is the Great General who, as it were, lays Himself down on our path; and in order to turn back we must trample Him under our feet.

The Abundant Life *November 14*

AS FREE, NOT MISUSING LIBERTY

As free, and not using your liberty for a cloke of maliciousness, but as the servants of God. 1 Peter 2:16.

Let us think today about the misuse of freedom. As a young fellow was running down the street with a long pole on his shoulder, he rounded a corner in a hurry, and the end of his pole struck a man on the nose. "What do you think this is?" demanded the man who was hurt.

"Well, it's a free country, isn't it?" said the runner.

"Yes, but your liberty ends where my nose begins."

To seek personal satisfaction and gain at the expense of another simply because I am legally free to do so, is truly a misuse of freedom.

"But," says one, "surely I can do as I please if I am only hurting myself." This is false reasoning. No one lives to himself. Take, for example, the matter of eating. Surely that is a personal matter, and in this area one should be free to do as he pleases. It is no one's business what I eat. A little thought reveals the fact that what you eat affects your health. If you become ill, you then immediately become an object of someone's care. Many a child has caused countless sleepless nights for his parents by what he ate. This is not limited to the physical. Many times decisions that bring heartache to loved ones are thought to be of no concern to others.

Insisting on one's rights in certain circumstances may be a misuse of liberty. "Well, I had the right of way, didn't I?" says someone in an auto accident. Maybe he did, but it is very possible to have the right of way and still get killed. I may have the right to foreclose a mortgage on a widow, but that might not be the Christian thing to do in the light of the golden rule.

Then too, our influence must be considered. I may feel free to do certain things on the Sabbath day that are not clearly defined in the minds of others; but if my action is a stumbling block for someone else, I had better reconsider. Let us not misuse our liberty.

The Abundant Life   *November 15*

THAT YOUR JOY MIGHT BE FULL

These things have I spoken unto you, that my joy might remain in you, and that your joy might be full. John 15:11.

The story is told of a little girl who was riding with her daddy in the country for the first time. She had heard about cows and had seen a few pictures of them, but this was the first time she had actually seen one face to face. They stopped to look more closely at one that was grazing in the field; and finally the little girl said to her daddy, "Daddy, that cow must be a Christian."

"Why do you say that?"

"Well, because she has such a long face."

This probably never happened, and perhaps no little girl ever said such a thing; but it is true that many have thought that Christianity makes people gloomy, and that if you were having a lot of fun as a Christian, it was probably wrong. This is not the Christianity of Jesus. He said, "These things have I spoken unto you, that my joy might remain in you, and that your joy might be full."

"Whatever is done to the glory of God is to be done with cheerfulness, not with sadness and gloom. There is nothing gloomy in the religion of Jesus. If by a mournful attitude Christians give the impression that they have been disappointed in their Lord, they misrepresent His character, and put arguments into the mouth of His enemies. Though in words they may claim God as their Father, yet in gloom and sorrow they present to the world the aspect of orphans.

"Christ desires us to make His service appear attractive, as it really is."—*Thoughts From the Mount of Blessing* (1956), p. 88.

"The life in which the fear of the Lord is cherished will not be a life of sadness and gloom. It is the absence of Christ that makes the countenance sad, and the life a pilgrimage of sighs. . . . Christ dwelling in the soul is a wellspring of joy. For all who receive Him, the very keynote of the word of God is rejoicing."—*Christ's Object Lessons,* p. 162.

SERVE THE LORD WITH GLADNESS

Serve the Lord with gladness: come before his presence with singing. Ps. 100:2.

Once an artisan, who served a rich Eastern master, became indebted to an unmerciful creditor and was threatened with slavery. It was impossible for the poor man to pay the debt, and it worried him so that his work was falling off every week. One day his master spoke about this to the steward. "Why, sir," the steward replied, "that poor fellow cannot possibly do good work. He cannot manage his tools, for his hands tremble, nor can he see well what he is doing, since his eyes are often filled with tears. He often sits down as if in despair and sighs heavily, and sometimes he makes himself drunk to forget his misery. A heavy debt is pressing upon him, sir; and until it is paid, he will not be able to do one good piece of work."

"Tell him, then, that I have paid his debt," the generous master said. The steward delivered the message. You can imagine the joy of that poor man as from that moment fresh vigor was poured into his veins; his hands trembled no more, nor were his eyes dimmed with tears. He swung his hammer with a will. He served his master with gladness, and his heart was filled with singing.

Why should not this be our experience? Our debt, too, has been paid, and we have a generous, loving master to serve.

A man who was converted met one of his old associates one day, and the latter remarked, "I hear you have given up all your pleasures."

"No," replied the other, "I never knew what pleasure was till now."

> "This is my Father's world;
> Why should my heart be sad?
> The Lord is King; let the heavens ring!
> God reigns; let the earth be glad."
>
> —MALTBIE D. BABCOCK

The Abundant Life   *November 17*

HOW GOOD AND HOW PLEASANT

Behold, how good and how pleasant it is for brethren to dwell together in unity! Ps. 133:1.

The Christian life is a life of joy and gladness because of the fellowship that Christian men and women can experience. Psalm 133 is a song that was sung by the Israelites on pilgrimage to Jerusalem to attend the annual feasts. The widely separated members of Israel thus felt themselves united with each other and they sang with joy in their hearts. The fellowship they enjoyed is said to be like precious ointment on the head.

The anointing oil of the sanctuary was an ointment composed of many precious ingredients—myrrh, cinnamon, sweet calamus, and cassia with olive oil as a base—and it was said to have had a very delightful fragrance. It was a rich perfume, rather than a musty oil, as we Westerners might imagine. How like that is the fragrance of brotherhood and fellowship! We are drawn to a circle where the atmosphere of peace, unity, and concord prevails much as we are attracted by the fragrance of a rose, a lilac, or carnations. Fellowship is like the dew of Hermon descending upon the mountains of Zion—vital, refreshing, life giving, absolutely essential to thirsty plants. Without it heat would become intense and the ground hard; vegetation would perish.

Life without fellowship is dry and hard. Every thirsty soul longs for the comradeship that fellowship in Christ supplies abundantly. There is nothing exclusive about the dew. No one can keep the dew wholly unto himself, for it falls upon all. So where the spirit of Christian fellowship exists all are blessed with joy and gladness.

Note this little song in Moffatt's translation, "How rare and lovely it is, this fellowship of those who meet together!—sweet as the sacred oil poured on the head, that flows down Aaron's beard, down to the very collar of his robe; vital as dew of Hermon, that falls on the hills of Sion. For in this fellowship has the Eternal fixed the blessing of an endless life" (Ps. 133:1-3).

The Abundant Life   *November 18*

WITH JOY SHALL YE DRAW WATER

Therefore with joy shall ye draw water out of the wells of salvation. Isa. 12:3.

He who seeks to satisfy his soul's thirst in the world apart from Christ, is like a man endeavoring to satisfy his thirst by putting an empty cup to his lips. Some, despising such a one for his ignorance, have thought to satisfy their own thirst by using a variety of golden and bejeweled empty cups. In the search for happiness apart from Christ, the soul only turns from one empty cup to another. Apart from Christ there is nothing that really quenches the thirst. The dull and heavy soul may be content with an empty appearance of happiness, but as Dr. Salter puts it, "Let the wit, the great scholar, the fine genius, the great statesman, the polite gentlemen, lay all their heads together, and they can only show you more and various empty appearances of happiness. Give them all the world into their hands, let them cut and carve as they please, they can only make a greater variety of empty cups. For, search as deep and look as far as you will, there is nothing here to be found that is nobler and greater than high eating and drinking and rich dress and applause and vanity, unless you look for it in the wisdom and laws of religion."

The Christian can with joy draw the water of life from the wells of salvation and find it satisfying to the depths of his soul.

We are told that travelers in the desert, dying of thirst, cry in vain for water and see visions of fountains and groves rising before them—a mirage of oases, with lakes of cool crystal water—but they are only optical illusions. So it is in a life apart from Christ. But in Christ Jesus we have the invitation to come to the waters and drink. "The water that I shall give him shall be in him a well of water springing up into everlasting life" (John 4:14).

There is real joy in drawing water from the wells of salvation—not simply a mirage but a reality, a wellspring of life, a well of water from which you can continue to draw with increasing satisfaction.

The Abundant Life   *November 19*

BE YE THANKFUL

And let the peace of God rule in your hearts, to the which also ye are called in one body; and be ye thankful. **Col. 3:15.**

To ask a man to *be* something is more difficult than to say, "Do something" or "say something" or even "give something." To merely say, "Thanks," when you do not mean it, is either sarcasm or hypocrisy. True thanksgiving must be the outflowing of gratitude and praise from the heart. Some may say, "How can I be thankful when I feel I have nothing for which to be thankful? Be thankful? Not for what I've gone through!" Shall we be two-faced about this matter of thanksgiving?

The unthankful man is blind. Of the factors that blind us—attitudes of mind that destroy the spirit of gratitude—the most common is self-centeredness. The self-centered person considers all blessings as due him. He says, "I had it coming to me." He can never be thankful for what he has, because someone else has more. This self-centeredness manifests itself at times in self-pity, and eclipses all blessings. No state is more destructive of gratitude than self-pity. It is also manifested in a critical attitude toward others—an attitude that always sees an ulterior motive in every act of kindness. "Why should I be thankful? He's doing that just because he expects a raise!" "Well, the only reason he helped me out is that he's trying to make a hit with my sister."

Another gratitude-destroying factor is a false sense of values. He who evaluates life in terms of physical and material prosperity is ungrateful if he is poor, or ill, or in trouble. "Why should I be thankful? We lost everything we had in the fire, and through some technicality there is no insurance." If we could view present experiences in terms of tomorrow and the over-all picture, we might be extremely grateful.

Only when self is crucified and Christ is enthroned within can we truly be thankful. Instead of pitying self, the Christian rejoices in a new self-confidence dedicated to service; and this true sense of personal worth fills one with humility and gratitude in being able to serve. Then the goal is not getting, but giving with a thankful heart.

The Abundant Life   *November 20*

GIVING THANKS ALWAYS

Giving thanks always for all things unto God and the Father in the name of our Lord Jesus Christ. Eph. 5:20.

In a time of great despondency among the New England settlers, it was proposed to proclaim a fast. An old farmer arose, spoke of their provoking Heaven with their complaints, reviewed their mercies, showed that they had much to be thankful for, and moved that instead they should appoint a day of thanksgiving. Ever since, we in the U.S.A. have had Thanksgiving Day.

We should give thanks always and not just for the things that make us happy, but for all things; because in the end all things work together for good to those who love the Lord.

"And is this then the only way,
    The feasting and the fun,
Just to give thanks for one short day
    Then feel that all is done?

"The Pilgrims feasted long ago,
    The bitter with the sweet;
Theirs was a thanks we cannot know,
    Yet faith made it complete.

"We walk the road their courage blazed.
    We reap what they have sown;
Yet can we praise as they have praised,
    For freedom, faith, and hope?

"Then thank the Giver all the way
    For sun and shadow too.
You'll find that then Thanksgiving Day
    Will last the whole year through."

—*Author Unknown*

The Abundant Life   *November 21*

MAGNIFY GOD WITH THANKSGIVING

I will praise the name of God with a song, and will magnify him with thanksgiving. Ps. 69:30.

Is it not true that we are more pleased with sincere expressions of gratitude than we are with actions and gifts prompted by ulterior motives? Our heavenly Father, too, is far more interested in thanksgiving and gratitude than in the most expensive of sacrifices and burnt offerings. The psalmist goes on to say, "This also shall please the Lord better than an ox or bullock that hath horns and hoofs. The humble shall see this, and be glad: and your heart shall live that seek God" (Ps. 69:31, 32).

This being true, no matter what our station in life, we can be assured that through praise and thanksgiving we please and magnify our heavenly Father.

How can we magnify God? We are admonished, "Forgetting our own difficulties and troubles, let us praise God for an opportunity to live for the glory of His name. Let the fresh blessings of each new day awaken praise in our hearts for these tokens of His loving care. When you open your eyes in the morning, thank God that He has kept you through the night. Thank Him for His peace in your heart. Morning, noon, and night, let gratitude as a sweet perfume ascend to heaven."—*The Ministry of Healing,* p. 253.

Note again: "The revelation of His own glory in the form of humanity will bring heaven so near to men that the beauty adorning the inner temple will be seen in every soul in whom the Saviour dwells. Men will be captivated by the glory of an abiding Christ. And in currents of praise and thanksgiving from the many souls thus won to God, glory will flow back to the great Giver."—*Christ's Object Lessons,* p. 420.

Could this be accomplished by the spirit of thanksgiving? May God help us today to praise the name of the Lord with a song and to magnify Him with thanksgiving.

The Abundant Life   *November 22*

ENTER INTO HIS GATES WITH THANKSGIVING

Enter into his gates with thanksgiving, and into his courts with praise: be thankful unto him, and bless his name. **Ps. 100:4.**

There is so much to be thankful for. In fact, we are told, "In every thing give thanks: for this is the will of God in Christ Jesus concerning you" (1 Thess. 5:18). John Oxenham prayed:

> "For all things beautiful, and good, and true;
> For things that seemed not good yet turned to good;
> For all the sweet compulsions of Thy will
> That chastened, tried, and wrought us to Thy shape;
> For things unnumbered that we take of right,
> And value first when they are withheld;
> For light and air; sweet sense of sound and smell;
> For ears to hear the heavenly harmonies;
> For eyes to see the unseen in the seen;
> For visions of the Worker in the work;
> For hearts to apprehend Thee everywhere;—
> We thank Thee, Lord."

Praise and thanksgiving have therapeutic value. "Nothing tends more to promote health of body and of soul than does a spirit of gratitude and praise. . . . It is a law of nature that our thoughts and feelings are encouraged and strengthened as we give them utterance. While words express thoughts, it is also true that thoughts follow words. If we would give more expression to our faith, rejoice more in the blessings that we know we have,—the great mercy and love of God, —we should have more faith and greater joy. . . . Then let us educate our hearts and lips to speak the praise of God for His matchless love. Let us educate our souls to be hopeful and to abide in the light shining from the cross of Calvary."—*The Ministry of Healing,* pp. 251-253.

The Abundant Life   *November 23*

Let Us Sing Unto the Lord

O come, let us sing unto the Lord: let us make a joyful noise to the rock of our salvation. Ps. 95:1.

The abundant life is the life filled with songs of praise, thanksgiving, hope, faith, and love. "Let praise and thanksgiving be expressed in song. When tempted, instead of giving utterance to our feelings, let us by faith lift up a song of thanksgiving to God. . . . Song is a weapon that we can always use against discouragement. As we thus open the heart to the sunlight of the Saviour's presence, we shall have health and His blessing."—*The Ministry of Healing,* p. 254. And why? "When heaven comes in touch with the earth, there is music and song—'thanksgiving, and the voice of melody.' "—*Education,* p. 161.

Men have received great blessings through songs. As a burglar, discouraged and dissatisfied, was walking the streets of a city he heard a gospel song that led him into a hall. As he listened to the song and the message that followed, new light dawned upon his soul; and he became a new man in Christ. Later he said, "It was the song that drew me in." Songs of faith and hope and love draw men to Christ.

A minister received a call to work in a certain city. He hesitated to accept since there were so many problems involved and he felt very inadequate. Early one morning as he thought about the difficulties he heard a neighbor whistling in his garden. On the wings of the melody came these words:

> "He leadeth me! O blessed thought!
> O words with heavenly comfort fraught!
> Whate'er I do, where'er I be,
> Still 'tis God's hand that leadeth me."

This minister always felt that God inspired that song to give him the courage necessary to make the right decision.

May God give us a song in our hearts today.

The Abundant Life — *November 24*

FORSAKE NOT THE ASSEMBLING OF YOURSELVES TOGETHER

Not forsaking the assembling of ourselves together, as the manner of some is; but exhorting one another: and so much the more, as ye see the day approaching. **Heb. 10:25.**

The abundant life is a life of Christian fellowship through which life's greatest joys are experienced, and life's greatest blessings are mediated. It is when fellowship is broken that most of life's problems arise and that personality ills develop. A man at war with himself, with others, and with God, soon destroys himself. A man at peace with himself, with others, and with God, finds that through fellowship God has brought many blessings to mankind. This being true, no therapy is more effective than the restoration of fellowship.

Psychiatrists and psychologists are finding group therapy very much worth while in restoring patients to mental and emotional health. The value of meeting together and sharing in group discussions and in worship cannot be overemphasized. That's why Paul tells us, "Let us bestow thought on one another with a view to arousing one another to brotherly love and right conduct; not neglecting—as some habitually do—to meet together, but encouraging one another, and doing this all the more since you can see the Day of Christ drawing near" (Heb. 10: 24, 25, Weymouth's translation).

Some may say, "I can be a good Christian without going to church." But Christian association in worship keeps aglow within our hearts the warmth of Christian love. Taking advantage of church services and activities contributes immeasurably to living the abundant life.

A story is told of a New England pastor who visited a missing parishioner in his home, and found him sitting before an open fire. Without saying a word the minister took the tongs, lifted a glowing coal from the fire, and laid it aside on the hearthstone. In silence they watched it die out, whereupon the man exclaimed, "You needn't say a single word. I'll be there next Sabbath."

The Abundant Life   *November 25*

O Come, Let Us Worship

O come, let us worship and bow down: let us kneel before the Lord our maker. Ps. 95:6.

The abundant life is a life that is refreshed, strengthened, and vitalized through worship. There can be no abundant life apart from a firm and living contact with the source of life. Many Christians have too narrow a concept of worship. It is unfortunate to think of it in terms of mere ritual, long prayers, or long and uninteresting reading. Whether at home or at church, such worships are not worship at all, for they are not refreshing and vitalizing. Worship should be like drinking from a crystal-clear stream. It should be like resting in the mountains, in view of the majesty and splendor of the snow-capped peaks mirrored in a quiet lake; like gazing into a fountain that broadens and deepens with our gaze. It is like relaxing quietly in the shadow of a mighty rock as the storm rages around.

Raymond Cummings Brooks puts it this way: "Worship serves its purpose when it helps to give our spirits cathedrallike dimensions, when it makes us aware of the vast possibilities which are inherent in our universe, in ourselves, in our fellows, and in our common life. It is an attempt to make the best possible adjustment to that which a man believes to be the greatest possible concern. It is the way we cultivate those attributes of mind and habits of conduct that make possible for us and through us for our fellows the light and warmth and invigorating power of the Eternal. It is an attempt to get beneath all shame, pretense, and make-believe, and become actually aware of the deepest reality about ourselves and about our world."

An unknown author writes concerning the church: "This is the place where reverent souls may meet with God and gather strength and grace to face the future hours with less of fear and more of joy and hope. This is the place where lonesome heart may meet with friend and much of hurt and doubt by love shall be dispelled and all of life shall happier be and blest."

The Abundant Life   *November 26*

WORSHIP THE CREATOR; GIVE GLORY TO HIM

Fear God, and give glory to him; for the hour of his judgment is come: and worship him that made heaven, and earth, and the sea, and the fountains of waters. Rev. 14:7.

Too often when we think of God and the judgment, we tremble with fear; and a life motivated by fear is not the abundant life. However, fearing God is by no means incompatible with the abundant life if one's life is hid in Christ. "Praise ye the Lord. Blessed is the man that feareth the Lord, that delighteth greatly in his commandments" (Ps. 112:1). "Blessed is every one that feareth the Lord; that walketh in his ways. . . . Happy shalt thou be, and it shall be well with thee" (Ps. 128:1, 2). These two texts show that *blessing, delight,* and *happiness* are perfectly compatible with *the fear of the Lord.* When we are in harmony with our Creator, we have nothing to fear. Our fear of God is an attitude of love and respect, mingled with wonder and awe. A God as great as He, and as loving, overwhelms the soul and inspires true worship.

The abundant life also gives glory to God. You ask, "How can we give glory to God? What is glory? We cannot add to His brightness." God's glory is His character. "The Word of God reveals His character. He Himself has declared His infinite love and pity. When Moses prayed, 'Show me Thy glory,' the Lord answered, 'I will make all My goodness pass before thee.' This is His glory. The Lord passed before Moses, and proclaimed, 'The Lord, The Lord God, merciful and gracious, long-suffering, and abundant in goodness and truth, keeping mercy for thousands, forgiving iniquity and transgression and sin.' He is 'slow to anger, and of great kindness,' 'because He delighteth in mercy.'"—*Steps to Christ* (Pocket ed.), p. 10.

We give glory to God, then, by manifesting His character in our lives and by sharing with others the truth about God and His true character. We give glory to Him by clarifying in men's minds the truth about His wonderful love. This is abundant living.

The Abundant Life   *November 27*

In the Beauty of Holiness

Give unto the Lord the glory due unto his name; worship the Lord in the beauty of holiness. Ps. 29:2.

The abundant life is the beautiful life, the holy life. "The choicest productions of art possess no beauty that can compare with the beauty of character, which is the fruit of the Holy Spirit's working in the soul." —*The Ministry of Healing,* p. 37.

This loveliness of character, this beauty of holiness, we do not naturally possess. Speaking of John, the beloved, we read, "John did not naturally possess the loveliness of character that his later experience revealed. By nature he had serious defects. He was not only proud, self-assertive, and ambitious for honor, but impetuous, and resentful under injury. He and his brother were called 'sons of thunder.' Evil temper, the desire for revenge, the spirit of criticism, were all in the beloved disciple. But beneath all this the divine Teacher discerned the ardent, sincere, loving heart. Jesus rebuked his self-seeking, disappointed his ambitions, tested his faith. But He revealed to him that for which his soul longed,—the beauty of holiness, the transforming power of love."—*The Acts of the Apostles,* p. 540.

Too often we misunderstand holiness. What is holiness? "Holiness is not rapture: it is an entire surrender of the will to God; it is living by every word that proceeds from the mouth of God; it is doing the will of our heavenly Father; it is trusting God in trial, in darkness as well as in the light; it is walking by faith and not by sight; it is relying on God with unquestioning confidence, and resting in His love."—*The Acts of the Apostles,* p. 51. F. D. Huntington once said, "Holiness is religious principle put into action. It is faith gone to work. It is love coined into conduct; devotion helping human suffering and going up in intercession to the great Source of all good."

May God help us today to worship the Lord in the beauty of holiness, thus giving unto Him the glory due His name.

IN SPIRIT AND IN TRUTH

God is a Spirit: and they that worship him must worship him in spirit and in truth. **John 4:24.**

A woman seeking the abundant life is talking to the Master. She does not realize to whom she is speaking at first, but soon recognizes that she is in the presence of One who understands the secrets of her heart. Immediately she seeks to evade conviction by resorting to controversy. So many in their search for the abundant life find that the quest leads to the worshipful life; but when they stand on the threshhold of new insights, technicalities of religious forms and ceremonies eclipse the light of truth, and they go away disappointed.

"The woman saith unto him, . . . Our fathers worshipped in this mountain; and ye say, that in Jerusalem is the place where men ought to worship. Jesus saith unto her, Woman, believe me, the hour cometh, when ye shall neither in this mountain, nor yet at Jerusalem, worship the Father. . . . True worshippers shall worship the Father in spirit and in truth: for the Father seeketh such to worship him" (John 4:19-23).

The worship that really contributes to the abundant life is worship not only motivated by the right spirit but also founded in truth.

To very few did Jesus reveal plainly that He was the long-looked-for Messiah, but to the woman of Samaria, He said, "I that speak unto thee am he." "That which had been withheld from the Jews, and which the disciples were afterward enjoined to keep secret, was revealed to her."—*The Desire of Ages,* p. 190. She at that moment had a taste of the abundant life, and the wonderful revelation was almost overpowering.

To such worshipers, Christ draws near. "As the mother watches for the smile of recognition from her little child, which tells of the dawning of intelligence, so does Christ watch for the expression of grateful love, which shows that spiritual life is begun in the soul."—*Ibid.,* p. 191. To all who respond He gives the abundant life, freely.

The Abundant Life   November 29

With Reverence

Wherefore we receiving a kingdom which cannot be moved, let us have grace, whereby we may serve God acceptably with reverence and godly fear. Heb. 12:28.

The abundant life is filled with reverence and godly fear, knowing that the kingdom of God is secure. There is wonderful confidence and strength in an appreciation of the greatness of God and His abiding presence. "True reverence for God is inspired by a sense of His infinite greatness and realization of His presence."—*Education,* p. 242.

In a message to our youth, we read, "One of your strong temptations is to irreverence. God is high and holy; and to the humble, believing soul, His house on earth . . . is as the gate of heaven. The song of praise, the words spoken by Christ's ministers, are God's appointed agencies to prepare a people for the church above, for that loftier worship into which there can enter nothing that is impure, unholy."—*Messages to Young People,* p. 265.

Nothing mars the abundant life more subtly than irreverence, which often leaves a permanent scar. A group of boys once learned unholy words to the melody of a favorite hymn, thinking it was smart. When undetected, they would sing these words to each other during worship service. At least one of those boys is in the ministry today; and even yet when that hymn is sung, if his attention is not focused on the message—the true thoughts of the written words—the old irreligious words come floating into his mind on the wings of the melody. If they should go unchecked, surely the Spirit of God would be grieved and that minister's worship for that day would be ineffective.

The psalmist reminds us of the greatness of God when he calls us to worship in Psalm 95, verse 3, "For the Lord is a great God, and a great King above all gods." Habakkuk reminds us that "the Lord is in his holy temple: let all the earth keep silence before him" (Hab. 2: 20). Nothing that is sacred, or pertains to the worship of God, should be treated with carelessness and indifference.

The Abundant Life   *November 30*

GROWN UP AND POLISHED

That our sons may be as plants grown up in their youth; that our daughters may be as corner stones, polished after the similitude of a palace. Ps. 144:12.

The abundant life is characterized by maturity and culture. "That our sons may be as plants grown up in their youth." Some people never seem to grow up. Even in adulthood their childish reactions manifest themselves in complaining, pouting, nagging, and faultfinding, in jealousy and hostility, in temper tantrums and unreasonable demands of various kinds. The maturing process is most easily effected while we are young, but it is very difficult later in life.

The abundant life is the maturing life. Paul says, "When I was a child, I spake as a child, I understood as a child, I thought as a child: but when I became a man, I put away childish things" (1 Cor. 13:11).

"That our daughters may be as corner stones, polished after the similitude of a palace." The hope expressed is that both our sons and daughters may be mature, polished, and cultured, but an interesting thought is brought to light in the choice of symbols. Why should not our sons be the cornerstones and our daughters the plants? The psalmist emphasizes here the importance and influence of Christian womanhood. The stability and tone of a society can be measured by the status and character of its women. Many a man living the abundant life can be thankful for a mother who nourished him as a tender plant.

Polishing is important in living the abundant life. One cannot live the abundant life without true refinement and culture. Someone has said, "If our religion does not clothe us in the refinements of common courtesies, it will fail to win the interest and attention of the men of the world."

"Small kindnesses, small courtesies, small considerations habitually practiced in our social intercourse, give a greater charm to the character than the display of great talents and accomplishments," said M. A. Kelty.

DECEMBER

Life Everlasting

December 1

Everlasting Life

Who shall not receive manifold more in this present time, and in the world to come life everlasting. Luke 18:30.

One day a pious old man was walking along the street with a New Testament in his hand when a friend who met him said, "Good morning, Mr. Price. What are you reading?"

"Ah, good morning," replied he. "I'm reading my Father's will."

"Well, what has He left you?" said his friend.

"Why, He has bequeathed me a hundredfold more in this life, and in the world to come—life everlasting."

All during this year we have been considering various aspects of life in their true perspective. We come now to a consideration of the reward at the end of the journey, of the future.

How long is everlasting life? That we cannot comprehend, although there have been many interesting illustrations to describe it.

Someone has said that if the world were changed into a steel ball, and an ant came once every hundred years to walk on it for a short day, eternity would have only begun when the little creature had succeeded in wearing it all away.

Another has said, "Add together ages of ages, multiply them by the leaves on the trees, the sands on the seashore, the dust of the earth, and still you will be no nearer the end of eternity than when you first began your calculation."

The attainment of mere endlessness alone, however, is not sufficient motivation. In fact, it might be very undesirable. For everlasting life to be appealing, it must be worth while. Two conditions are important: Our lives should be worth extending, and our future challenging enough to create anticipation. The first, Christ seeks to make possible for us now; and the second is assured, since Christ's plans for the future surpass all human expectations.

Life Everlasting   *December 2*

I Am the Resurrection and the Life

Jesus said unto her, I am the resurrection, and the life: he that believeth in me, though he were dead, yet shall he live: and whosoever liveth and believeth in me shall never die. Believest thou this? John 11: 25, 26.

In a certain American city there lived a man and his wife who had three sons—all of them in the service of their country. Within two weeks there came three Government slips indicating that each of those boys had been killed in action or was missing. It was a terrible blow.

It was close to Easter, and the week preceding there was a good deal of speculation all over the neighborhood as to whether those parents would be in their regular place the next Sabbath morning. When Sabbath morning came they were there. In the congregation that morning was a small boy who was sitting in the pew immediately behind the bereaved father and mother. He had heard of the tragedy, and he watched them all through the service. He saw them open their hymnbooks and rise and sing with the congregation. He saw them bow their heads reverently while the pastor prayed. He saw them take part in the responsive reading on the triumph of Christ over death. He was puzzled. Then came the offering call; and as the deacons passed the plate, the boy's keen eyes saw that father, who was a comparatively poor man, put a crisp, new ten-dollar bill on the plate. The boy could contain himself no longer. He pulled his father, who sat beside him, down to his level and whispered, "Dad, they must believe it."

"What do you mean, son?"

"Why, they must really believe in the resurrection. They're here. They sang. They read the Bible; and just think, Dad, they even gave ten dollars. Boy, they really must believe it."

Obviously, life everlasting means a life that extends beyond the grave. For the Christian, this first death is but a sleep, a quiet rest in the land of the enemy. He who believes in Christ will awaken from that sleep never to die again. This hope takes the sting out of death.

Life Everlasting   *December 3*

I Have the Keys

I am he that liveth, and was dead; and, behold, I am alive for evermore, Amen; and have the keys of hell and of death. Rev. 1:18.

Is our hope of life everlasting only wishful thinking, or is there a sound basis for it? When Jesus says, "I have the keys that will unlock the tomb," we can believe what He says. God's word is certain. We can have confidence in Jesus' words; because, first of all, He lived what He taught. Many philosophers have expounded beautiful truths, but only Jesus was able consistently to live what He taught. This gives us confidence in Him.

Second, His life was the remarkable fulfillment of scores of Old Testament prophecies concerning His birthplace, His being born of a virgin, His tribe and family, His career, the nature of His work, the time of His appearance and His death. He was what He said He was.

Third, His own death on the cross gives Him the right to the keys. This may sound like a strange basis for hope. Can you conceive of the faith of the Nazi being based upon the death of Hitler? No wonder the cross is foolishness to some. The crucifixion can be understood only in the light of the great controversy and Christ's atonement, through which the character of God as well as the nature of sin and the character of Satan were made manifest. Christ earned the right to forgive the sins of, and to give eternal life to, every man who accepts Him.

Fourth, He demonstrated the fact that He had the keys to the tomb. Three times He brought the dead to life again, and the empty tomb on the glorious resurrection morning silently witnessed the truth of His word. He alone of all religious leaders can point to an empty tomb and say, "I have the key." This is an amazing truth. Christ calmly based His entire claim upon His ability to arise from the grave. He said, "I will rise again," and did; thus you and I can believe.

Fifth, He has ascended into the very presence of God, whence He says, "I am he that liveth, and was dead; and, behold, I . . . have the keys of hell and of death."

Life Everlasting *December 4*

Not Hurt of the Second Death

He that hath an ear, let him hear what the Spirit saith unto the churches; he that overcometh shall not be hurt of the second death. Rev. 2:11.

Christ is addressing the church in Smyrna, symbolic of the church of God that lived during the time of pagan persecutions from about A.D. 100 to about A.D. 313. Significantly, He introduces Himself to these people by saying, "these things saith the first and the last, which was dead, and is alive" (Rev. 2:8). The people of God suffered greatly during those days. To them He says, "Fear none of those things which thou shalt suffer: behold, the devil shall cast some of you into prison, that ye may be tried; and ye shall have tribulation ten days: be thou faithful unto death, and I will give thee a crown of life" (Rev. 2:10). In this setting, then, the promise becomes very precious. Not only were they to be rewarded with a crown of life, but they were also to be saved from the second death.

In going through times of difficulties such as the church at Smyrna suffered, and such as many Christians today are suffering, the persecuted ones often wonder, "How long will the tribulation last?" To them Jesus says, "I know; I understand. I am the first and the last; and, not only that, I know what you are going through. I was dead, and I am alive. I have been through what you are going through. Believe Me; I am with you." What a wonderful Saviour Christ is, and what a wonderful promise He makes! To the aged, facing the grave, or to the young man on the battlefield, the promise is satisfying. To all of us, everywhere, the thought is comforting.

"He that overcometh shall not be hurt of the second death." From that death there will be no resurrection. At the time of the second death he that hath the power of death, Satan, will be destroyed as well. The second death will be the death of death, if you please; for death shall be no more. This is the promise to the overcomer.

Thank God for this wonderful hope that is ours.

Life Everlasting *December 5*

An Everlasting Kingdom

Thy kingdom is an everlasting kingdom, and thy dominion endureth throughout all generations. Ps. 145:13.

The nature of everlasting life in the hereafter intrigues us. We can evaluate it only in terms of life as we know it. Here on earth we are not only members of Christ's spiritual kingdom but also citizens of a literal kingdom. Sometimes there is conflict between the requirements of the two kingdoms, and we suffer as a result. What about the future?

The Lord's kingdom shall be one kingdom. The kingdoms of this world shall become the kingdom of our Lord and of His Christ. His kingdom shall be an everlasting kingdom, for "the Lord is King for ever and ever" (Ps. 10:16).

The greatest earthly kingdom does not compare with the glory of the everlasting kingdom. Listen to the voice of an emperor whose glory had passed away, as he talks to his general. "Yes, our life once shone with all the brilliance of the diadem and the throne. . . . But disasters came. The gold gradually became dim. The reign of misfortune . . . has effaced all brightness. We are mere lead now, General Bertrand; and soon I shall be in my grave. Such is the fate of great men. . . . Our exploits are tasks given to pupils by their tutor who sit in judgment upon us, awarding us censure or praise. . . . I die before my time; and my dead body too must return to the earth to become food for worms. Behold the destiny near at hand of him who has been called the great Napoleon. What an abyss between my deep misery and the eternal reign of Christ which is proclaimed, loved, adored, and which is extending over all the earth. Is this to die? Is it not rather to live?"

What a glorious day that will be when all the kings of the earth will bring their honor and glory into the city of the great king! Their glory then will be lost in the glory of King Jesus and that of the Father and of all the holy angels. Think too of all the fears and sorrows that will be o'er when there will be no more strife among nations and no more war. Oh, Thou King of kings, come quickly!

Life Everlasting   *December 6*

TO SIT WITH CHRIST ON HIS THRONE

To him that overcometh will I grant to sit with me in my throne, even as I also overcame, and am set down with my Father in his throne. Rev. 3:21.

Life everlasting with Christ is not to be a life of endless ease, an empty, purposeless life; for we are told that we shall not only live but also reign with Him. Dominion over all the earth is to be restored to man (Micah 4:8), and he will again assume his position of rulership. This reigning with Christ will not be an authoritarian leadership. Jesus said, "Ye know that they which are accounted to rule over the Gentiles exercise lordship over them; and their great ones exercise authority upon them. But so shall it not be among you: but whosoever will be great among you, shall be your minister; and whosoever of you will be the chiefest, shall be servant of all. For even the Son of man came not to be ministered unto, but to minister, and to give his life a ransom for many" (Mark 10:42-45). The rulership that is ours, then, is that of superior service. We will have everlasting opportunities to serve.

We are to sit with Christ in His throne even as He is set down with His Father in His throne. When Christ sits upon His throne of glory we shall sit with Him in the same relationship that He now sustains to His Father—that is, a priest upon His throne. We shall be kings and priests representing God to the universe through all the ages to come. Note the following statement:

"He 'shall sit and rule upon His throne; and He shall be a priest upon His throne.' Not now 'upon the throne of His glory'; the kingdom of glory has not yet been ushered in. Not until His work as a mediator shall be ended, will God 'give unto Him the throne of His father David,' a kingdom of which 'there shall be no end.' Luke 1:32, 33. As a priest, Christ is now set down with the Father in His throne."—*The Great Controversy*, p. 416.

It is in this relationship that we shall sit with Christ on His throne. What a wonderful privilege will be ours!

Life Everlasting   December 7

All Things New

And he that sat upon the throne said, Behold, I make all things new. And he said unto me, Write: for these words are true and faithful. Rev. 21:5.

We all enjoy having something new. Whether it is receiving a new toy, a new doll, a new game, or wearing a new suit, driving a new car, or moving into a new house, it is always a pleasant experience. Not only do we enjoy new tangible possessions, but we also appreciate new experiences, new opportunities, new insights, new beauties, new pleasures, and new friends. Just think what it will mean to have *all* things new!

The new, however, to be satisfying, must be understood in terms of what we know. We do not want the new things to supplant all that is good in the old, such as old friends and loved ones, or old memories that are pleasant and beautiful. Everything that is desirable in the words *new* and *more* will be experienced by the redeemed.

"There, immortal minds will contemplate with never-failing delight the wonders of creative power, the mysteries of redeeming love. There will be no cruel, deceiving foe to tempt to forgetfulness of God. Every faculty will be developed, every capacity increased. The acquirement of knowledge will not weary the mind or exhaust the energies. There the grandest enterprises may be carried forward, the loftiest aspirations reached, the highest ambitions realized; and still there will arise new heights to surmount, new wonders to admire, new truths to comprehend, fresh objects to call forth the powers of mind and soul and body."—*The Great Controversy,* p. 677.

Now, is this just wishful thinking? Who says all things will be new? Ah, "he that sat upon the throne" says it. Does He really mean it? Oh, yes, He says, "Write: for these words are true and faithful."

Let us pray for new insights and experiences in things divine today so that we may be prepared to enjoy those things new hereafter.

Life Everlasting *December 8*

THE TABERNACLE OF GOD IS WITH MEN

And I heard a great voice out of heaven saying, Behold, the tabernacle of God is with men, and he will dwell with them, and they shall be his people, and God himself shall be with them, and be their God. Rev. 21:3.

Life everlasting is often considered as being lived as a spirit with God in some far-off heaven that seems unreal and ethereal, some place beyond the reach of the human. The future life, to be appealing, however, must have a reality that is understood in the light of what reality means to us. We find it difficult to think of reality apart from material structure. Though it is true that reality transcends structure, it does not ignore it; for God created a material universe in which His moral universe lives and moves. All of us agree that fellowship and love are realities that satisfy the heart, but even these are not separated entirely from physical bodies and places. Although the word *home* connotes qualities of mind and heart that cannot be measured by rules and scales, it is also associated with a spot on earth and some kind of structure.

The joys of the redeemed will also be experienced within the structure of a physical universe. John saw this earth renewed by the power of God—a very real world; he saw, too, the Holy City, New Jerusalem, coming down from God out of heaven as a great voice declared, "Behold, the tabernacle of God." It was a literal city containing mansions prepared by our Lord. Although it has features we cannot completely fathom now, the reality of it as we know reality increases the joy of anticipation in our hearts as we look forward to a home therein. Of course, the most wonderful aspect of today's promise is the thought that in the earth made new and in this wondrous city, God will dwell with men and be their God and they shall be His people.

"The throne of God and of the Lamb shall be in it; and his servants shall serve him" (Rev. 22:3).

Read again the description of that city in Revelation 21 and 22.

No More Sorrow

And God shall wipe away all tears from their eyes; and there shall be no more death, neither sorrow, nor crying, neither shall there be any more pain: for the former things are passed away. Rev. 21:4.

Tears are wiped away when the causes are removed, when suffering is relieved, when wounds are healed, and when hearts are comforted. There is no more sorrow where there are no more causes for heartache. In the earth made new there will be no more war, for example, with all its attending suffering and sorrow, no more sad partings. There we may probably go our several ways, yet we shall know that we shall meet again, and all will be well in the meantime. There will be no more broken promises, for all will keep their vows. There will be no more blasted hopes, for there will be no false hopes, and we shall not hope in vain. All our hopes will be fulfilled, for no sin will interrupt or block their realization. There will be no more unwanted children and minority groups who feel rejected and lonely, for all will be adopted into the royal family of the universe and will enjoy the fellowship of the saints of old and of all the other members of the heavenly family as well. There will be no more disappointments, for there will be no more sin. In so far as past sorrows are concerned, earth has no sorrow that heaven cannot heal.

It is difficult for us to imagine what the world would be like without tears and sorrow. Everlasting life without this hope, however, would be unbearable; for as someone has said, "Whole years of joy glide unperceived away while sorrow counts the minutes as they pass." In this life sorrow plays its important part. It has a work in molding and fashioning our characters; for "sorrows are our best educators. A man can see further through a tear than a telescope." This is true only because of sin; and when sin is over, sorrow, having done its work, will be no more. For then "sorrow and sighing shall flee away" (Isa. 35:10).

Life Everlasting   *December 10*

No More Sickness

And the inhabitant shall not say, I am sick: the people that dwell therein shall be forgiven their iniquity. Isa. 33:24.

There are very few people in this world who can say, "I have never been sick." When this mortal puts on immortality, none shall ever again say, "I am sick." What a wonderful thought!

In heaven there will be no more headaches, backaches, or toothaches; no more fever, nausea, or dizziness; no more arthritis, rheumatism, or neuritis; no more cancer, tuberculosis, or pneumonia; no more epidemics with quarantine and isolation wards; no more operations, wearisome treatments, or painful injections; no more broken bones, torn ligaments, or bruised muscles; no more pain of any kind. Not only will physical diseases be no more, but mental ills will no longer afflict the children of God. There will be no more mental agony, no more depressing, melancholy thoughts to harass the mind, no more hallucinations and terrifying nightmares, no more lapses of memory or strange mental quirks.

You, dear reader, can add your own illness to this list. There will come a time when you never again will say, "I am sick."

Have you ever wondered what doctors and nurses will do in the earth made new? Those who practice medicine enjoy the study of physical forces, chemical reactions, and natural laws. In this life they have just begun to understand a few of these laws. In heaven they will have the opportunity to delve more fully into the secrets of creative power. We read: "There, when the veil that darkens our vision shall be removed, and our eyes shall behold that world of beauty of which we now catch glimpses through the microscope; when we look on the glories of the heavens, now scanned afar through the telescope; when, the blight of sin removed, the whole earth shall appear in 'the beauty of the Lord our God,' what a field will be open to our study! There the student of science may read the records of creation and discern no reminders of the law of evil."—*Education*, p. 303.

Life Everlasting   *December 11*

ALL WILL BE CHANGED

Behold, I shew you a mystery; We shall not all sleep, but we shall all be changed, in a moment, in the twinkling of an eye, at the last trump: for the trumpet shall sound, and the dead shall be raised incorruptible, and we shall be changed. 1 Cor. 15:51, 52.

In any thoughtful consideration of the life hereafter many questions arise. There are great laws that govern the physical universe, some of which we understand partially. Others are still a mystery. With the increase of knowledge, many changes in our concepts have been necessary. Some changes have been sudden and revolutionary with the discovery of new facts.

When Christ comes, we shall all be changed to adjust to the universe in its larger aspects and relationships. Some things in nature will change. The results of sin will be destroyed. The process of death and corruption in the natural world will give place to the process of life and incorruption. Flowers will no longer fade and die as now. They will probably simply dissolve, and a perfect cycle will be experienced. No more thorns and thistles will prick and discourage the gardener. No decaying odor so repulsive to our sense of smell will counteract the fragrance in the pure atmosphere of a world without death.

The greatest change, however, will be the change in us, when this mortal body puts on immortality and this corruptible frame of ours puts on incorruption. Notice the text says, "*We* shall all be changed." Obviously, there must be a change if we are to be able to experience interplanetary travel, for example, to say nothing about intergalaxy transportation. We are told that the redeemed will follow the Lamb whithersoever He goeth in the universe. The Master Creator-Scientist will effect this change to a new system far more efficiently than any change we have experienced in this world. We are, of course, not talking about character change, which will be made before Christ comes, but a physical change, the change to which we are all looking forward.

Bodies Like Unto His Glorious Body

Who shall change our vile body, that it may be fashioned like unto his glorious body, according to the working whereby he is able even to subdue all things unto himself. Phil. 3:21.

What will you and I be like in the hereafter? Paul posed this question in 1 Corinthians 15:45, "But some man will say, How are the dead raised up? and with what body do they come?" Back of this question is the idea that no one wants to lose his identity. Paul points out that in nature when we plant wheat, the new body is wheat in the harvest. You can always depend upon receiving in the harvest just what you plant. Likewise, in the resurrection we shall be able to identify one another. The apostle says, however, that our resurrected bodies will be of a different nature because of the different environment in which we shall live and move. "Even in this world, all flesh is not identical. The flesh of human beings, animals, fish and birds is different in each case. There are bodies which exist in this world, and bodies which exist in the heavens. These bodies are not, as it were, in competition; the splendour of an earthly body is quite a different thing from the splendour of an heavenly body. . . . There are illustrations here of the raising of the dead. The body is 'sown' in dishonour; it is raised in splendour. It is sown in weakness; it is raised in power. It is sown a natural body; it is raised a spiritual body. . . . The first man came out of the earth a material creature. The second Man came from Heaven and was the Lord Himself. For the life of this world men are made like the material man; but for the life that is to come they are made like the One from Heaven" (1 Cor. 15:39-48, Phillips' translation).

Our resurrected bodies will be like unto Christ's glorious body after His resurrection—a real body of flesh and bones. When Jesus appeared to the disciples in the upper room, they recognized Him by His voice and characteristics that distinguished Him from every other person they had known. They felt Him; He was a reality. That is the way you and I will be in the earth made new.

Life Everlasting   *December 13*

EYES AND EARS OPENED

Then the eyes of the blind shall be opened, and the ears of the deaf shall be unstopped. Isa. 35:5.

What a thrilling thought for those who are blind and deaf! Just think what it will mean to those who live in silence or in darkness every day, to have the silence broken by the sound of the trumpet and the voice of our Lord and to have the darkness dispelled by the Light of the world at His coming and to be able to look into His face. We who have both of these senses cannot fully appreciate this hope.

There is also in our text the revelation of a hope that will appeal to all, even to those who have full use of both eyes and ears. Think how blind and deaf we really are, all of us, how much there is that we do not see or hear even in this life. And concerning the hereafter, Paul reminds us, "Eye hath not seen, nor ear heard, neither have entered into the heart of man, the things which God hath prepared for them that love him" (1 Cor. 2:9). For example, when our ears are opened, "there will be music there, and song, such music and song as, save in the visions of God, no mortal ear has heard or mind conceived."—*Education,* p. 307.

When the veil that interposes between the visible and invisible world will be drawn aside, wonderful things will be revealed. Among the most wonderful will be the privilege of seeing the angels and conversing with those celestial beings who unseen have been our companions on earth. "Every redeemed one will understand the ministry of angels in his own life. The angel who was his guardian from his earliest moment; the angel who watched his steps, and covered his head in the day of peril; the angel who was with him in the valley of the shadow of death, who marked his resting place, who was the first to greet him in the resurrection morning—what will it be to hold converse with him, and to learn the history of divine interposition in the individual life, of heavenly co-operation in every work for humanity!"—*Ibid.,* p. 305.

Life Everlasting   *December 14*

STREAMS IN THE DESERT

Then shall the lame man leap as an hart, and the tongue of the dumb sing: for in the wilderness shall waters break out, and streams in the desert. **Isa. 35:6.**

Three beautiful pictures are here presented by Isaiah. Each involves a marvelous transformation, each presents a delightful contrast: a crippled man leaping as an agile deer, men once speechless singing, and streams of water flowing in a desert. Combine all three and you have a dismal picture of an old man bent and lame, unable to express his loneliness and despair, limping along a desert trail in search of water; then suddenly a stream of water breaks forth from a mighty rock, and the whole landscape is transformed and blossoms as a rose. The lame man is made whole; and renewed in youthful vigor, he leaps as an hart, his tongue once dumb is loosed, and he sings from his heart joyful songs of praise and thanksgiving to his Creator. What new hope and courage this brings to the weary traveler! The thought of it alone is to us as a stream in the desert even now.

We are reminded of the song by George F. Root:

> "O the way is long and weary,
> And our bleeding feet are sore;
> Is it far to Canaan's land?
> Is it far to Canaan's land?
> In the desert we are longing
> For its shelter more and more.
>   Is it far, is it far to Canaan's land?
>
> "We are weary, faint, and sore,
> We are weary, faint, and sore,
> Sadly wand'ring thro' the wilderness,
> And o'er the desert sand;
> We are weary, oh, so weary,
>   Is it far, is it far to Canaan's land?"

Life Everlasting   *December 15*

Shall Not Hurt nor Destroy

They shall not hurt nor destroy in all my holy mountain: for the earth shall be full of the knowledge of the Lord, as the waters cover the sea. Isa. 11:9.

Hurt and destruction among men as well as in the animal kingdom will be no more in the earth made new, for the earth shall be full of the knowledge of the Lord. Jesus, the Creator, will be the ruler.

> "The wolf shall dwell with the lamb,
>   and the leopard shall lie down with the kid,
>   and the calf and the lion and the fatling together,
>   and a little child shall lead them.
> The cow and the bear shall feed;
>   their young shall lie down together;
>   and the lion shall eat straw like the ox.
> The sucking child shall play over the hole of the asp,
>   and the weaned child shall put his hand on the adder's den.
> They shall not hurt or destroy in all my holy mountain;
>   for the earth shall be full of the knowledge of the Lord
>   as the waters cover the sea" (Isa. 11:6-9, R.S.V.).

Hurt and destruction come through ignorance, particularly the ignorance of the knowledge of God. When the earth is made new, all shall know Him, from the least to the greatest. We read: "The great controversy is ended. Sin and sinners are no more. The entire universe is clean. One pulse of harmony and gladness beats through the vast creation. From Him who created all, flow life and light and gladness, throughout the realms of illimitable space. From the minutest atom to the greatest world, all things, animate and inanimate, in their unshadowed beauty and perfect joy, declare that God is love."—*The Great Controversy,* p. 678.

Life Everlasting   *December 16*

THE PAST FORGOTTEN

For, behold, I create new heavens and a new earth: and the former shall not be remembered, nor come into mind. Isa. 65:17.

So many of us have a poor memory when it comes to remembering what we should remember and too good a memory for the things we ought to forget. We are all too conscious of the mistakes of the past that have defeated us, and we cannot seem to forget some of the hurts of days gone by. Many such experiences haunt our dreams in the night and block the flow of our energies in the day.

The memory of an evil deed lingers long in a selfish mind and heart and not only affects our interpersonal relationships but also our health as well. The inability to forget the past has ruined many a fellowship that had wonderful possibilities for happiness. Many a marriage has failed for this very reason. Because of their unwillingness to forgive and forget, some people have even declared that they will not enjoy heaven if certain individuals are to be there.

In the earth made new, however, no unpleasant memories will spoil the happiness of the redeemed; and this will not be true because God will blot out certain brain cells. In the first place heaven's inhabitants will all be converted and transformed men and women. No selfish hearts will be there. And in the second place, the redeemed will have settled all their questions during the millennium. At that time the records will have been gone over, and life's questions will have been answered and settled so satisfactorily that the former will not be remembered, nor come into mind. Each will understand one another's hearts and motives, and the joy of loving hearts will not be marred by the unpleasant memories of the past. All will be thankful for the wonderful love of God and together will share in planning a future unspoiled by sin.

The expulsive power of a new affection will erase the past and spur us on to greater heights and new experiences in a glorious fellowship together throughout eternity.

Life Everlasting   *December 17*

BUILD AND EAT

And they shall build houses, and inhabit them; and they shall plant vineyards, and eat the fruit of them. Isa. 65:21.

Life in the hereafter will be filled with real activities. It will be no idle inactive existence, but a constructive satisfying one. Building something and eating tasty food constitute two of life's greatest joys. What would life be like without something constructive to do or without the pleasure and joy of eating? To be able to build a home and live in it without fear of being evicted, with no heavy mortgage hanging over him, is a joy everyone longs to experience. This would be especially so if one could build a house just as he wanted it, with all the little extras that make a home beautiful, practical, and livable. Add to this the pleasure of landscaping it according to your own individual taste and of having a garden of beautiful flowers and good things to eat, knowing that no pests, weeds, or storms will destroy any of it, and you have a picture of Paradise beautiful.

Perhaps you say that this would be a carpenter's or a farmer's paradise, and that you are not interested in building houses or planting vineyards. It may be that you have driven nails and poured concrete long enough. Perhaps you have worked many long hours in the vineyard, and look forward to the day when such labor will be no more. Take courage! Much of the hard labor in this life is due to disease, pests, and weeds, which are the result of sin. With these gone, weary toil and trial will be no more.

"There will be no weariness in doing the will of God and offering praise to His name. We shall ever feel the freshness of the morning, and shall ever be far from its close."—*The Great Controversy*, p. 676.

No longer will the sun beat down mercilessly to scorch men. No longer will one grow weary and bent with age, for all will renew their strength in the vigor of everlasting youth. What a joy it will be to build and plant and eat under such circumstances!

Life Everlasting   *December 18*

As the Days of a Tree

They shall not build, and another inhabit; they shall not plant, and another eat: for as the days of a tree are the days of my people, and mine elect shall long enjoy the work of their hands. Isa. 65:22.

Among the disappointments that characterize the present life are those that come from not being able to enjoy the fruit of one's labors. Often men with high ideals and dreams of great achievement work hard—a whole lifetime—to accomplish an objective and then die without seeing the fruition of their hopes. This is especially true in the experiences of pioneers in almost every worthy field of endeavor.

Longevity, fruitfulness, restfulness, and beauty characterize the life everlasting for the redeemed. Several psalms deal with the thought, "as the days of a tree are the days of my people."

> "And he shall be like a tree planted by the rivers of water,
>   that bringeth forth his fruit in his season;
> his leaf also shall not wither;
>   and whatsoever he doeth shall prosper.
>
> "The ungodly are not so:
>   but are like the chaff which the wind driveth away.
> Therefore the ungodly shall not stand in the judgment,
>   nor sinners in the congregation of the righteous.
>
> "For the Lord knoweth the way of the righteous:
>   but the way of the ungodly shall perish" (Ps. 1:3-6).
>
> "The righteous shall flourish like the palm tree:
>   he shall grow like a cedar in Lebanon.
> Those that be planted in the house of the Lord
>   shall flourish in the courts of our God.
> They shall still bring forth fruit in old age;
>   they shall be fat and flourishing" (Ps. 92:12-14).

Life Everlasting   *December 19*

Not Labor in Vain

They shall not labour in vain, nor bring forth for trouble; for they are the seed of the blessed of the Lord, and their offspring with them. Isa. 65:23.

It is a wonderful thought to realize that in the life hereafter there will be no fruitless, fatiguing toil and labor. This alone would make life everlasting worth while. But far more important than this are our family relationships, and dearer to our hearts than anything else in this world are our children. They are the only things in this life that we can take with us into the hereafter. Therefore we want to see them with us. The promise in our text for today is that our offspring will be with us.

This is a promise we can claim. Listen to our text in Moffatt's translation: "They shall not work in vain, nor rear their children to die suddenly, for they are a race whom the Eternal blesses, and with them shall their children live."

Those who have lost little ones here will rejoice in the thought that on the resurrection morning angels of glory will carry the resurrected little ones to the arms of their mothers, and what joy will be theirs to bring up these little ones in a world in which there is no sin, no death, no cruel foe to tempt or to bring suffering or insecurity. They will no longer rear their children to die suddenly. No longer will we see a mother bend over a little casket and cry out, "I can't let you go." No longer will parents seek to calm a suffering child in vain as they watch him die before their eyes while they stand helplessly by, their own hearts breaking with anguish.

It is not clearly revealed what kind of family relationship will be experienced in the hereafter, but this much we do know: "There the redeemed shall know, even as also they are known. The loves and sympathies which God Himself has planted in the soul shall there find truest and sweetest exercise."—*The Great Controversy,* p. 677.

Life Everlasting   *December 20*

Before They Call I Will Answer

And it shall come to pass, that before they call, I will answer; and while they are yet speaking, I will hear. Isa. 65:24.

In this present sinful world delays and disappointments interfere with our plans and spoil our happiness. Many times God allows them that we might learn certain lessons. Often our plans fail that God's plans for us might succeed. However, not everything that happens is God's will, although nothing can happen to defeat it ultimately. How often we call unto God and seem to get no answer! Is anybody listening? We wonder, because in our blindness we cannot see.

God *is* listening when we pray even though we do not feel that He is. His delays are for a purpose, as was the delay on the part of Jesus when He heard that Lazarus was sick. He deliberately waited two days, and let Lazarus die, to show His power over death and to give us hope and assurance. In the world to come, circumstances will be different. Sin and disappointment will be no more, and man and God will be one again even as Jesus and God are one.

Today Isaiah gives us a wonderful insight into the heart of God, who longs for the fellowship of His people. He wants to serve them. As Jesus came not to be ministered unto but to minister, so God enjoys ministering to His created beings more than we realize.

In any type of service, he serves best who sees what there is to be done and who does it without being told. Such servants are rare. In our relationship with God and Jesus, however, the term "servant" is not adequate. Jesus said: "Ye are my friends. . . . Henceforth I call you not servants; for the servant knoweth not what his lord doeth: but I have called you friends; for all things that I have heard of my Father I have made known unto you" (John 15:14, 15).

The finest of interpersonal relationships exist when two friends or lovers anticipate each other's needs and make each other happy by seeking to meet those needs in advance. This is the relationship that will exist between God and His people in the earth made new.

Life Everlasting   *December 21*

Seed and Name Remain

For as the new heavens and the new earth, which I will make, shall remain before me, saith the Lord, so shall your seed and your name remain. Isa. 66:22.

A man's name is generally very dear to his heart. All of us appreciate being called by name, and we want our names to stand for something worth while—some worthy achievement. Such statements as, "I saw your name in the paper last night," or, "I saw your name on the honor roll," strike a responsive cord in our hearts, but having our names removed from an important list is an unpleasant experience.

Some men go to great lengths to immortalize their names, and we find them on monuments, buildings, or tombs. Certain names endure through the centuries. Some family names, however, become extinct for lack of sons to perpetuate them. In the life everlasting this will no longer be true. There will be no death to cut off one's seed or name, and each name will be great because it represents one of the redeemed of earth for whom Christ died. Each name will remain, not just on a tombstone, not just in memory, but as an ever-living person.

Someone may say, "But will we not each have a new name in heaven?" Yes, we will; for we read, "To him that overcometh will I give to eat of the hidden manna, and will give him a white stone, and in the stone a new name written, which no man knoweth saving he that receiveth it" (Rev. 2:17). This name, however, refers to a character, a condition of heart, that we alone will know. So far as knowing one another is concerned, we shall know as we are known. Jesus said, "Many . . . shall sit down with Abraham, and Isaac, and Jacob in the kingdom" (Matt. 8:11). They were known as Abraham, Isaac, and Jacob here in this world. We shall know one another. Our seed and our name will remain throughout eternity.

Is my name worthy to remain? Does it stand for the kind of character that will be a blessing to all with whom I come in contact?

Life Everlasting — **December 22**

From One Sabbath to Another

And it shall come to pass, that from one new moon to another, and from one sabbath to another, shall all flesh come to worship before me, saith the Lord. Isa. 66:23.

Just think what a Sabbath worship service will be like in the New Jerusalem! To see the angels of heaven gathered together, an innumerable company, and to see the redeemed of all ages stand on the sea of glass, will be an inspiring sight. To hear the music of the heavenly angelic choir, the song of Moses and the Lamb sung by the redeemed, the special song that only the 144,000 can sing, as well as the great oratorio chorus, "Worthy Is the Lamb," in which every being will join, will be an experience that will thrill the soul.

More wonderful yet will it be to hear God, the Father, and Jesus Christ teach the Sabbath school lesson and preach the sermon. No one will sleep then, for no one will be weary, and the ministers will be most challenging. No irreverence will mar the service, and no noisy trucks and airplanes will disturb the period of meditation.

"Hail, peaceful day! divinely blest! Sweetly thy glories would we sing,
Memorial of that sacred rest, Of vast creation's mighty King:
This hallowed time to man was given, A foretaste of the bliss of heaven.

"Hark! through the shining courts above What rapturous praises echo now!
Around that holy law of love Seraphs in adoration bow;
Let earth, responsive to the strain, Exalt alone Jehovah's name.

"O come, thou bright, immortal day! When at His temple all adore,
And own His universal sway From age to age, forevermore;
Then Zion shall in triumph reign, And Eden bloom on earth again."

—Annie R. Smith

They Shall See His Face

And they shall see his face; and his name shall be in their foreheads. Rev. 22:4.

What do you see in a face? Chesterfield wrote, "Look in the face of the person to whom you are speaking if you wish to know his real sentiments, for he can command his words more easily than his countenance." Since one can show approval or disapproval so readily in one's face, even God uses this terminology to express Himself in terms of hiding His face or lifting up His countenance upon us.

Just think what it will mean to see the fullness of His love revealed in a countenance hidden since man's fall. Ever since Adam hid his face from the Lord, sin has separated man from God, and now at best we see through a glass darkly, but then we shall see face to face.

When Jesus comes some will cry for the rocks and mountains to fall on them to hide them from His face. The redeemed, however, will look up and rejoice in His coming and be glad to look on His face. No longer will they want to hide, for their sins will have been forgiven and their characters will be like the Saviour's.

The men who will see His face are the men in whose foreheads His name is written. The Father's name stands for three things: His title, His character, and His authority. When the saints stand on the sea of glass with the Father's name written in their foreheads, they will reflect His character, they will have been adopted into the royal family and thus carry the family name, and they will be invested with all the authority behind that name, for they shall be sons and daughters of the Most High, kings on His throne with Him. They will be a people who have uppermost in their minds the character of their heavenly Father and the desire to glorify Him. They shall see His face.

Is the Holy Spirit writing that name in your forehead and mine today? Are we seeking to reflect His image so we can look upon His face and live? A glorious privilege that will be.

Life Everlasting   *December 24*

Everlasting Joy

And the ransomed of the Lord shall return, and come to Zion with songs and everlasting joy upon their heads: they shall obtain joy and gladness, and sorrow and sighing shall flee away. Isa. 35:10.

> "And a highway shall be there,
>   and it shall be called the Holy Way;
> the unclean shall not pass over it,
>   and fools shall not err therein.
> No lion shall be there,
>   nor shall any ravenous beast come up on it;
> they shall not be found there,
>   but the redeemed shall walk there.
> And the ransomed of the Lord shall return,
>   and come to Zion with singing,
>   with everlasting joy upon their heads;
> they shall obtain joy and gladness,
>   and sorrow and sighing shall flee away."
>
>   (Isa. 35:8-10, R.S.V.)

Here Isaiah paints a picture to encourage the souls of weary travelers. Everlasting happiness will be theirs and ours when we hear the words, "Enter thou into the joy of thy Lord."

Of course, the privilege of walking the golden streets and living in the beautiful mansions will be no small source of pleasure, but the greatest happiness will be that of entering into the joy of our Lord. His joy is that of fellowship with the redeemed. The redemption of lost souls will be the most satisfying reward to the Saviour, and it will be our greatest source of gladness. To have someone come up to you in heaven and say, "You know, if it had not been for you, I wouldn't be here. Thank you so much," will thrill your heart through and through. Fellowship with these and face-to-face communion with God and our Saviour will bring joy everlasting.

Life Everlasting / *December 25*

Everlasting Light

The sun shall be no more thy light by day; neither for brightness shall the moon give light unto thee: but the Lord shall be unto thee an everlasting light, and thy God thy glory. Isa. 60:19.

Long ago on the hills of Judea, one night, to certain shepherds the angel of the Lord came, "and the glory of the Lord shone round about them. . . . And suddenly there was with the angel a multitude of the heavenly host praising God, and saying, Glory to God in the highest, and on earth peace, good will toward men" (Luke 2:9-14).

That memorable flash of light was only a faint reflection of the everlasting light heralding the coming of the true Light of the world, veiled in human flesh. When the veil is lifted and His glory shines forth in all its splendor in the earth made new, who will be able to stand? We think of the words of Thomas Binney in this connection:

> "Eternal Light! Eternal Light!
>   How pure that soul must be
> When, placed within Thy searching sight,
> It shrinks not, but with calm delight
>   Can live, and look on Thee.
>
> . . . . .
>
> "There is a way for man to rise
>   To that sublime abode:
> An offering and a sacrifice,
> A Holy Spirit's energies,
>   An Advocate with God:
>
> "These, these prepare us for the sight
>   Of holiness above;
> The sons of ignorance and night
> May dwell in the eternal Light,
>   Through the eternal Love!"

Life Everlasting   *December 26*

My New Name

Him that overcometh will I make a pillar in the temple of my God, and he shall go no more out: and I will write upon him the name of my God, and the name of the city of my God, which is new Jerusalem, which cometh down out of heaven from my God: and I will write upon him my new name. Rev. 3:12.

Have you ever wondered in what sense Jesus would have a new name? How will that name be written upon the overcomer? Listen to a parable:

An ugly thorny brier grew in a ditch, scratching everything that touched it. "Ah, me," it sighed, "I can't think why I was made. I have no beauty or worth. If only I were a bunch of violets or an oak or even the corn beyond the hedge, I would be of value; but I'm only a brier!"

One day a gardener transplanted the brier in a beautiful garden. It felt ashamed, and was embarrassed because of its ugliness. "If that gardener had only known what I am, he wouldn't have brought me here. He can never get any good out of me. I can tell him that." As if he knew what the brier had been thinking, the gardener laughingly said, "If I can't get any good out of thee, maybe I can put some good into thee!" and he went away.

The lonesome brier wished itself back in the ditch again, to hide its ugliness. One day the gardener grafted a bud into the brier's bark. As the bud grew steadily the gardener cut away the old thorny growth until all the old brier top was gone. The new growth began to bud and blossom.

Soon many came to see the new rose growing where once a rough brier had been, and they admired its color and fragrance. All praised the gardener. The brier had a new name, a rose; for it had a new character. The gardener had a new name, too, in the field of horticulture.

The great Gardener of the universe will be seen in a new light through the transformation of human briers into beautiful roses, and thus upon such His new name will be written.

Life Everlasting   *December 27*

SHINE AS STARS FOREVER

And they that be wise shall shine as the brightness of the firmament; and they that turn many to righteousness as the stars for ever and ever. Dan. 12:3.

"And they that be wise shall shine." The marginal reading for the word "wise" is "teachers." The original word in Hebrew lends itself to that concept. The word translated "wise" here is translated "understand" in Daniel 11:33, where we read, "and they that understand among the people shall instruct many: yet they shall fall by the sword, and by flame, by captivity, and by spoil, many days."

Today's promise is written especially for teachers, who will shine throughout all eternity. You say, "But I'm not a teacher." Yes, you are. Once you understand something wonderful you cannot refrain from sharing it with others. To see the results of that sharing throughout eternity will constitute one of the greatest joys of the redeemed. You never forget the one who shared with you the knowledge of God. Nor will those forget you with whom you have shared that glorious truth. You do not now see the full results of sharing your faith, as teachers never see the full results of the influence of their lives and teaching. In the hereafter, however, we shall see; and then all "that turn many to righteousness" will shine "as the stars for ever and ever."

The following prayer for his teacher by a native who appreciated her will be then fulfilled: "Oh, Lord, bless de teacher who come so far to 'struct us in de way to heaven. Rock her in de cradle of love. Backen de word of power in her heart dat she may have souls for her hire and many stars in her crown in de great gettin'-up mornin' when de general roll is called; and when all de battle is over, may she fall all kivered wid victory, be buried wid de honors of war, and rise to wear de long white robe in glory, and walk de shinin' streets in silver slippers down by de golden sunrise, close to de great white throne; and dere may she strike glad hands wid all her dear scholars and praise You, Lord, forever and forever! For Jesus' sake. Amen."

Life Everlasting December 28

IN THE AGES TO COME

That in the ages to come he might shew the exceeding riches of his grace in his kindness toward us through Christ Jesus. Eph. 2:7.

The more we think of the wonders of the life everlasting, the more we marvel at the love of God and the riches of His grace in His kindness toward us in Christ Jesus. Throughout eternity we shall be the trophies of His grace, ever revealing His goodness in us. Our being there will bear this testimony, for only His grace will make it possible.

We are like Sammy, who presented himself for admission to the church. The officers hesitated, thinking he did not understand the doctrines of the gospel and conversion. They decided, however, to examine him. "Do you think, Sammy," said the pastor, "that you have been born again?"

"I think I have," was the answer.

"Well, if so, whose work is that?"

"Oh, God did a part; and I did a part."

"Ah, what part did you do, Sammy?"

"Why, I opposed God all I could; and He did the rest."

The Holy Spirit had been Sammy's teacher. He knew the work of grace in his heart that had created him anew in Christ.

Throughout eternity only one reminder of sin will remain. Listen: "One reminder alone remains: Our Redeemer will ever bear the marks of His crucifixion. Upon His wounded head, upon His side, His hands and feet, are the only traces of the cruel work that sin has wrought.... 'He had bright beams coming out of His side: and there was the hiding of His power.' Habakkuk 3:4, margin. That pierced side whence flowed the crimson stream that reconciled man to God—there is the Saviour's glory, there 'the hiding of His power.' ... The tokens of His humiliation are His highest honor; through the eternal ages the wounds of Calvary will show forth His praise, and declare His power." —*The Great Controversy,* p. 674.

Shall we not now begin to show the exceeding riches of that grace?

Life Everlasting   *December 29*

PLEASURES FOREVERMORE

Thou wilt shew me the path of life: in thy presence is fulness of joy; at thy right hand there are pleasures for evermore. **Ps. 16:11.**

Sin can give temporary pleasure, but not real joy. Its paths lead away from God to death. The path of life leads to God, to fullness of joy and pleasures forevermore. In contrasting heavenly and worldly pleasures F. G. Pilkington has written: "The pleasures of the world surfeit without satisfying, while heavenly pleasures satisfy without surfeiting. The surfeited nature of the sensualist requires a constantly increasing stimulus to rouse his used-up powers, but with each advance in Christian enjoyment, there is an increased power to appreciate heavenly joys. The pleasures of the world are like the kiss of Judas given but to betray. The pleasures of heaven make the soul bright and beautiful as when the face of Moses was transformed by the vision of God."

Life's greatest pleasures do not come from the gratification of passing desires, but result from careful preparation and development. What you are has more to do with genuine pleasure than what you do. Christians can never enter into certain "pleasures" because such activities do not help to prepare them for the pleasures of the redeemed.

"The Lord Jesus is making experiments on human hearts through the exhibition of His mercy and abundant grace. He is effecting transformations so amazing that Satan, with all his triumphant boasting, . . . stands viewing them as a fortress impregnable to his sophistries and delusions. They are to him an incomprehensible mystery. The angels of God . . . look on with astonishment and joy, that fallen men, once children of wrath, are through the training of Christ developing characters after the divine similitude, to be sons and daughters of God, to act an important part in the occupations and pleasures of heaven."—*Testimonies to Ministers,* p. 18.

Life Everlasting   *December 30*

TO EAT OF THE TREE OF LIFE

He that hath an ear, let him hear what the Spirit saith unto the churches; To him that overcometh will I give to eat of the tree of life, which is in the midst of the paradise of God. Rev. 2:7.

"In the midst of the street of it, and on either side of the river, was there the tree of life, which bare twelve manner of fruits, and yielded her fruit every month" (Rev. 22:2).

Ellen G. White saw the tree of life in vision and wrote, "On one side of the river was a trunk of the tree, and a trunk on the other side of the river, both of pure, transparent gold. At first I thought I saw two trees. I looked again, and saw that they were united at the top in one tree. . . . Its branches bowed to the place where we stood, and the fruit was glorious; it looked like gold mixed with silver. . . . We all went under the tree and sat down to look at the glory of the place, when Brethren Fitch and Stockman . . . came up to us and asked us what we had passed through while they were sleeping. We tried to call up our greatest trials, but they looked so small compared with the far more exceeding and eternal weight of glory that surrounded us that we could not speak them out, and we all cried out, 'Alleluia, heaven is cheap enough!' and we touched our glorious harps and made heaven's arches ring."—*Early Writings*, p. 17.

One of the privileges of the redeemed will be the monthly visit to the New Jerusalem to partake of the fruit of the tree of life and to worship. (See Isa. 66:23.) Worship will not be confined to the Sabbath day. All life's joys will be experienced in an atmosphere of worship.

As Mrs. White in vision saw Jesus leading His people to the tree of life, she said, "Language is altogether too feeble to attempt a description of heaven. As the scene rises before me, I am lost in amazement. Carried away with the surpassing splendor and excellent glory, I lay down the pen, and exclaim, 'Oh, what love! what wondrous love!' The most exalted language fails to describe the glory of heaven or the matchless depths of a Saviour's love."—*Ibid.*, p. 289.

Life Everlasting   *December 31*

He Shall Be Satisfied

He shall see of the travail of his soul, and shall be satisfied: by his knowledge shall my righteous servant justify many; for he shall bear their iniquities. Isa. 53:11.

Try to visualize the scene of the coronation of the Son of God at the close of the millennium, when all beings who have ever lived are gathered about the throne. Christ, the saints, and the New Jerusalem have come to earth; and the wicked have been raised.

"Far above the city, upon a foundation of burnished gold, is a throne, high and lifted up. Upon this throne sits the Son of God, and around Him are the subjects of His kingdom. . . . Above the throne is revealed the cross; and like a panoramic view appear the scenes of Adam's temptation and fall, and the successive steps in the great plan of redemption. . . . Each actor recalls the part which he performed. . . . With all the facts of the great controversy in view, the whole universe, both loyal and rebellious, with one accord declare: 'Just and true are Thy ways, Thou King of Saints.' . . . The hour has come when Christ occupies His rightful position. . . . It was for the joy that was set before Him—that He might bring many sons unto glory—that He endured the cross and despised the shame. And inconceivably great as was the sorrow and the shame, yet greater is the joy and the glory. He looks upon the redeemed, renewed in His own image, every heart bearing the perfect impress of the divine, every face reflecting the likeness of their King. He beholds in them the result of the travail of His soul, and He is satisfied. Then, in a voice that reaches the assembled multitudes of the righteous and the wicked, He declares: 'Behold the purchase of My blood! For these I suffered, for these I died, that they might dwell in My presence throughout eternal ages.' "—*The Great Controversy,* pp. 665-671.

To live in anticipation of that dramatic moment, to share this hope with all with whom we come in contact, and to walk each day in fellowship with Him who makes this possible—*This Is Life.*